# Conflicts over Resource Ownership

# Books from
# The Lincoln Institute of Land Policy

The Lincoln Institute of Land Policy is a school that offers intensive courses of instruction in the field of land economics and property taxation. The Institute provides a stimulating learning environment for students, policymakers, and administrators with challenging opportunities for research and publication. The goal of the Institute is to improve theory and practice in those fundamental areas of land policy that have significant impact on the lives and livelihood of all people.

**Constitutions, Taxation, and Land Policy**   Michael M. Bernard

**Constitutions, Taxation, and Land Policy—Volume II**
Michael M. Bernard

**Federal Tax Aspects of Open-Space Preservation**   Kingsbury Browne

**Taxation of Nonrenewable Resources**   Albert M. Church

**Conflicts over Resource Ownership**   Albert M. Church

**Taxation of Mineral Resources**   Robert F. Conrad and R. Bryce Hool

**World Congress on Land Policy, 1980**   Edited by Matthew Cullen and Sharon Woolery

**Land Readjustment**   William A. Doebele

**The Rate of Return**   Edited by Daniel M. Holland

**Incentive Zoning**   Jerold S. Kayden

**Building for Women**   Edited by Suzanne Keller

**Urban Land Policy for the Reagan Years**   Edited by George Lefcoe

**Fiscal Federalism and the Taxation of Natural Resources**   Edited by Charles E. McLure, Jr., and Peter Mieszkowski

**State Land-Use Planning and Regulation**   Thomas G. Pelham

**The State's Role in Property Taxation**   Edited by H. Clyde Reeves

**Land-Office Business**   Gary Sands

**The Art of Valuation**   Edited by Arlo Woolery

# Conflicts over Resource Ownership

## The Use of Public Policy by Private Interests

**Albert M. Church**
University of New Mexico

**LexingtonBooks**
D.C. Heath and Company
Lexington, Massachusetts
Toronto

**Library of Congress Cataloging in Publication Data**

Church, Albert M.
  Conflicts over resource ownership.

  Bibliography: p.
  Includes index.
  1.  Natural resources—Government policy—United States.  I.  Title.
HC103.7.C478            1982            333.7'0973            82–47942
ISBN 0–669–05712–6

*Copyright © 1982 by D.C. Heath and Company*

Published simultaneously in Canada

Printed in the United States of America

International Standard Book Number: 0–669–05712–6

Library of Congress Catalog Card Number: 82–47942

*To Michael and Eric*

# Contents

# Figures and Tables

# Acknowledgments

This book and research would not have been possible without the financial support of the Lincoln Institute of Land Policy. I am grateful for the institute's continuing interest in natural-resource policy and in my work. I owe particular thanks to Arlo Woolery, Matt Cullen, and Will Knedlick.

Most of this work was accomplished while I was on sabbatical from the University of New Mexico as a visiting scientist at the Massachusetts Institute of Technology (spring 1981). The Taxation, Resources, and Economic Development (TRED) meetings supported by the Lincoln Institute of Land Policy in the fall of 1981 ("Fiscal Federalism and the Taxation of Natural Resources") presented a productive environment for the exchange of ideas. Numerous people read sections of this book and made worthwhile suggestions. Robert Shelton was particularly helpful. Finally, Jenifer Zamora's typing skills were absolutely necessary to complete this task.

# 1 Overview

This book is about the competition among private interests over the receipt and control of natural-resource revenues. It also addresses the private interests' use of public policy. The central hypothesis is that effective resource ownership and control are shared among many private interests, and these arrangements are determined by historical, social, judicial, legislative, and economic institutions. The policies and management of these institutions determine who controls resource use and resource revenues, and thus they determine both the formal and informal property-ownership rights. These interest groups include consumers, legal owners of natural resources, elected officials, government bureaucrats, trade associations, and residents in resource-producing jurisdictions. The means used to obtain property rights to the income from natural resources and control over when and how they are used are derived from influencing the social, economic, and political institutions, which are in both the private and the public sector.

The public policies that have had and are likely to continue to have the greatest influence are public ownership, taxation, and direct regulation. This book concentrates on their use by local, state, and national governments. This competition gives rise to interjurisdictional and regional competition, and it is expected that interest-group and interjurisdictional squabbles will continue and perhaps expand.

These institutions change over time in response to world politics and economics, war, election outcomes, changes in technology, and innumerable other economic, psychological, political, and social factors. The effect of the competition among private interests and their use of the public sector may be better understood by observing recent events and studying the characteristics of natural resources and how they affect human behavior. Tracing how and why these institutions have changed over time implies a multidisciplinary and heuristic approach. However, this study is unbalanced, for it stresses the economist's approach. Since the stuff of economics is analyzing how resources, both natural and man-made, are allocated among alternative uses and evaluating how they should be used, this bias is not debilitating. Although economists normally assume that institutions are given and constant, a growing literature concerns how institutions affect resource allocation.

1

The purpose of this book is to pull together descriptive and theoretical material and to review economic theory and modeling techniques in a new way that makes this information comprehensible to those lacking a background in economics. The people who can benefit are public-sector policymakers and their advisers and those who affect and are affected by the institutions that control natural-resource development and use. This information will aid them in evaluating public policy and the techniques used to forecast its formation and effects from a broad perspective.

Resource allocation describes what goods and services are produced, how they are produced, and who consumes them. Economists classify allocation systems as market oriented or command oriented. In the market system, individual decisions are voluntary, and they determine both prices and resource allocation. In command systems, allocations are involuntary. The ownership, tax, and regulatory authority of the public sector is one such means of control. Most economists champion the market as a mechanism that works and should be relied on in most cases to allocate resources.

The fundamental paradigm describing how markets function is supply, demand, and the forces of market equilibrium. Supply reveals the behavior of producers in response to technological factors and various prices for their product and for the inputs they must purchase. Demand reveals the behavior of consumers in response to the prices of goods and services and anticipated income. Furthermore, individuals are owners of the elemental factors of production, which consist of their labor, and the services of land, natural resources, and man-made capital accumulated in the past. When consumer behavior (demand) and producer behavior (supply) are put together, a market clearing price arises at equilibrium, where the amount produced equals the amount demanded. Not only is each separate commodity market thought to approach an equilibrium price and quantity, but all markets taken together are believed simultaneously to approach equilibrium, and these equilibriums determine the allocation of all resources.

One major role of economists is to describe how markets operate individually and simultaneously and to identify the key factors that determine supply, demand, and equilibrium. Abstract or theoretical models are used to describe general properties, and empirical data are employed to quantify and to test for the predictive and explanatory accuracy of these models. Once this is accomplished, the effects of factors external or exogenous to the models may be simulated to observe how they are likely to effect market equilibrium and resource allocation.

A second role for economists is to specify which resource allocations are better and which are worse. The criterion that is most widely used as an objective is that the welfare of individuals should be maximized. This criterion can be used to specify the efficient use of resources. When efficiency is achieved, no other resource allocation results in a higher level of satisfaction of people's preferences for a given initial distribution of ownership in natural and man-made wealth and a legal system to enforce agreements and contracts. It can be shown that this efficient resource allocation corresponds to a situation in which the number of voluntary exchanges among owners, producers, and consumers is maximized. By implication, interference with exchange and voluntary behavior reduces economic efficiency. Since markets and negotiations over price, quantity, and quality are how trade and exchange take place, free and competitive markets in which no individual or organization acts in a way that influences market prices ensures an efficient resource allocation. This is the fountainhead of economists' faith in markets as a device to allocate resources.

Taxes affect the costs and rewards associated with exchanges and thereby indirectly regulate resource allocation. Government regulation and ownership directly affects resource allocation. Public policy may impede or aid markets in achieving efficiency. The heart of economic policy evaluation is to determine how taxes and regulation can be employed to enhance economic efficiency or, at a minimum, to minimize their distorting effects on market-determined resource allocation.

When an individual or an organization possesses sufficient market power to affect prices or when individuals or institutions directly affect another and an involuntary exchange takes place, markets are said to fail in achieving efficiency. In these situations, public policy can be used to affect resource allocation directly by regulation or indirectly in markets by taxes and fiscal measures designed to ensure that efficiency prevails. The standard textbook approach in evaluating public policy is to determine situations in which markets fail and to derive least-cost policies that minimize the loss of efficiency because of the failure. With this welfare-economics approach, public-policy effects on resource allocation and the extent to which it enhances or reduces efficiency can, in theory, be measured. How public policy is actually determined and what makes it change goes far beyond the abstract goal of resource efficiency because people singly and in organizations establish, enforce, and change public policy.

The tax and regulatory powers represent the power to coerce, and these powers result in reallocation of resources. They also affect the distribution of income and wealth and property rights to natural and man-made resources. Since these policies are established and enforced in the political and judicial environment, they themselves are the result of competition, exchange, and power. The overriding motive for private interests to influence public-sector ownership, tax, or regulatory policies is gains or losses of income and wealth. The perceived change in financial and social well-being can be used to explain why people act. The methods used and the induced changes in the ownership and control of natural-resource ownership and income is what we analyze here.

The devices and institutions employed in this competition are not always straightforward or clearly discernible. A transparent grab for the prize does not always work, particularly when the public sector is involved. The successful players know that it is more productive to claim that the public interest is at stake and that the recommended policy will aid society or some large segment in it. The supporting private interests, nevertheless, design the policy primarily to benefit themselves, but often in an obtuse or even deceitful way. They plan that those who lose because of the policy will be unaware of what is happening. This is accomplished in two ways. First, the losers should be a large, diffused group in which none suffers great losses. The second tactic is to conceal the desired effect through obfuscation, accomplished by means of public claims to rightness and social responsibility, private lobbying with elected officials and bureaucrats, and designing the policy so that its superficial and apparent effects are to benefit a large segment of society. The result is complex and circuitous legislative and administrative regulatory policy.

Thus the beneficiaries of public policy are frequently small in number and their gains are great. Consequently these interests have an incentive to organize and to expend time and resources to obtain enactment of the desired policies. This means both distributing some of the benefits to others whose aid may be helpful in the competition and spending on resources that will make for more-effective lobbying, including campaign contributions and occasionally direct payments and bribes to decision makers. These activities use up resources that might otherwise be spent in more-productive activities. In the process of securing gains, this public-sector coercion reallocates resources, and the distortion produces losses in welfare.

Up to this point, this discussion could apply to any commodity or resource that is positively or negatively valued by producers and consumers. However, natural-resource wealth and income are particularly susceptible to the effects of taxation and regulation. The most important is that nearly all natural resources are immobile, and this fixity eliminates the most-effective means at owners' disposal to prevent losses by moving to a different legal jurisdiction. A second reason is that owners of natural resources and extractive firms have experienced enormous increases in wealth since 1973, which stands as an attractive target for those wishing to share and use the public sector as their instrument in altering the income and wealth distribution established in prevailing institutions. Thus public policy affects the allocation of resources among competing uses and, with it, economic efficiency and the distribution of income.

The discussion thus far has presented a possible interpretation of the history of natural-resource ownership and control, and it forecasts continuous competition among consumers, resource owners, extractive firms, and federal and state governments over resource-based wealth. The outcomes from this competition, aside from exacerbating interjurisdictional conflicts, are uncertain. Thus there are alternative futures whose implications need to be understood. Those dealing directly as interested parties and public policymakers and indirectly as observers and analysts require some guides in order to analyze these alternatives.

The basic paradigm of economics is supply, demand, and market equilibrium. The preferences of consumers are expressed in a demand function, which indicates the quantities they are willing to purchase at various prices and how other variables, including income and the prices of other commodities, affect this relationship. A demand function may be specified for any commodity; examples include safety and reduction of risk, views and environmental aesthetics, the value of knowing that certain irreplaceable natural wonders such as the Grand Canyon and Yellowstone Park exist, and a value on love and other personal attachments. The supply function reveals the quantities of a commodity people are willing to produce or give up at various prices. These include commodities that are part of the natural or man-made endowment. The cost of alternatives and personal preferences determines the characteristics of the supply relationship and commodities that are produced, and the cost of the next-best alternative that is not produced determines the characteristics of the supply relationship. Both supply and demand reveal opportunity cost in monetary terms, for underlying the concepts is the notion of a trade-off: having more of one thing requires that something must be given up.

A market that allocates resources efficiently ensures that no opportunities for a resource that would produce goods and services that are more highly valued is bypassed. However, market failures frustrate this goal and may require coerced intervention by the public sector. The method conventionally used to verify that government intervention enhances efficiency is called *cost-benefit analysis*. With this technique, individual and collective preferences and willingness to pay that are not revealed by private markets and those costs that are not reflected in price due to market failure are estimated so that total social costs and benefits of alternatives can be quantified. If social benefits exceed social costs and the free market fails to provide for the optimal amount of a commodity, direct government production or incentives to the private sector can be used to achieve resource efficiency. To do this, the policymaker not only needs to know that private markets fail and the cost of that failure in terms of misapplied resources but how direct and indirect intervention will affect private markets. Cost-benefit analysis requires an understanding of how markets function. Quantified economic models that are sensitive to changes in public policy are necessary in order to predict the responses to public policy and to evaluate the need for and effectiveness of alternative public policies, including the option of doing nothing.

Economic model building entails two interrelated tasks. The first is theoretical: defining producers and consumer behavior and deriving specific economic and physical relationships that describe this behavior. The purpose of the theoretical model is to define the problem being analyzed clearly and to deduce certain hypotheses and explanations that can be tested empirically. The second task is to carry out empirical testing and estimation. If the theoretical hypotheses stand up, the model is accepted, and a policymaker may have some confidence in it. If the model performs poorly, it should be rejected.

One of the difficulties in working with models is that complex problems are not easily reduced to understandable and manageable dimensions. In trying to resolve this problem, one school of thought holds that the integrity and rigor of the theoretical model is paramount; among these are the economists and pure scientists. In order to achieve this end, pure models are necessarily highly simplified and abstract, which makes their operation and interactions clearly understandable and interpretable. The drawback with this pure approach is that the problem must be narrowly defined and the underlying assumptions highly restrictive and unrealistic, thus limiting the ability of the models to analyze complex policies and issues. The second school of thought deviates from traditional pure models by incorporating relationships and hypotheses from various disciplines and striving to use all of the information from empirical data. These models tend to entail many relationships whose interactions cannot be solved analytically and may not be understood a priori. Computer simulations of alternative scenarios using the model are made to produce outcomes that are interpreted for policy implications. The drawback to this approach is that it is difficult to discern what causes the predicted outcomes, which are sometimes counterintuitive. Exercises of simulating past events with models have revealed gross inaccuracies. Although the difference between theoretically based models and empirically based simulation models is not always distinct, it is the basis of much discord and mistrust among model builders and a contributing factor to the misunderstandings among model users.

A related factor that results in the misinterpretation and misapplication of economic models is the inadequate or, more often, nonexistent communication and understanding between model builder and user. The user must understand the basic premises upon which the model is built, its key assumptions and limitations, and the techniques used to estimate it empirically. Another cause of misunderstanding between builder and user is the purpose of a model. Model users generally fall into two classes: those who want to predict and those who wish to conduct policy analysis. Model builders are generally interested in the process of constructing the model and in its acceptability within their discipline more than in its use. This divergence creates a gulf that is unlikely ever to be removed; at best the resulting misconceptions can be reduced.

The hypothesis developed in this book is that conflicts among resource owners, consumers, and a myriad of special-interest groups that use government power to affect natural-resource ownership, revenues, and control will continue to escalate despite the avowed intention of the federal government to deregulate and to allow private markets to function relatively unhindered. This forecast is based on two observations. The first is that the quantity and quality of renewable and nonrenewable natural-resource reserves are diminishing, and thus market prices for privately and publicly owned natural resources are rising or are expected to rise. The public's awareness of both diminishing reserves and rising prices has changed its expectations and has made each special-interest group more willing to fight for its perceived share of natural-resource-based wealth and benefits. The second reason is that large-scale changes in international and national institutional arrangements have taken place that are shifting the focus of regulatory and tax policy to the subnational level of government. This has been caused in part by the pullback on the federal level and in part by the growing aggressiveness at the state and local levels.

Resource-based conflicts take on many guises, ranging from disputes over legal ownership to complex regulations and tax codes that in effect transfer control of resource development and ownership of resource revenues to the public sector, which then redistributes them by lowering other taxes and various public-expenditure and subsidy programs. Adopting an inclusive view of the resource-competition hypothesis requires definitions of what natural resources and their ownership entails and a brief review of past-resource-ownership institutions and policies. Legal ownership of natural resources is vested with government, individuals, and other private entities (trusts, partnerships, and corporations). Privately owned natural resources are restricted to those individuals who are able to monitor and control them. The resources include land, fuels, and nonfuel mineral rights and certain rights to surface and groundwater. Public ownership of natural resources includes these rights, as well as the stewardship of the natural environment, which is not owned in the strict legal sense. Its components include navigable waterways, fisheries, wildlife species stocks, the atmosphere, and what might be more encompassingly called the ecosystem. These natural resources are the responsibility of society at large and as such are delegated to government entities. Public authorities are responsible for protecting the health, safety, and welfare of society under the police powers of the state. This implies that government is granted a portion of the bundle of rights making up private property.

Public policy does not evolve spontaneously to serve the hypothetical but undefinable public interest. Rather it is determined by the interplay of special interests, elected officials, and bureaucrats. Bureaucrats are the managers of publicly owned resources. They exercise control by means of creating and disseminating information and administering legislative man-

dates that grant varying degrees of discretion. Many observers have noted
that the public sector is frequently ineffective in managing the natural
resources under its ownership, much less carrying out its stewardship and
police-power responsibilities in regulating the entire spectrum of natural
resources.

Market-oriented economists point out that publicly owned natural
resources are often ineffectively managed because government agencies are
assigned multiple goals that are ambiguously defined or defined too narrowly, moreover, their performance is not monitored or regulated. One way
to mitigate these conflicts and inefficiencies is to have the public sector emu-
late the private sector. For example, Baden and Stroup of Montana State
University (1981) have proposed that environmental groups such as the
National Audubon Society, the Sierra Club, and the Wilderness Society
acquire legal title to large tracts of government wilderness lands. These
economists are concerned that in the political climate of the 1980s, "environmental concerns will be swept away in a rush to supply the U.S. with
vital resources." Thus government management objectives may become
dominated by short-run considerations. Baden and Stroup cite the example
of the Audubon Society's Rainey Wildlife Sanctuary where wildlife thrives,
yet oil wells on the site supply the society with nearly $1 million in annual
revenues. They maintain that this private ownership may be more efficient
than public ownership because the constituencies and goals of private
groups are more clearly defined.

Nevertheless there are valid reasons to believe that the private sector
fails to use natural resources effectively, and the power of the state is necessary to ensure that goals of economic efficiency and equity are achieved.
This basis for this position is distinction made by economists between private and public commodities. The economist's definition of a private good
is one whose possession, use, and control affect only that owner and others
who voluntarily agree to be so affected. Under the narrowest definition,
when one person consumes a private good, it precludes others from doing
so, whereas public goods can be consumed by one or more persons without
diminishing the ability of others to enjoy them. Few commodities fit this
polar (public-private) definition. Although it is relatively easy to think of
purely private goods, such as eating ice cream at home, examples of purely
public goods are less obvious. The usual textbook example is national
defense, for no matter how much one person is protected and enjoys it, her
consumption has no effect on any other person's consumption, and it is
impossible to prevent other people from consuming the security it provides.
Most goods and services supplied by the private and public sectors, however, display both private- and public-good attributes. Garbage pickup service is an example. Each individual receives the purely private benefit of
trash removal, and the entire municipal population benefits as well because

of the associated control over vermin and insect populations and the reduction in potentially bothersome smells, all of which are public goods. It is also a service that is supplied to either the public or private sector, but its public-good attributes mean that regulations exist in most jurisdictions that these services be available and used.

Ownership gives one the legal title and right to possess, whereas the ability to exploit, sell, develop, or otherwise control natural resources or other commodities is only partially vested with legal owners. Legal and social institutions and economic realities grant others various degrees of control, which taken together with ownership rights are called a *bundle of rights.* Government policies enacted under its police powers can take away, modify, or transfer the bundle of property rights. Direct regulatory involvement is one method; examples include zoning and siting reviews and requirements, building and operating permits, licenses, health codes, and air- and water-emissions controls for pollutants. Government fiscal policy consists of both receipts (taxes and fees) and expenditures. It indirectly affects the bundle of property rights. Taxes place a fiscal burden on persons or property, alter prices, and affect how much is produced and consumed. Government expenditures on roads, parks, and utilities are amenities that generally increase the value and the bundle of rights of landownership nearby or in the jurisdiction because they make real property more accessible, developable, and the area a more desirable place to live and work.

The legal distinction between public and private ownership becomes blurred when the entire bundle of rights associated with real property and natural resources is considered. The economic definition of public and private goods is clear but becomes muddied when applied because many commodities simultaneously display characteristics of both public and private goods, and this is irrespective of who holds legal title. The word *ownership* is used to denote portions of the bundle of property rights, and *public* and *private goods* are used to refer to their economic definition.

This explanation of public and private goods is deficient, however, because it does not specify key characteristics. Excluding people from consuming public goods is impossible or at best difficult and expensive, whereas use and access to private goods is controlled by their owners, although the legal ownership of the bundle of rights may be divided among different private individuals and the state. Furthermore, consumption of a public good is involuntary, whereas consumption and exchange of private goods is entirely voluntary. The first difference makes it clear why use and access to surface water and groundwater and the air are primarily but not exclusively a public good. It would be impossible or extremely costly to prevent people from navigating on rivers and bodies of water or from using the environment. Groundwaters are hydrologically interconnected so that control of one well or the land surface is not sufficient to preclude others from pumping from an aquifer at another location. This is also true of mineral rights to oil and gas-bearing subsurface strata, and mining from seawater for the material is somewhat mobile in situ and can be transferred from one location to another. However, rights to hardrock and other minerals that are stationary in the earth's crust and mining from the seabed are almost exclusively private goods because exclusion and control are possible.

A key attribute of a public good is its involuntary consumption. This is an implication of the definition of a public good and the attribute of no exclusion. When an owner is unable to control use and consumption by others, that aspect of the good is public and can be used by others without the owner's permission. This is an involuntary transfer. With a purely public good such as national defense, consumption by additional individuals in no way hinders consumption by others; also everyone consumes the same amount, although they may value it differently. It is said of a pure public good that if additional people consume it, there is no additional cost. With impure public goods (mixed public- and private-good characteristics), additional parties may consume the impure good but at a cost, for at some point congestion takes place. Take a swimming pool as an example. Although it is relatively easy and cheap to exclude people, making the pool a private good, additional individuals may be allowed to use it without diminishing the consumption of those who are already in the water and may even increase it. However, beyond a certain number of users, the pool becomes crowded, which means that as additional swimmers are allowed in, the satisfaction and consumption of others may diminish. The same is true of hiking and wilderness areas on publicly or privately owned land, but in this case it is harder to exclude users; thus the mix of private- and public-good attributes is different.

These examples illustrate that public goods are not necessarily provided only by the public sector, although most government activities display both private- and public-good attributes. The involuntary-consumption aspect of public goods depends on the inability to exclude people from using and consuming them, for the corollary is that people are forced to consume the public good.

The nadir of involuntary consumption is polluted air, which is more appropriately labeled a "public bad." There is no way to avoid consuming it, save moving to a cleaner environment or entering into voluntary agreements with others to reduce airborne emissions, which would in turn reduce smog. Although this kind of voluntary arrangement is not easily made, if concluded it would turn the involuntary public-good characteristic into a private good to the extent that emissions of pollutants were reduced after voluntary negotiations.

The pollution example is one of a mixed public and private good. A major source of air pollution is exhaust emissions from automobiles. The transportation services of the privately owned automobile are private goods. However, the bundle of rights associated with using an automobile is restricted by traffic laws, availability of highways, and other factors. Further, this commodity produces a public bad by exhaust emissions. This partial public bad is consumed involuntarily by others; the public portion is called an *externality* by economists. Externalities are defined as an involuntary exchange where third parties are affected but do not directly enter negotiations. Air-, water-, and land-pollution externalities associated with the extraction, processing, and consumption of natural resources are believed by many to be pervasive. The example of air pollution originating from the combustion of natural gas, oil, gasoline, and coal is an obvious one.

It can be argued that the externality and public-good aspects of certain activities are accounted for in private negotiations among the affected parties. However, reaching voluntary agreements and complying with them becomes more unlikely as the publicness of an activity increases. A large contingent of economists maintains that externalities stemming from resource extraction are particularly ill suited to being negotiated privately and that direct and indirect government intervention is required.

A brief history of the ownership of the bundle of rights associated with natural resources is a prerequisite to the hypothesis developed in this book. When the European colonists arrived in the New World, they were confronted with virgin resources on an unimaginable scale. A primary motivation for the long and risky sea voyages and venturing forth into unknown lands was to discover and claim wealth. The colonists hoped to discover undeveloped natural wealth (in many cases to steal developed wealth from established cultures—for example, the pillaging of the Aztec and Peruvian gold) and to transport it to European markets. This exploitation motive was pursued both individually and collectively by means of active support and direct subsidization by home governments. During the sixteenth through the mid-twentieth centuries, colonization occurred in nearly all non-European portions of the globe. In retrospect, it is possible to say that some of these adventures were more successful in capturing wealth and in establishing Western culture and stable governments than others. The twentieth-century reaction of anti-imperialism and nationalism has resulted in wars and other social and private costs.

In the initial stages of colonization, the costs of securing control over natural resources were almost exclusively those of discovery and excluding other adventurers. Since these activities were carried out under the auspices of the state and in many cases were subsidized by European governments, title and ownership was taken in the name of government. Mercantile licenses and land grants were made to individuals at the pleasure of these governments. Thus from the earliest colonies, the proceeds from natural-resource exploitation were shared by monarchies and their agents by means of taxes, licenses, and outright ownership and to a smaller extent directly by private individuals.

Discovery of natural resources and the technology to exploit and use them determined the extent of the natural endowment, and these conditions were changing rapidly over the years. Resource-rich colonies would supply raw materials to the home country and become markets for finished products. The natural-resource wealth was exploited, often ruthlessly and with respect to the shortest time frame, and financial and man-made capital and labor were imported to the colonies to make this possible. The United States was fortunate enough to secure early political freedom (including release from foreign ownership), and Canada, Australia, and New Zealand were granted growing political and economic freedoms. Regardless of the legal forms of political and economic freedom, policymakers realized that the trade flows of exchanging natural resources for European finished goods and capital would have to continue. Leaders also realized that the natural wealth was beneficial only to the extent that it was exploited. To accomplish this, they sought to transfer this wealth as rapidly as possible to private hands. Individuals seeking their own best interests could convert natural resources into marketable products and produce the associated income flows faster than alternative development methods.

The environmental policy of the eighteenth and nineteenth centuries in the United States was to exploit the country's natural bounty. Land and mineral rights were given (land under the various Homestead Acts and other transfer programs and minerals under claimstaking and the General Mining Law) to those who would develop and exploit them. Because the stages of discovery, development, and exploitation were turned over to the private sector, the income flows from natural resources stayed within this sector, with only insignificant amounts siphoned into the public sector in the form of royalties, sales revenues, and taxes. Regulations regarding when, how to, and how much exploitation could take place were nonexistent or minimal. The rule of the marketplace was relatively unfettered, and the extent of markets expanded dramatically as new lands were settled and transformed into a rich agricultural base, and minerals and timber resources were discovered and extracted. Capital to support these activities continued to flow from the European continent. The New World developers became adept at selling ownership in land and natural resources in order to raise capital. In many instances, however, this ownership failed to include control and benefits from the exploitation, as in the case of selling and reselling ownership in the vast ranches and mineral rights in the western United States where clear title and control was never delivered. Canals, railroads, and other large-scale projects were financed with bonds and other financial instruments sold in Europe. When financial collapses occurred, as they often did, the resource and investment remained because it was immobile.

Western territories were managed by the federal government, with the primary motive to secure these regions from control by Indian populations and to encourage transfer to private ownership. Maintaining federal control ensured that the transfer took place and that the West remained subservient to the national government, which was dominated by the populous eastern states. Conditions, such as control of native population and the existence of "responsible" political leadership, were imposed before the territories were admitted as states, many designed to ensure this subservient status. The growth of the federal budget and federal regulatory agencies during the nineteenth and twentieth centuries ensured that the relationship would continue as it had in the past.

During this period, however, a countermovement decrying the needless destruction and overly ruthless exploitation of natural resources began to form. It originated in the 1890s under the leadership of John Muir and other well-known conservationists. In 1893 President Benjamin Harrison decreed that 13 million acres be placed under federal protection, and William McKinley added 21.4 million acres to that total. In the early part of the twentieth century, the movement grew, in large part due to the political and economic support of the gun-making and ammunition industries whose interests were to preserve game and wildlife so that it was available to sportsmen and so there would be a market for their products. The movement, supported by Theodore Roosevelt, succeeded in preserving some of the unique natural scenic wonders, under the auspices of the national park system, from being ravaged by extractive activities. Concerns were also raised about the exhaustibility of oil and certain nonfuel minerals, and these concerns were translated into federal restrictions on leasing (the Mineral Leasing Act of 1920) and regulation of publicly owned natural resources. Perhaps the importance of the conservation movement was that it was another indication that Americans in the late nineteenth and twentieth centuries were beginning to question their faith in relying so heavily on unrestricted private markets.

The financial and resource-extraction-related excesses and destruction lent additional support to those who questioned unfettered markets. Antitrust legislation, labor laws, and bank and securities regulations were all responses to the distrust. With the onset of the Great Depression of the 1930s, distrust of economic markets turned to temporary abhorrence. The response was massive intervention by the federal government in fiscal affairs, regulatory activities, and income redistribution. The details of these actions need not be repeated here, but the large-scale government intervention and its ensuing regulation of the economy during World War II have left a legacy that has given the political conservatives decades of struggle.

Distrust of market forces was reemphasized and expanded during the ecology and environmental movements of the last half of the 1960s and 1970s. The first signs of the destructive impact of humans on the ecosystem were popularized by Rachel Carson in *Silent Spring*. Air- and water-pollution problems in urban areas and in suburban and rural areas near industrial sites caused by pesticides and herbicides, industry, electric-power generation facilities, and dumps (including potential risks of spills and accidents of toxic and nuclear materials) created an awareness of how industrial, agricultural, and consumption activities affect the environment. The Clean Air Act and Clean Water Act of 1970, their subsequent amendments and extensive implementation regulations, and associated legislation and judicial interpretations represent direct control of private markets on a massive scale. Economists would interpret these regulations as an effort to correct for environmental externalities associated with using the land, air, and water as a free dumping place for by-products of production and consumption. This movement also made the public at large aware that natural resources encompass the natural endowment of minerals, timber, and fish, which are used directly by humans, as well as the atmosphere, hydrological, and ecosystems, which support all life.

Concerns of the environmentalists regarding long-run effects of population growth, resource extraction, and pollution on people and the earth's ecosystems were produced by simulations of likely future implications of population and economic growth. The most acclaimed efforts were made by Meadows et al. (1972) and Forrester (1971) of MIT who projected ecological disaster and collapse of the system's ability to support an overpopulated earth burdened by exhausted nonrenewable resources and severe pollution. The public awareness of these and other gloomy forecasts were followed by the 1973 Middle East war, the oil embargo, and the dramatic oil-price increases of 1973–1974 and in the aftermath of the Iranian revolution. (Between 1973 and 1979, the world price of a barrel of oil, unadjusted for inflation, rose from less than two dollars to over thirty-six dollars.) The oil-price increases served to cause and exacerbate the 1974–1975 worldwide recession and to underpin unprecedented continuous inflation. During this period, there were speculation and enormous price increases, followed by instability first in competing fuels—coal, and natural gas—next in timber and nonfuels minerals, followed by speculation in gold and silver as hedges against inflation, and finally with strategic materials (chromium, cobalt, and other materials). This instability made it appear to many that private markets could not be trusted to establish prices and allocate resources. The pessimistic forecasts of the modelers coupled with the Organization of Petroleum Exporting Countries (OPEC) oil cartel, which had disrupted private markets and government economic policies throughout the world, provided additional impetus to those factions, which were predisposed to distrust the operation of markets and the evidence convinced others.

President Nixon had imposed price and wage controls on the economy in mid-1971 in order to control inflation. In 1974 price controls were removed from all commodities except for oil and natural gas. The effect of domestic price regulation was to transfer income to consumers in the form of lower prices for domestic oil and gas by restricting owners' and producers' bundle of rights by forced subsidized prices. It was clear, however, that the benefits would be short-lived because domestic production fell as a result and imports increased. Historical accident, academic modelers, unstable markets, and the conservation and environmental movements all contributed to distrust of private markets. The political response was direct regulation and indirect regulation by taxation.

The combined effects of environmental, land-use, health, and other regulations requiring environmental impact and siting studies and expenditures for air- and water-pollution-control devices, health and safety techniques, land reclamation after timbering and mining, and the associated license fees caused a slowdown in exploration and development activities, lengthened development times of projects, and increased costs because of regulatory delays, productivity declines, and increased fees and taxes. Price regulations on domestic oil and natural gas imposed additional burdens, which brought exploration of new reserves to a near standstill.

Past exploration activity, however, had produced a stock of known reserves that could be extracted at relatively low costs because capital expenditures to find and develop them had been made in the past. Once an investment is made, its owner will use it as long as revenues exceed the actual outlays required to continue using it. Investment in extracting nonrenewable resources differs in that depletion (analogous in certain respects to depreciation for other capital investments) is determined entirely at the behest of the owner, whereas depreciation of man-made capital stocks is determined primarily by the passing of time (obsolesence) and, to a lesser degree, by actual use. Consequently the owner of a natural resource evaluates the profitability of current extraction vis-a-vis future extraction. The decision depends in large part on expectations of future prices and costs. Because the future is uncertain and therefore introduces additional risk and because most businesses have borrowed to make past capital investment, and this requires a cash flow to service debt, the prevailing bias is to produce as long as extraction creates a positive cash flow (sales revenues minus required cash outlays). Because a developed stock of nonrenewable resources existed, domestic production of fuels continued, albeit at an ever-declining rate. The United States shifted from a coal-based to an oil-based economy in 1949. Concurrently the international oil companies found immense reserves in the Middle East that could be extracted at costs far below those prevailing domestically. The United States became a net oil importer in 1948. It took a number of years to realize that Nixon's Project Independence (1974) coupled with regulated price was totally ineffective and that dependence on foreign oil seemed destined to continue to grow.

After years of lobbying, oil prices were allowed a phased deregulation in 1980, to be fully deregulated by President Reagan in 1981, and in 1977 natural gas started its path toward deregulation. The immediate impact on natural-gas prices was moderate because the base-regulated price, which increases commensurately with inflation, was established before the 1979 OPEC oil-price increase. The effect on oil prices at the consumer level was also moderate because by 1980 nearly half of U.S. consumption was imported and 1981 arrived with a temporary world oil glut. However, domestic wellhead prices increased for high-cost deregulated natural gas and for newly discovered deregulated oil sources. The 1980 windfall-profits tax (due to expire in 1987) takes a bulk of the profits created by deregulation from established fields; thus its burdens on newly discovered oil are light. Further state and local severance taxes are deductible from the tax (which in effect subsidizes these revenues), and royalties paid to state and local governments and Indian tribes are exempt from it. These provisions and higher market prices have created a windfall in state resource revenues. The intent of the federal government's policy in the 1980s of accelerated leasing of coastal offshore oil and gas tracts and onshore coal lands in the western states and deregulation of prices coupled with lowered tax rates on new discoveries was to encourage domestic exploration and development. These policies had some effect, at least initially.

In 1979 natural-gas discoveries exceed consumption for the first time in ten years. Exploration and development of fuels accelerated rapidly, and undervalued known reserves were recognized on Wall Street as evidenced by dramatic acquisitions and takeovers in 1980 and 1981. The Fuel Use and Implementation Act of 1980 impels electric utilities and certain industries to convert to steam coal. However, federal policy has impediments to coal use—primarily regulations pertaining to occupational health, reclamation of strip-mined land, and environmental controls on coal burning—which have reduced miners' productivity. Also the costs of mining and using coal have increased. Nevertheless, rising petroleum prices and projections of growing coal demand, particularly low sulfur, strip-mined western coal whose work force is not controlled by the United States Mine Workers, has created optimistic projections regarding future coal use and prices, particularly in the West. Although excess capacity burdened the domestic coal industry throughout the 1970s, western coal output expanded continuously.

In some areas, this growth has not been unconditionally welcomed. Western coal development has created boom towns that demonstrate much of the instability, transience, and fiscal problems of past resource-related booms. Coal strip mining, transportation, and processing for domestic electricity and export have produced undesirable social and environmental externalities, which western state residents believe they should be compensated for. In 1975 Montana enacted a 30 percent maximum severance tax on coal, and five other western states have followed Montana's lead by increasing coal taxes. Deregulation of oil and natural-gas prices and tax laws that have encouraged state taxation have created a tax windfall for producing states, reversing the previous price regulations and other controls that had shifted income from producing to consuming states. The effect of these changes has been to shift implicit income transfers created by regulation and explicit tax and regulatory powers from federal auspices that benefited consuming states to state hands that have benefited resource-rich state residents.

The western state policymakers realize that the fiscal bonanza from oil and natural-gas production will be short-lived because of diminishing resource quality and the increasing cost of discovery and development. Foreign sources, alternative technologies, and conservation mean that economic exhaustion of U.S. oil will most likely occur by the end of the century. Gas will be next, and economically recoverable coal reserves will eventually be depleted. Farsighted leadership realizes that this natural-resource wealth is valuable, and its extraction creates jobs and indirect economic activity for the entire region. At some point in the future, the resource and its associated tax revenue and economic base will no longer exist. Consequently states took steps to ensure that some of the exhaustible natural-resource wealth was converted into financial wealth that would be held in trust for future state residents. In order to accomplish these ends, the political realists know that current residents must be compensated as well, and this was carried out by state subsidies and aid to energy-impacted areas and resource-tax revenue-based reductions in personal and corporate income taxes. The late 1970s and 1980–1981 period may be a precursor of efforts among resource-rich states to capture ever-larger portions of resource revenues from diminishing natural capital stock, converting these to financial capital that can be preserved and grow through prudent investment so that future residents may benefit from this original resource endowment.

Thus the ownership and control of natural-resource wealth has come full circle in North America. Originally the European colonists seized these resources for their various governments as though they were free goods and sought to exploit the renewable (agriculture, timber, hunting) and nonrenewable natural wealth as rapidly as possible. Colonial and subsequent independent governments saw the wisdom of transferring resource ownership to private hands and providing supportive tax laws and a regulatory environment in order to encourage development and economic growth. Until the advent of modern technology and increasing real resource prices, only those resources that could be exploited and transported most cheaply were depleted. While fur-bearing animals were reduced nearly to extinction, for example, the bulk of the resource base was left virtually intact until the late nineteenth century. A diminishing low-cost resource base, extractive excesses, and environmental externalities coupled with a proconsumer bias culminated in a mid-twentieth-century political climate that produced regulations on price, development, and harmful by-product emissions. These returned much control from the private sector back to the national government. In the 1970s, price and other deregulation, resource scarcity (increasing costs and prices), and a national goal of reducing dependence on foreign sources resulted in a transfer of control and development (including revenues) back to private hands. The resulting vacuum allowed state governments to pursue a larger share of resource revenues and control over development and exploitation. In this process, the resource-rich western states and Canadian provinces are evolving out of their politically and economically subservient roles as suppliers of cheap resources to exercising their tax and regulatory muscle. They are also planning to wean themselves from economies based on exporting natural-resource wealth by creating private and public financial wealth for financing these and other projects in an effort to retain and control ever-larger shares of national wealth. This socialization of resource revenues and wealth entails redistributing some benefits immediately to their constituencies and retaining some for future generations.

Details of how institutions and property rights affecting oil and natural-gas prices and development in the United States and Canada have changed recently are provided in chapter 2. The recent events surrounding taxation and regulation of energy resources in the United States and Canada are described and interpreted in the framework of the private-interest competition over natural-resource income and wealth. The contrasts between the two countries are revealing in that one may be viewed as a precursor of events in the other. In chapter 3, the economic literature concerning public and collective choice is fit into the hypotheses of natural-resource competition. Further, the nature of income and wealth associated with natural-resource property rights is described in detail, and their unique susceptibility to tax and regulatory powers is developed. This leads to theoretic models of public choice. In one model, no legal or institutional barriers to government power are considered. In the second, the limitations and powers of federal, state, and local government jurisdictions are assumed to exist. These institutions impose constraints, and their effect on how interest groups use public power for private purposes is analyzed. Chapters 4 and 5 explain what economic models can accomplish, when they should be used, and how to use them. It is important for policy analysts to understand the limitations and capabilities of models so that they may interpret the predictions made from models and determine how suitable they are for simulating the effects of policy and evaluating these effects.

In this book, I defend no particular policy position and therefore make no conclusions. However, it can be surmised that the general course of deregulation of energy resources and prices and reduction in other distorting taxes and regulations is a correct one. The political risks are that the effect of more-efficient resource use, such as conservation, and enhanced incentives to search for and discover new reserves takes time. Also changes in public policy create uncertain situations, which various interest groups attempt to exploit for their own benefit. State and local government tax and regulatory institutions will continue to play a significant role in this process, and their primary goal of maximizing benefits for special interests and jurisdiction residents is predictable. The policy question facing the national government becomes, At what point do regional self-interests conflict sufficiently with national resource policy that new limitations on subnational governments become necessary?

There are several macroeconomic goals conventionally prescribed for national government: full employment, economic growth, price stability, and a socially fair distribution of income and wealth. The economic-efficiency criterion is implicit in the first three of these goals, and tax and regulatory policies at all levels of government may be used to promote all goals. In order for analysts and policymakers to ascertain how seriously national policy and economic goals may be interfered with by private interests and other units of government, they need quantifiable information. Regretably there is little information about the extent to which tax and regulatory policies distort the allocation of natural resources, particularly at the subnational level, and comprehensive studies of who benefits and who loses from these policies are even scarcer. Proposals to limit state severance-tax rates, design of changes in the oil windfall tax and phased deregulation of natural gas, and changing the distribution of mineral royalties paid to the federal government would alter the economic distortions and the income redistribution in uncertain degrees.

Tax and regulatory-related distortions in resource allocation and effects on the distribution of income and wealth are interdependent, with the sole exception being when a policy leaves resource allocation undisturbed and affects only prices. However, in all other cases, public policy affects how, when, and where natural resources are extracted and used. Although a policy may directly affect use of a particular resource in one jurisdiction or in one use, the repercussions cascade and stimulate or inhibit the development of resources in other jurisdictions, affecting the use of substitute commodities and inputs into production, as well as the technology of those processes. These changes in the location, technology, and timing of resource discovery, development, and use may reduce the output of the economy, its economic efficiency, and affect its ability to satisfy human wants. Welfare economics is capable of measuring the dollar value of these losses if more information were available. Furthermore, changes in resource allocation mean that markets are affected and cause prices to change. These indicate how the consumer (uses of income) and owners of resources, firms, and purchased inputs (sources of income) are affected and thus how the value of their real income and wealth is altered. In order for policymakers to make informed judgments, they have less need to know the immediate effects of these policies, although these are the aspects that are most frequently emphasized in public debate. They have a greater need to understand the ultimate effects after markets have adjusted and repercussions have been internalized. However, resource allocation takes time, and so it is understandable why elected officials concentrate on the initial and superficial impacts. Elections occur all too frequently for the incumbent, and consequently this makes politicians' time horizons short. Additionally the ultimate repercussions of policy are often circuitous and difficult to predict a priori or to analyze ex post. It is easier and more understandable to assert what a policy will do than to anticipate carefully both immediate and longer-term effects. From the political standpoint, it is preferable to have more people believe that they will benefit and to deceive those who will be losers.

An essential factor that determines how markets have responded to regulatory and tax changes is time. Resource allocation and income distribution effects change over time because past investments made by extractive firms constrain present and future managerial decisions. The immediate effect of an altered regulatory or tax environment occurs in management decisions for previously developed sites. The decision maker can vary the rate of extraction and the ore cutoff grade (the lowest-quality ore which is extracted) within the bounds established by the local geology and the technology embodied in plant and equipment. At the limit, a previously operating unit can be shut down or opened up.

Over a longer time span, existing equipment depreciates, and resource exhaustion occurs at developed sites. Management decision making determines the location, technology, and extent of new investment. As investment occurs, far larger adjustments occur in resource allocation, and these alter the degree of resource distortion and redistribution of income. On a grander scale, regional shifts in income and wealth and, more specifically, government's share may have greater repercussions. These include increasing the level and quality of government services, reducing other taxes (because of Alaska's oil tax and royalty income, noncorporate taxes have been nearly eliminated), and encouraging industries not based on natural resources to locate in resource-rich jurisdictions. Low taxes and superior government services attract both people and industries, and other indirect or direct subsidies to industry attract capital and jobs. When the high-wage-paying industries migrate, per-capita incomes rise, which in turn attracts job seekers. Induced changes in location may entail allocation distortions and may alter the geographical distribution of income and wealth. This possibility is one of the major criticisms of state energy severance-tax policy made by representatives of consuming states. Beyond assertions and posturing, little is known about the magnitude of these various distortions or the income redistribution caused by the regulatory and tax-induced market adjustments that occur over time. However, the literature surveyed and the economic analysis described throughout this book supports several qualitative implications.

The critical role that time plays in the market-adjustment process must be recognized. Short-run responses to regulatory and tax-policy changes are constrained by the human inertia of detecting the implication of changes, making decisions and implementing them, and by the remaining life of investments made under the previous circumstances. This implies that taxes and regulation initially may be effective in capturing and redistributing natural-resource-based revenues. However, as investment and other decisions are made and adjustments implemented, these policies will be less effective. Furthermore, not only will the policies be mitigated, but gains may be dissipated as new institutions arise. On the other hand, the initial magnitude of resource distortions will grow as adjustments occur; this is most true for the induced migration of people and capital. These dynamic factors lead to the conclusion that the national government should concern itself primarily with the longer-range distortions than with the shorter-range income-redistribution effects as the basis for policymaking.

Furthermore the federal tax and regulatory policies of the past fifty years have induced their own set of distortions, which need to be reduced. As these changes occur, such as deregulation of energy prices and allocation, simultaneous steps should be taken so that subnational governments are not used in ways that frustrate moves to more-efficient resource use. However, more needs to be known about resource markets before major policy changes are made. The earlier transition in the twentieth century to low-entropy, low-cost energy of oil and natural gas permitted unprecedented economic growth. The backward transition to less-efficient and dirty coal and the high cost of discovery and recovery of oil and natural gas will be difficult and vulnerable to critics of the market-oriented resource-allocation system. Wise government policies can reduce impediments to the transition and pave the way for the ultimate transition to renewable-energy resources and to new technologies.

# 2

# Case Studies of Energy Tax and Regulatory Policies in the United States and Canada

The hypothesis that the income from the extraction and processing of natural resources is particularly vulnerable to being singled out and diverted through government tax and regulatory activities is central to this book. Because natural resources are nonuniformly distributed and fixed but their consumption is determined largely by the geographic distribution of population; regional competition over the control and income from these resources is expected. The events surrounding the Middle East war and oil embargo of 1973 created enormous increases in the value of known reserves of oil and natural gas and, to a lesser extent, for other natural resources. These changes, reflected in corporate profits and wealth for the owners of mineral rights, became ever more irresistible targets for those wishing a share. The energy shortages created by government regulations led to further intervention by the federal government—first in an effort to cushion the blow of dramatic and unanticipated price changes and second to carry out so-called national energy policies designed to provide for future supply and demand. In this chapter, energy taxation and regulation in the United States and Canada are described in order to illustrate how the regional competition over natural-resource incomes has escalated and how these policies have been employed as redistributive mechanisms.

Applying the regional-competition hypothesis to the historical evolution of all natural-resource tax and regulatory policies in the United States and Canada from their beginnings is a monumental task. In order to make this practical, I review here only the case of energy taxation and regulation, emphasizing post-1973 events. The reason for narrowing the scope of these case studies is that many separate groups have an interest in this competition, so there are a multitude of agents and objectives and thus a complex interplay of political, legal, social, and economic forces. I hypothesize that the objective of each competing group is its own economic self-interest. However, prevailing legal, economic, and other constraints are complicating factors, which evolve gradually. Constitutional constraints may be viewed as the most static, yet they and the powers of the political jurisdictions defined by them are in a constant state of flux. This is particularly true for Canada, whose constitution was in the process of reformulation during this period. Clearly legislative constraints are yet more uncertain, for laws and regulations are variables that change slowly and reflect the power of various interest groups. Thus, tracking how legislatures, the courts, and their constituents have behaved over time is informative. Finally, historical precedents impose constraints that decay gradually, and these require acknowledgment and scrutiny as well. The flux in energy prices (both world prices and domestic regulated prices), technology, new discoveries, and public policy, including taxation and regulation, makes for a complex story. The case studies of the United States and Canada illustrate how this competition within the public and private sectors proceeded before and after the OPEC oil embargo. The studies highlight the political and economic techniques employed in the competition and how the institutional barriers and fixed and overlapping jurisdictions forced the participants to work within these constraints.

Unfortunately, the case studies are unable to show what would have occurred had these institutions not been present. A related difficulty with the case-study approach is that cause and effect are difficult to discern because of the large number of factors affecting actual events. Nevertheless, the saga of energy resource conflicts in the United States and Canada provides insight into how competition for rents has proceeded over time.

## The U.S. Case

The comparative histories of natural-resource development, regulation, and taxation illustrate both differences and similarities between the United States and Canada. Low cost and plentiful renewable and nonrenewable natural resources were instrumental to the growth and development of the agricultural and industrial bases in both countries. However, the United States managed to throw off both political and economic colonialism earlier in its history. Furthermore, federal-state relationships and constitutional constraints have resulted in a somewhat different pattern of regional competition and search for resource rents in the two countries. In the U.S. case study, the regulatory and tax treatment of oil and gas are discussed first, followed by a review of the effect of the 1973–1974 oil-price shocks and federal and state responses to them. Next, coal is discussed in a similar way; and finally, other nonrenewable and renewable resources are briefly mentioned.

Starting shortly after its first discovery and successful development, oil and later natural gas enjoyed special tax and regulatory treatment. The reasons for this are complex, but in large part they can be explained by the enormous economic rents that were created as the economy converted from coal as the primary energy source to a petroleum base during the twentieth century (1949 in the United States). Oil received preferential federal leasing, tax, and regulatory treatment starting in the early twentieth century. This came about in part in response to the formation of giant nationwide, later to become multinational, corporations of extraordinary power. Antitrust laws were never successfully invoked against the captains of the oil industry, who were also successful in incorporating preferential concessions into the tax code soon after the advent of the corporate income tax. Although the initial dollar savings from tax preferences were small because corporate income-tax rates were low until World War II, once installed they became institutions that grew in significance as the tax rate was increased to approximately 50 percent by the 1940s. Congressmen from the oil-rich states had acquired seniority and crucial chairmanships by that time, so that the tax advantages became unassailable. Import quotas were initiated in 1959 when cheap foreign oil was seen as a threat to domestic producers.

The restrictions on foreign crude were invoked for the stated purpose of national defense. The argument was made that excessive dependence on imported oil and on long and vulnerable supply lines would diminish the ability of the United States to fight a war and to remain independent of foreign pressures. The restrictions were designed to foster growth of the domestic industry, and at the same time certain identified domestic reserves were designated for national defense purposes, to be held as a strategic reserve until war or emergency. The effect of artificially reducing the supply of imported oil, which at the time was cheaper to extract and transport than domestic oil, was to increase the price of petroleum in the United States. Numerous economists (such as Stigler 1974 and Brannon 1979) have pointed out that a tariff or import tax would have achieved the same ends more efficiently for the nation but would have been less lucrative for domestic producers.

Import quotas caused domestic crude oil prices to exceed imported oil by about $1.25 per barrel and hastened depletion of domestic reserves. Crediting foreign tax payments against the U.S. corporate tax liabilities caused U.S. capital to flow into foreign exploration and development, which indirectly benefited foreign consumers by lower prices. A related mandated subsidy was the Jones Act, passed in the 1920s. It requires that all marine shipments between U.S. ports be on tankers that are American-built, -owned, and -manned. An updated version of this law, the cargo preference bill, requiring 30 percent of imported oil to be treated similarly has been in and out of the Congress since 1975. President Eisenhower established the import quotas by proclamation (imports were limited to 12 percent of U.S. production), which were not rescinded until 1974 by President Nixon due to the pressure for additional imports and the impracticality of enforcing the quota in the face of falling U.S. production. By 1977 imports accounted for 45 percent of U.S. consumption (Mead 1978).

A second regulatory device used to create and protect industry rents and profits was the advent of state commissions that regulated the oil-production rate (so-called allowables) and siting of wells (density of wells) over known oil reserves (called *unitization laws*). The first and most powerful of these was the Texas Railroad Commission. In the 1930s the Interstate Oil Compact allowed states to regulate oil production, and the Conally Hot Oil Act established an enforcement mechanism. By 1945, twenty-one states regulated oil production. For example, from 1960 to 1965 the Texas Railroad Commission set a maximum allowable production rate at 27 to 29 percent (Mead 1978). Although formed for the purpose of conserving the state's nonrenewable oil resource by regulating pumping rates to ensure maximum recovery from each field, the effect and ultimate purpose of the regulations were to serve industry. Restricting pumping rates below maximum capacity reduced total output below what it would have been in the absence of regulation in a free market. A lower output meant higher prices to consumers, and a situation in which market price exceeded the cost of discovering and pumping another barrel of oil (restricted by regulatory commissions)—hence higher economic rents for the industry. State commissions controlled the number of producing wells, and federal import limitations protected producers from the entry of new firms and foreign competition. The sale and leasing of government-owned mineral rights also became part of this control, and states imposed relatively modest taxes on the industry. Once formed, the constituency of those who benefited was economically and politically powerful.

Technology forced the flaring or burning of natural gas by-products until the 1940s when pipeline technology and costs allowed for the collection, drying, and distribution of natural gas. The timing was not good for producers, for the pipelines were built to supply gas as a substitute fuel during World War II when price regulation and rationing prevailed. Natural gas became regulated in 1938 by Congress, to the benefit of consumers, as had certain other industries during the war years. In 1954, the Supreme Court held that Congress had intended price controls to cover the wellhead price of natural gas in interstate commerce.

In large part due to the lobbying efforts of the oil industry, the federal income tax code grants extractive industries several unique concessions. The first is the depletion allowance. Although it went through a period of frequent change in the 1920s and 1930s (Page 1977), the depletion allowance was founded on the concept that the nonrenewable resource is depleted analogously to how man-made (reproducible) capital depreciates, and this required recognition in the tax code.

The tax law allows for cost or percentage depletion. In cost depletion, the expenditures made to drill and develop an economically exploitable reserve (successful wells) are amortized over the expected lifetime of the well (or mine). In percentage depletion, as the resource is extracted, a percentage of its value is deducted from the corporate income tax base as an expense of depletion. A confirmed reserve is worth more than the costs of developing it because of the "dry holes" produced in the process, and increasing resource prices make percentage depletion more attractive than cost depletion particularly for oil and gas where a 27.5 percent rate prevailed until 1976. The effect—to lower the effective corporate tax rate and attract investment—results in lower prices and greater production and consumption than would have occurred in its absence.

The depletion deduction is limited to 50 percent of a company's profits. Originally the maximum provision was applied on a company-wide basis, but in 1958 it was redefined to apply to the operating unit, which restricted its scope somewhat. In 1978 approximately 511,000 barrels of crude and 3 billion cubic feet of natural gas were granted percentage depletion; in 1979 the figures were 360,000 barrels and 2.2 billion cubic feet of gas.

The long-standing criticism of the allowance among economists (Harberger 1955) and finally among legislators led to changes, resulting in the 1975 Tax Reform Act (Mead 1978). Major oil and gas producers were no longer allowed to use percentage depletion, and the rate gradually drops to 15 percent for nonintegrated independent producers by 1984. Depletion rates for other exhaustible resources were untouched but were granted lower percentage rates. The depletion provisions were tightened further by the 1976 and 1978 Tax Reform Acts.

The second major tax benefit for nonrenewable resources is the expensing of exploration and certain development expenditures. Although these expenditures are actually capital investments because an exploitable reserve produces revenue over many years, the tax law permits for their immediate deduction. For oil and gas, all intangible drilling expenses, such as labor and materials, which are used up in the process of drilling wells, can be expensed. These account for roughly one-half the cost of such wells. The effect is like an interest-free loan from the federal government because the immediate expensing lowers today's tax bill and defers it to the future. Brannon (1979) estimates that the provision is equivalent to a 23 percent investment tax credit (reduction in a company's tax liability by 23 percent of such expenditures) on a successful well and a 5 percent credit on an unsuccessful well when the corporate income tax rate is 48 percent. The National Academy of Sciences reported in 1980 that comparing exploration and drilling investment treated in a theoretically correct accounting sense versus the current tax treatment shows that the value to the taxpayers of this tax concession is twelve cents for every dollar of tax revenues lost if the interest rate is 10 percent and fourteen cents for every dollar if the interest rate is 15 percent.

Brannon (1979) estimated the simultaneous effect of the depletion and expensing provisions on data from 1958 through 1960. The two provisions were deemed to be equivalent to an investment tax credit ranging from 75 percent for sulfur and iron ore to 5 percent for sand, gravel, and calcium carbonate. He estimated the overall effect on gas and oil at 18 percent, coal at 30 percent (which increases as more production comes from capital-intensive western strip mines), and 46 percent for uranium. He also evaluated the effect on alternative energy sources based on a version of the 1978 House energy bill of 32 percent for geothermal steam production for power plants (due to the proposed 22 percent depletion rate and other tax incentives), zero for solar energy, and a relatively low but unspecified rate for oil shale. The differential effects clearly favor conventional energy sources and serve to encourage investment, production, and consumption of them. Brannon added that these provisions are not effective because they reward the larger, more-successful producers without providing sufficient incentive for exploration; have little effect on making marginal deposits feasible; and by rewarding successful ventures and increasing their profits but not affecting unsuccessful ones, increases the variation in the rate of return, thereby increasing risks.

Another tax benefit particularly helpful to oil companies is the foreign investment tax credit. Income taxes paid to foreign countries can be used to reduce U.S. obligations, with a maximum as the amount that would have been due under U.S. tax laws. The effect is to exempt 46 percent (the U.S. maximum corporate tax rate in 1980) of foreign subsidiary profits from taxation and thereby subsidize foreign countries and encourage them to levy corporate income taxes. However, oil and gas multinational companies may not consolidate their income with the income from other business enterprises for the purposes of the foreign tax credit, and the carry-back provisions are limited. Furthermore, energy industries are subject to a 15 percent minimum tax on all items receiving preferential tax treatment.

The investment tax credit, inaugurated in the Kennedy tax cut and changed numerous times since, benefits the resource industries because their technology is more capital intensive than in manufacturing. The effect of a credit is to lower the effective tax rate. Resource industries also benefit differentially from the lower taxes that prevail both for individuals and corporations on capital gains. Much oil and gas exploration has been carried out by independents who would then sell their leases and equity interests to the major oil companies. Complex ownership provisions allow some wealthy investors to enjoy the lower capital gains rate. Coal royalty income is taxed at the capital gains rate instead of the ordinary income rate. The effect of those provisions is to lower the effective corporate income tax rate on resource firms (Church 1981) and to induce more and riskier investment into these industries than would otherwise by the case (Page 1977).

The effect of tax-preference items (called *tax expenditures* in the federal budget) is to reduce the effective corporate income tax rate below its nominal rate. In 1978 the U.S. Treasury undertook an exhaustive analysis of corporate tax returns from 1972 and computed effective tax rates for nineteen industries (table 2-1). The natural-resource industries clearly enjoy preferential federal tax treatment.

Another way to estimate the effect of the special tax provisions is by calculating the tax revenue forgone because of these provisions. Those are known as tax expenditures, and those for President Carter's proposed 1981 budget are shown in table 2-2. However, these forgone taxes measure only a small portion of the ultimate economic losses due to artificially low prices and too-rapid depletion stimulated by the tax concessions.

Another source of benefits to the oil and gas industry and other nonrenewable-resource industries is the transfer of ownership from the federal government to private hands on preferential terms. Of course, this process also went on for renewable resources as well, but it had terminated at the

**Table 2-1**
**Effective Tax Rates on U.S.-Source Income**

| Industry | Effective Tax Rate (%) |
|---|---|
| Manufacturing, not classified elsewhere | 42.0 |
| Paper and allied products | 38.4 |
| Credit dealers, brokers, insurance agents | 38.3 |
| Wholesale and retail trade | 38.0 |
| Communications | 36.1 |
| Electric, gas, and sanitary services | 35.3 |
| Lumber and wood products (nonfurniture) | 34.6 |
| Primary metals: Ferrous | 33.7 |
| Contract construction | 33.4 |
| Services | 31.6 |
| Transportation | 30.1 |
| Primary metals: Nonferrous | 29.4 |
| Real estate | 28.4 |
| Agriculture, forestry, fisheries | 28.1 |
| Unclassifiable businesses | 27.7 |
| Mining, not classified elsewhere | 25.6 |
| Petroleum and natural gas | 24.7 |
| Coal mining | 19.4 |
| Banking | 18.6 |

Source: U.S. Department of Treasury, Office of Tax Analysis, *Effective Income Tax Rates Paid by United States Corporations in 1972* (Washington, D.C.: Government Printing Office, 1978).

**Table 2-2**
**Tax Expenditures Relating to Energy in Fiscal 1981 Budget**
*(billions)*

| Expenditure | Amount |
| --- | --- |
| Expensing of exploration and development costs | $2.565 |
| Excess oil percentage depletion over cost depletion | 3.020 |
| Capital-gains treatment of royalties on coal | 0.100 |
| Residential energy tax credits | 0.460 |
| Alternate conservation and new-technology tax credits | 0.495 |
| Investment credits on electric and gas utility investments | 2.816[a] |

Source: Executive Office of the President, *Special Analysis: Budget of the United States Government* (Washington, D.C.: U.S. Government Printing Office, 1980).
[a]Estimated by one-sixth of tax expenditures for Investment Tax Credit.

end of the nineteenth century in the case of agricultural land and forests (under the various homestead acts and other provisions), and regulations concerning the fishing industry had restricted access somewhat to that resource.

From the founding of the United States, government policy has been to transfer ownership of mineral rights to private hands. This includes the location, prospect permitting and leasing, or transfer of all mineral and surface rights. Locatable minerals, which include metals, semiprecious stones, and uranium on federal lands, are regulated by the 1872 General Mining Law. The law provides for free access for prospecting, protection for registered mining claims (which are secured by three annual expenditures of $100 or more on labor or improvements), a permanent transfer of ownership (a patent) if the claim is proved to be valuable ($500 spent on labor and improvements) for $5 per acre, and no assessment of royalties or reservations.

Under the Mineral Leasing Act of 1920 (a product of the early twentieth-century conservation movement) prospecting permits are awarded for unknown resources, and competitive leasing is established for known resources. Upon discovery of a valuable resource, the prospector is given exploration rights and a preference-right lease. This act applies to coal, oil, natural gas, phosphates, sodium, onshore sulfur, and potassium (potash) on federal lands. The act is administered by the secretary of the interior, who is directed to ensure that leasees show diligence in developing the resource leading to production in order for the lease to be maintained. The secretary's authority extends to lease provisions, which may include token royalties if profitable production would otherwise prove impossible. Otherwise competitive leasing is achieved in preferential bidding and auctions where a bonus payment is made to secure the lease. Offshore leasing, established in 1953, requires competitive leases by bonus bids; oil, natural gas, and some sulfur are affected (Tiesberg 1980). Onshore oil and gas leasing conveyed ownership to private hands on a preferential basis until relatively recently. A moratorium on coal leasing was established in 1971 until 1980. New lease activity was accelerated in 1981 as the Reagan administration, under Secretary of the Interior Watt, planned to accelerate regulations on disposition of federal lands. It may be concluded that the majority of federally owned mineral rights were disposed of (excepting offshore areas) long before the advent of recent events at what would now be considered near-sacrifice prices. These lease provisions are summarized in table 2-3.

The natural-gas industry, which developed during the World War II and postwar period (in 1940, 2 trillion cubic feet were produced, and by 1955 this had expanded to 14 trillion cubic feet), did not fare as well as the oil industry at the hands of the federal government. The Federal Power Commission (FPC), established in 1938, was dominated by consumer-state interests and took the position of maintaining low gas prices and encouraging conversion to natural gas by industry and consumers. The FPC began to regulate the wellhead price of gas going through interstate pipelines in 1954, and this power was upheld by the U.S. Supreme Court. Producers were willing to sell gas at low rates because it had been a worthless by-product, and large reserves had previously been discovered as an offshoot of the search for oil. The FPC policies kept natural gas at equivalent-energy prices below oil and electrical energy, and adaptation to the fuel continued rapidly so that by 1980, 27 percent of U.S. energy came from this source.

In 1968, natural-gas consumption exceeded new reserves discovered for the first time. From then until the advent of phased price decontrol, the industry primarily relied on an inventory of past reserves because the regulated price was less than the cost of discovering and developing new resources. The low price continued to induce consumers to switch to this fuel and not to pursue conservation since it was cheaper to buy gas than to make investments in insulation and more efficient equipment, and other alternatives. The next benchmark came in the winters of 1976-1977 and 1977-1978 when shortages arose. The intermittent-service clauses in industrial contracts were invoked, and curtailments shut down many midwestern employers. "Shortages" is a misnomer because these problems were artificial ones caused by federal regulatory policy. Whenever prices are regulated at below the cost of replacement, consumers demand more than producers are willing to discover and develop. The problems would have been eliminated at any time that prices were decontrolled and allowed to increase to the level determined in the marketplace. Although the industry had been clamoring for decontrol, these winters of shortages made consumers seek and obtain further government regulations, which ensured supplies to resi-

**Table 2–3**
**Major Provisions of Federal Law Governing Leasing of Federal Lands for Energy-Resource Development**

| Land Category | Resource | Type of Lease | Bonus Bid | Royalty | Distribution to States |
|---|---|---|---|---|---|
| Outer continental shelf | Oil and gas | Competitive | Yes | Not less than 12.5%, usually 16.67% | None |
| Public domain | Oil and gas: | | | | States except Alaska get 50%. 40% goes to reclamation fund and 10% to general fund. For Alaska, 75.6% to state and 16% to Alaska native fund. No restrictions on use but priority to be given to energy areas |
| | In known geological structure | Competitive | Yes | Not less than 12.5% | |
| | Other | Noncompetitive | No | Maximum of 12.5% | |
| | Coal: | | | | |
| | Before 1976 | Noncompetitive | No | 5 cents per ton | |
| | After 1976 | Competitive | Yes | Underground 8%; surface mined, 12.5% | |
| Acquired lands | Oil and gas: | | | | Distribution same as for other receipts on same category of land. For national forest land, 25% goes to states, to be spent on roads and schools in affected counties |
| | In known geological structure | Competitive | Yes | Not less than 12.5% | |
| | Other | Noncompetitive | No | Maximum of 12.5% | |
| | Coal: | | | | |
| | Before 1976 | Noncompetitive | No | 5 cents per ton | |
| | After 1976 | Competitive | Yes | Underground, 8%, Surface mined, 12.5% | |

Source: Cuciti and Galper (1981).

dential users to the detriment of industrial and commercial users. The regulations in effect were transferring profits and economic rents that would have gone to producers and owners of leases to consumers because market prices would have been higher in the absence of FPC regulations.

Price regulation fell on oil in the summer of 1971 when President Nixon established price and wage controls for the entire economy. Phase IV of the controls expired in 1974, and with it the entire structure, save oil-price and product regulation, which continued under the ironically named Emergency Petroleum Conservation Act (1973) and the Emergency Policy and Conservation Act of 1975, which extended price controls through May 1979 and with presidential discretion through September 1981. President Carter called the portion of the regulations relating to allocating low-cost, "old" crude oil or equivalent-dollar payments among refiners (entitlements) and production and prices among distributors and wholesalers "an administrative nightmare" (Mead 1978).

The 1973 war in the Middle East and the OPEC embargo brought about the most significant changes. Although OPEC was founded in 1960 in Baghdad under the authorship of Juan Pablo Perez Alfonzo of Venezuela, its diverse political and economic interests had prevented it from taking any effective actions previously. Its original purpose was to establish a safety net designed to prevent the deterioration of oil prices. In 1959 the major multinational oil companies chose to exercise their power to cut oil prices unilaterally and without warning to the exporters, which were dependent on these tax and royalty earnings. The multinational oil companies exercised this power again in 1960, and these acts were the driving force behind OPEC's formation (see Stobough and Yergin 1979). In 1969 Colonel Qadaffi rasied Libya's oil price by 25 percent (or 40 cents a barrel) as a unilateral act of defiance. The October 1973 Arab-Israeli war and the oil embargo were instrumental in curtailing production and tripling world oil prices to $5.40 per barrel. The Iranian revolution, the fall of the shah, and resulting cutbacks in production allowed OPEC to increase per-barrel prices from $14.54 in October 1979 (although some price cutting had been taking place before this time) to $30 by October 1980. At this time the non-Communist world's demand for oil was approximately 50 million barrels per day, of which OPEC supplied 21 million. (For insight into the economic effects of OPEC see Griffen and Steele 1980; and the potential for other international resource cartels, see Labys 1980 and Klass, Burrows, and Beggs 1980).

Rising energy prices, inflation, and shortages of petroleum products mixed with unforeseen and unforeseeable events were due primarily to ill-advised decisions made in the public and private sectors since World War II (see Stobaugh and Yergin 1979). Tax and regulatory policies have worked at cross-purposes. They have resulted in an overreliance on imported oil, subsidized consumption of oil and natural gas, and intransigent economic and political factions who have benefited in the past by receiving economic rents and preferential treatment and who are not willing to give them up without a fight. Under regulation, the price for so-called old oil (reserves developed prior to 1973) was approximately $5.25 per barrel, while the world price of oil soared to $35 in 1980 when domestic oil regulation was replaced with the windfall-profits tax. The regulated price for interstate natural gas (under the control of the Federal Power Commission and Federal Energy Regulatory Commission) remained at roughly half the equivalent price of oil, and this benefited consumers in the short run. Prior to 1978, intrastate gas fell under state regulatory commissions, most of which permitted significant in-state price increases that diverted gas to intrastate lines and stimulated the movement of people, jobs, and capital to gas-producing states.

The basic economics are relatively simple. Whenever market prices and the costs of production or consumption deviate, there is an incentive for individuals to alter their previous behavior; additionally the deviation creates economic rents that are sought after. When old regulated oil sold for $5.25 per barrel, the incentives for domestic producers and distributors were to cheat by redesignating oil from old wells to new oil whose price was near or at world prices; to plan exploration and development in view of expectations concerning what the deregulated prices for new and old oil might be; and to lobby to have the regulations changed. Paul Bloom, the enforcer at the Department of Energy (Paul L. Bloom, "Special Counsel for Compliance," *Wall Street Journal,* August 13, 1980), processed two-hundred accusations against fifteen top oil companies, amounting to $10 billion in claims. He settled many cases, with a total sum of $1.4 billion, and later gave $4 million in collections to charities. Producers manipulated inventories, pumped from existing wells, and lowered investment in discovery and development, which meant that U.S. production and oil and gas exploration and development investment in real dollars fell steadily during the 1973–1979 period. Although the price of imported oil continued to rise, people were willing to pay and import an ever-larger share of U.S. consumption. The effect of price regulation was to subsidize imports because the incentives were lacking for producers to increase domestic output. This allowed imports to fill the gap, and the lower total supply ended up increasing prices. (For a thorough examination of the economics, see Griffin and Steele 1980.)

Prices to consumers were lower because the old regulated oil price was averaged in with the price of new domestic and imported oil (price regulations carried all the way through refineries to the gas pump) so that consumers demanded more than they would have if they were paying world oil prices. The benefits of lower costs of crude to the large refiners with contracts for old oil were dissipated as they were forced to pay entitlements, which compensated smaller refiners. Some small independents could buy only new oil from unregulated domestic wells and imported oil. They lobbied for the regulations that allowed them to benefit from old price-regulated oil. The result was inefficient "teakettle" refiners, established solely to capture rents from the entitlements. One expert (Verleger 1979) estimated that the resulting inefficiencies would have totally dissipated the economic rents from old oil by the early 1980s had the controls not been eliminated. Regulation of refiners and distributors eliminated potential profits and discouraged investments needed to use heavy crude and to produce unleaded gasoline, causing further disruptions. The net effect of regulation was to shift economic rents, which without regulation would have been earned by U.S. producers, partially to U.S. consumers and primarily to oil-exporting countries. The consensus was that the benefits to consumers would be completely eliminated by 1985 because of distortions in investment.

Economists and others criticized the ill-advised regulations, with little initial impact, and suggested numerous schemes to reduce the power of OPEC and to bring prices and costs in line with each other (see Griffin and Steele 1980). Among the more obvious solutions was complete deregulation coupled with a tariff on imported oil, which would be computed to compensate for the risks caused by the dependence and loss of security due to oil imports and for the balance-of-payments problems it presented (Brannon 1979). It should be noted that President Nixon instituted a $0.21 per-barrel tariff on crude oil and $0.63 on refined products under powers granted by the Trade Expansion Act of 1962. In 1975 President Ford proposed and then withdrew a $3 per-barrel tariff, and President Carter recommended a $4.62 tariff in lieu of a defeated gasoline tax, but neither Nixon or Ford moved toward complete price deregulation.

Price regulation created resource dislocations on consumption as well. With domestic prices less than the cost of replacing the resource with new discoveries, excess consumption took place. More importantly, the price gave the wrong signals for investment decisions. For example, each time the gas lines disappeared, the demand for large, fuel-inefficient cars spurted. People continued to build and buy poorly insulated homes. Industries had less incentive to conserve, although they were the earliest and most effective in energy saving. Jorgenson (1970) showed that another industry response was to subsidize labor inputs for energy inputs. Such a substitution effect occurs whenever relative prices change and because it is technologically easier to substitute labor than capital for energy in the short run. This effect allowed the economy to create an unprecedented number of new jobs in the last half of the 1970s and to accommodate the baby boom generation, now reaching working age, and the record numbers of women entering the labor force. The substitution effect over the long run, however, is to substitute capital for energy that embodies more efficient technology, and then employment will grow more slowly.

It is apparent that energy price regulations on oil and natural gas distorted extraction, production, investment, and consumption decisions. It also reallocated economic rents, a far more important reason that various groups supported, fought, or approved the regulations. The OPEC producers extracted the greatest gains by capturing enormous economic rents and redistributed income to a historically unprecedented degree. The U.S. price regulation benefited consumers at the expense of fuel and energy producers, and in the shift, a significant portion of the rents flowed to the oil-exporting countries. As the world price of oil rose, these resource distortions and redistributed economic rents grew with increasing speed. Portions of the regulations were due to run out in 1980 and 1981, and the battle over deregulation became intense.

The National Energy Act of 1978 established the responsibility within the Department of Energy (DOE) for energy planning. *National Energy Plan II* (U.S. Department of Energy 1979a), released in 1979, laid out goals and an energy plan for the next twenty years. The short range was defined as 1979–1985. In this time span the objective of ensuring sufficient investment in conventional fuels was emphasized. The public-policy means of achieving this goal was through relaxing and removing regulations, tax, and other barriers that might inhibit oil and gas investment and production. This meant, above all, that the price of domestic natural gas and oil had to rise to reflect its replacement costs. Higher prices would serve to stimulate conservation as well. The midterm was defined in the plan as 1985–2000. Here the goals were enhanced recovery of oil and gas, shifting to high-cost reserves, and the direct and indirect use of coal energy (liquification, gasification, and magnetohydrodynamics, all indirect uses). The long run was defined as after the year 2000. During this period a transition to renewable energy (solar and geothermal) was anticipated (see also the *Global 2000 Report* by the Council on Environmental Quality, 1980 and the *World Coal Study,* 1980).

The report (U.S. Department of Energy 1979a) included a discussion of the fairness-and-equity issue by acknowledging that price regulation had helped consumers but in the short run only. It stated that the deregulation of oil and natural-gas prices and removal of other product regulations were necessary and that the proposed windfall-profits tax contained provisions such as the energy security trust fund, low-income assistance programs, and the minority set-aside program designed to compensate those poor who would be adversely affected. The plan also stated that capital expenditures for energy production would be enormous ($744 billion from 1977 to 1990 and, of all nonresidential business-fixed investment, energy accounted for 31 percent in 1977 although this was expected to decrease to 23 percent later). These investments would come in large part from the energy industry profits, which meant that deregulation and associated tax changes had to leave something for industry.

Oil and natural gas are close energy substitutes, and similar problems to those brought about by regulated oil prices affect natural gas. The regulatory body changed to the FERC, but the same regulations prevailed until the 1978 Natural Gas Policy Act was passed after a two-year legislative battle. President Carter had promised gas deregulation in a letter to the governor of Texas in 1978, but what he delivered and the economic rents that would have flowed to producers as profits and to the major producing states of Texas and Louisiana as taxes and royalties under deregulation were far different. The act (Wetzler 1980) unified the regulation of interstate and intrastate gas under the single umbrella of the FERC in 1979, deregulated the high cost of recovery gas, provided for escalation in gas prices under a complex set of incremental pricing rules, which placed heavier burdens on business, and included phased deregulation for gas discovered after April 1977 to be completed by mid-1985 with presidential authority to extend regulation for eighteen months.

The price of new (post-April 1977) onshore and offshore natural gas is to rise at a rate roughly commensurate with the rate of inflation. New gas is defined as coming from offshore leases and onshore wells:

1. 2.5 miles or more from the nearest marker well.
2. Any new well at least 1,000 feet deeper than a marker well closer than 2.5 miles.
3. New onshore reservoirs.
4. Stripper well production (less than 60,000 cubic feet per day).
5. Alaskan pipeline gas.

Furthermore high-cost gas under the act was decontrolled. This included:

1. Wells begun after February 1977 and production obtained from deeper than 15,000 feet.
2. Geopressurized brine.
3. Occluded gas from coal seams.
4. Devonian shale.
5. Other high-cost conditions on which the FERC rules.

When producers elect to accept high-cost gas prices, they must give up all credits, exemptions, and deductions under the federal income tax code. State severance taxes are allowed to be added to the price for all categories of gas and passed through to consumers. These prospects stimulated investment in deep wells. For example, Amoco Production earmarked more than one-third of its 1980 exploration budget for deep wells, and Conoco budgeted about $100 million. In 1976, 9,085 wells were drilled, and this rose to 14,681 in 1979. Production increased by 1.6 percent in 1979 and proved reserves continued to decrease, but at a slower rate (U.S. General Accounting Office 1981b).

The main effect of the 1978 act was to bring intrastate gas under federal price controls. The oil-price increases of 1979 made the act obsolete, for the 1980 ceiling price for regulated gas was $2.30 per thousand cubic feet (mcf), and high-cost gas sold for $4 per mcf, whereas the energy-equivalent price to $35 per barrel of oil would be $6 per mcf. This means that the complete deregulation of new gas in 1985 is when price increases on the order of two or more times will occur, and this event presents an enormous political problem because of rent redistribution. After 1985 prices will continue to rise as old gas reserves are depleted. It is estimated that old gas will be completely exhausted by 1988. A further problem is that pipeline companies purchased long-term gas contracts that promised producers a price tied to oil prices or other high-priced natural gas whenever decontrol occurs. Unless these contracts are modified, deregulated prices may increase more than was anticipated in 1980–1981. Furthermore, the complex rules and regulations are difficult to administer (see U.S. General Accounting Office 1980b), and there is no method to allocate gas as the act holds prices below true market price. Ideally the act should have provided for the rapid and orderly transition to deregulation with prices determined in free markets.

This position is supported both on theoretical grounds and from results of simulation models of energy markets. Simulations run by Robert S. Pindyck (1979) for 1977 through 1985 compare phased deregulation versus the policies prevailing in 1977 (with price increasing at 4¢ per mcf per year). These imply that with deregulation, consumers pay $54 billion more but that the overall value of the additional gas produced and consumed increases net benefits (consumer surplus) by $12 billion. Outlays on substitute fuel decline by $83 billion, and GNP shows a net increase of $86 billion, so that total net benefits to society total $126 billion. The simulations imply that without deregulation, society would pay $780 billion to save $54 billion from 1977 through 1985. However, the planned phased decontrol lies somewhere between these two extremes.

The negotiations over the windfall-profits tax and the deregulation of oil prices were heated, complicated, and took place largely behind closed doors. It is safe to say that the windfall-tax act was a quid pro quo for price deregulation. In 1979 President Carter elected to exercise the authority granted him in the Energy Policy and Conservation Act of 1975 and phase out oil-price regulations at the wellhead and throughout the distribution system. This included the entitlements programs for the equalization of crude-oil costs to refiners, which resulted in the teakettle refiners, which existed solely to secure the economic rents created by the program.

The windfall-profits tax enacted in 1980 (Public Law 96–223) was an excise tax on domestic production based on price increases due to decontrol and is limited to a maximum rate of 90 percent of company profits (Wetzler 1980). The tax per barrel is based on the difference between selling price and the base price established at the conception of the act in early 1979 for various classifications of oil and this base price is increased by inflation. Oil is classified into three tiers.

*Tier 1* is oil discovered before 1979, taxed at 70 percent for large producers and 50 percent for small non-integrated producers on their first 1000 barrels per day production with a base price of $12.81 per barrel.

*Tier 2* is oil from stripper wells (low production and high cost older wells), and National Petroleum Oil Reserves oil taxed at 60 percent for large producers and 30 percent for small producers' first 1000 barrels per day with a base price of $15.20 per barrel.

*Tier 3* is oil discovered after 1978, heavy oil and oil recovered by tertiary methods, is taxed at 30 percent with a base price of $16.55.

Secondary recovery involves water flooding and by maintaining pressure by reinjection of natural gas. Tertiary (enhanced) oil recovery includes steam flooding, surfactant injection and carbon dioxide injection. Production from state and local government owned land, Indian tribal lands, certain charities, and Alaskan newly discovered oil is exempt from the tax. Furthermore, state severance taxes enacted prior to March 31, 1979, are deductible from this tax up to a 15 percent rate as long as the tax is uniform on the entire price of each barrel of oil (Allen 1979). The tax is set to automatically phase out after 33 months and estimated tax revenue made in 1979 for 1980–1983 was $227.3 billion. This estimate excludes the impact of the tax on corporate income tax collections which will be reduced by the extent of the deductibility of the windfall profits tax. The exemption of state severance taxes and production from state and local government is estimated to produce $128 billion revenues from 1980–1990 (Church 1981).

The Economic Recovery Tax Act of 1981 changed the windfall-profits tax in several ways: the tax rate on tier 3 oil was reduced in a series of steps from 30 percent to 15 percent by 1986; stripper production (fewer than ten barrels per day) by independent producers was exempted; and the $1,000 royalty credit to owners was increased to $2,500 for 1981 with an exemption of two barrels per day, growing to three per day by 1985.

How does the tax affect the distribution of rents, and what is its effect on production? The U.S. Treasury estimated that the major oil companies would pay 90 percent of the taxes, but this does not determine who bears the final burden. A key determinant is how much the combined effect of deregulation and the three-tiered tax rate will affect domestic production and consumption. In the absence of quotas, the price of oil is determined by world demand and supply (determined in large part by OPEC), and U.S. policy changes would have little effect unless U.S. production increases dramatically. However, in 1979 the United States supplied only 14 percent of the world's oil. Those who are most knowledgeable in the industry maintain that the U.S. supply elasticity is low (meaning that for a 1 percent increase in price, the additional supply of oil increases by less than 1 percent). The effect of deregulation of stripper-produced oil in 1976 produced additional new supply consistent with an inelastic supply function. Furthermore, the three-tier system and the tax rates (70 to 30 percent) were selected so that the supply response would be uniform among the different classes. Thus one is forced to conclude that the combination of deregulation and the windfall-profits tax extracts the burden of price increases from all final consumers of petroleum products (all commodities with significant petroleum inputs such as plastics and fertilizers and those that are energy dependent) to the extent that domestic prices increase. Experience has shown that these increases have been relatively modest because of the small proportion of old oil produced in 1980 and the regulatory-induced inefficiencies (such as deferred production and refinery investment). Nevertheless, Brannon (1979) believes that consumers bear about two-thirds of the tax due to the decontrol aspect, which he calls the *price control tax*. Because the base prices were determined before the Iranian cutoff and price increases of 1979, stockholders of oil firms and royalty recipients are saddled with the remaining burden of the tax. The portion of the burden on consumers is diminished by the way in which the proceeds are to be spent. Originally 60 percent of the distribution of tax revenues was designated for income tax cuts, 25 percent for low-income assistance, and 15 percent for energy programs, but these were only guidelines and became symbolic and ignored. However, these tax revenues mean that other taxes do not have to be raised. Furthermore, a number of tax credits were passed, some of which directly benefit consumers and some of which indirectly benefit consumers if prices of goods and services fall as a result.

The effect on royalty recipients created unforeseen problems because a large proportion of leases are owned by ranchers, farmers, and other mid-del-income groups. This led to instituting a $1,000 credit to offset the tax, which was expected to aid 600,000 royalty owners. Several proposals for further tax relief were advanced, and the relief was enacted in 1981 by increasing the exemption and exempting stripper wells, which will enable those wells to remain profitable where they would otherwise have been shut down (estimated to be 180 million barrels over the next ten years). The 1981 act also reduced the windfall tax on newly discovered oil (found after 1978), which shifted $3.2 billion in revenues back to the industry.

The effect on oil output was uncertain. However lucrative, certain, and understood, decontrol policy for oil stimulated a more-extensive search for it, particularly in the Rocky Mountain overthrust belt, the Permian basin in Texas, the Williston basin in Montana and North Dakota, the Eastern Overthrust belt, the Michigan basin, the Gulf of Mexico, and eastern off-shore areas. Industry spent $50 billion on such activities in 1980, and drilling rigs in operation increased by 34.7 percent from 1979 ("Hunt for Oil Quickens," *Wall Street Journal,* October 15, 1980). In 1980, 65,000 new domestic wells, the most since 1956, were drilled, and 70,000 were anticipated for 1981. Verleger (1980) shows how the incentives for additional production by enhanced recovery on existing wells introduced by the windfall-profits tax (30 percent tax rate) is greater than in the absence of the tax. He utilizes the DOE's estimate of price elasticity of supply (the percentage change in output produced by a percentage change in price) from new wells as 0.38 and 0.124 for enhanced recovery from existing wells. He calculates that if oil prices increase by 5 percent, 8,870 barrels per day of additional oil would have been produced without the tax versus 9 thousand with the tax, a small net overall increase.

Mead and Deacon (1979) conclude that the tax reduces the incentive to produce, and Nobel Laureate Milton Friedman (1980) and the *Wall Street Journal* decried the tax for a number of reasons. Among the critical points that need to be determined is how the tax affects the after-tax cash flow to the industry, which is required for investment in discovery and development. Recommended provisions for tax exemptions for funds reinvested were deleted from earlier versions of the bill.

An additional complicating factor in oil and gas deregulation is the 1978 Power Plant and Industrial Fuel Use Act, which forbids new natural-gas-fired boilers for electric utilities and industrial plants and mandates conversion to coal for existing gas units by 1990. These regulations, supported by the coal industry, introduce additional inefficiencies. More high-cost gas was found in the 1977–1980 period than the DOE anticipated (the discovery rate had fallen continuously to a historic low in 1973), and production had fallen from 1973 through 1978. However, 1979 and 1980 production and discoveries showed growth. Energy consumers, producers, and some government officials began to express concern that mandatory conversion to coal would produce inefficiencies. Furthermore, a loophole was found in the act that could have caused an unanticipated increase in oil as a boiler fuel.

These descriptions of oil and natural-gas regulation illustrate what happens when special-interest groups make their preferences felt at the federal level and how previous policies, constitutional constraints, and pragmatic politics created incredibly tangled legislation whose precise final effect no one can be sure of. In 1980 the DOE issued a report on energy programs (price controls, conservation programs, supply stimulation, and tax preferences) estimating that the combined effect of such programs was to reduce prices in 1980 by 2 percent and probably to reduce them by 20 to 30 percent by 1990. The report concluded that the net effect of government policies on the supply of energy over the next ten years would be negligible. It pointed out that regulation, taxation, expenditure, and other policies work at cross-purposes and that the major determinant of production, consumption, and prices is the marketplace. However, it also concluded that the windfall-profits tax and other taxes raise public revenues and cause only slight decreases in supply, for these are effective in capturing economic rents, and that energy regulation reduces the inflation of energy prices by about 12 percent (another reason why decontrol is difficult to remove once it is in place). The report charged that the overall federal energy program is a waste of legislators', analysts', and political competitors' energy.

The effect of oil- and gas-price regulations, the 1973 and 1979 oil-price increases, and deregulation had an enormous impact on the personal incomes of residents of consuming and producing states. Price deregulation eliminated (although only partially for natural gas) an income transfer to consumers and shifted this benefit to the U.S. Treasury, state governments, and resource owners. These events have produced responses in both consuming and producing states.

## The States' Role

Oil- and gas-producing states and, to a lesser extent, mineral-producing states receive a significant proportion of tax revenues from special taxes they levy on the extractive industries. Variations in profits from extracting the various minerals and legal constraints have led most states to rely on severance and other taxes, such as property taxes and, for some, royalties from state-owned lands, and the corporate income tax, requiring separate accounting and other provisions to target energy firms and to pinpoint the most lucrative tax bases. The severance tax rate can be set selectively to single out those resources that are most able to pay. It is an excise, privilege, or occupational tax for the right to sever the mineral from the ground. Sometimes the tax is a license fee; though presumably designed to regulate the industry, it is also used to raise revenues. The first severance tax was enacted by Michigan in 1846 at a 4 percent rate on the value of output as a replacement for all other taxes, and in 1853 this was changed to a tax on the tonnage of coal, iron ore, and copper ore. Until the early twentieth century, most producing states levied property taxes on the value of mines. However, these taxes proved difficult to administer because of the problems associated with assessing the value of a mine that contained an uncertain reserve whose future value was problematical. By 1910 seven states had introduced severance taxes as a more-effective means of singling out particular minerals (Starch 1979; Church 1981). The depression of the 1930s and the conservation movement served to add more states to those using severance taxes.

There have been a number of challenges to the severance and other state taxes on several constitutional grounds. The commerce clause, which has been used as a basis to challenge state taxes, as have the due-process clause, the equal-protection clause, and the privileges-and-immunities clause, grants Congress the power to regulate commerce but provides no specifics. The Supreme Court has developed four tests to determine the validity of state taxes under this clause:

1. The tax's activity must have substantial nexus in the state, although a minimum connection has proved sufficient to meet the test.
2. The tax must be fairly apportioned to activities carried on by the taxpayer in the state, which has been reinterpreted from totally immunizing interstate commerce to burdening interstate commerce equally with intrastate commerce and apportioning in-state activities of corporations operating in the state by means of a variety of formulas even if they are inherently arbitrary.
3. The tax must not discriminate against interstate commerce by intentionally or unintentionally favoring local commerce.
4. The tax must be fairly related to services provided by the state. Except in the case of user charges, the Court has never heard a factual evaluation but has alluded to the "benefits of a trained work force and the advantages of a civilized society" as being sufficient.

The due-process clause limits the territorial reach of states' taxing authority and reiterates the nexus and fair apportionment under the commerce clause. The equal-protection clause prohibits the state from using "palpably arbitrary" classification criteria, although the latitude granted by the court is wide. The privileges-and-immunities clause is used to disallow taxes that impose greater burdens on nonresident citizens but does not apply to corporations. Finally, the severance tax has been attacked as breaching the validity of contracts when it falls on nonproducer royalty interests when the contract requires delivery to be "free of charge."

In 1922, the Supreme Court held that the Pennsylvania severance tax on anthracite coal extracted in the state was constitutional despite the fact that most of it was exported to other states and that bituminous coal was treated differently. The commerce-clause objection was held to be invalid because the activity was local and not in interstate commerce. The Court said that to interpret it as interstate activity would be to say that no activity could be subject to state taxation because interstate trade enjoyed tax immunity at the time. Although other challenges followed, the courts supported the right of states to levy severance taxes when they construed the activity to be local. Furthermore, the interpretation of strict immunity for interstate commerce was later relaxed by the Court, which further eroded challenges to these natural-resource taxes. Objections to natural-resource taxes based on other constitutional issues also failed to succeed whenever the tax satisfied the four-pronged test. The status of severance taxes for large fossil-fuel-producing states as of 1980 is shown in table 2–4.

Table 2–4 is incomplete in a number of respects. First, the relatively low mine-mouth value of coal relative to oil and natural gas means that the bulk of severance tax revenues comes from this latter source. For example, Starch (1979) estimates that these two resources produce 87 percent of state severance tax revenues, while coal produces only 8 percent. It is important to note that substantial revenues come from royalties for production from government lands, corporate income taxes, and property taxes. Furthermore, these rates are nominal and are subject to various special features and limitations, which alter the true effective tax rates.

As of 1979, twenty-five states taxed oil and gas production; the rates for oil ranged from 0.5¢ to 47.9¢ per barrel and for gas from 5.0¢ to 7.0¢ per mcf, and some states taxed the value of production (ad valorem) at rates ranging from 0.5 to 12.5 percent (see Church 1981; Morgan and Olson 1979). Four states imposed taxes on oil shale at 2 to 6 percent of the value of production. Conventional excise taxes are levied by states and the federal government on the transportation, conversion, distribution, and consumption of energy. These are not detailed here except to mention that excise taxes are frequently levied on pipeline companies (4 to 6 percent of gross

**Table 2–4**
**Severance Taxes on Fossil Fuels in Selected States, 1980**

| State | Oil | Gas | Coal |
|-------|-----|-----|------|
| Alaska | 12.25% | 10.0% | — |
| Kentucky | — | — | 4.5% |
| Louisiana | 12.5 | 7¢/mcf | — |
| Montana | 2.9 | — | 30.0 |
| New Mexico | 6.3 | 2.55% and 26¢/mcf | 6.5 |
| Oklahoma | 7.0 | 7.0 | — |
| Texas | 4.6 | 7.5 | — |
| Wyoming | 6.0 | — | 10.5 |

Source: U.S. Government Accounting Office (1981a).

revenues) and on utilities (0.25 to 6 percent of gross revenues). Relatively few states assess property taxes on producing oil and gas properties, but taxing of leasehold interest, leased acreage, and drilling and production equipment is commonplace. Royalty payments are taxed primarily as ordinary income to receiving individuals. Nineteen states provide various income tax credits and preferential property tax treatment for alternative energy equipment, such as solar and wind. States apply the corporate income tax to mineral companies, and most utilize the federal tax base or some variant of it apportioned to the activity that takes place in the state. A portion of federal revenues from royalty income is distributed to the states as detailed in table 2-3. In 1977 the states' share of royalties from production on federal lands was increased to 50 percent, and fees from other extractive-related activities are shared. Furthermore, the federal government makes certain payments in lieu of taxes in areas affected by federal installations and activity.

One tax that stands out in table 2-4 is Montana's 30 percent maximum rate on coal, which was invoked in 1975. In June 1978 several coal companies, out-of-state utility customers, and, ironically, because of the state's dependence on severance tax revenues, the city of Austin, Texas, challenged the tax in the Montana State District Court as violating the commerce clause. This challenge ultimately went to the U.S. Supreme Court, and the case sounded like an echo from the Pennsylvania case settled thirty years before. During the hiatus, the Court held that interstate commerce is not immune from state taxation and that it must pay its own way (Hellerstein 1981). The case was admitted to the jurisdiction of the Supreme Court in fall 1980 and decided in the summer of 1981.

In *Commonwealth Edison Co.* v. *Montana,* the Court relied on the four-pronged test to make its decision. The nexus and fair-apportionment provisions were never questioned; the decision relied on the discrimination and fair-relationship prongs. The plaintiffs maintained that the burden of the tax was borne almost exclusively by out-of-state consumers because 90 percent of Montana's coal is exported and tax revenues exceeded the benefits received from state-funded activities; thus coal paid more than its fair share (after property and income tax relief was passed in 1979, 20 percent of the state's tax revenue came from coal severance taxes). Of course, the fact that coal is physically exported does not necessarily imply that the tax is entirely exported because a portion of the burden may fall on resource owners (in Montana's case, approximately 75 percent of the coal comes from federal lands), labor, and suppliers of other inputs. The Court, unconvinced by the plaintiffs' arguments, noted the resident and nonresident consumers were treated equally and that state borders were irrelevant. Perhaps the Court's most-significant conclusion was that the state in providing police and fire protection, a trained labor force, and the "advantages of a civilized society" satisfied the "fairly related" test. A majority of the Court elected not be hear evidence relating to the quantitative estimates of benefits received compared with taxes paid. The Court refused to determine whether Montana provides a civilized society for the same pragmatic reason that hearing evidence on benefits received would put it in the business of judging quantifiable tax limits and, as the majority opinion pointed out, establishing tax rates is more properly carried out by the legislative branch of government.

The Court's pragmatism is further reinforced by research regarding tax exporting and the costs and benefits of energy development. For example, McLure (1969, 1978, 1980, 1981), Gillis and McLure (1975), Church (1981), Shelton and Morgan (1977), and others have examined the question of tax exporting, both theoretically and empirically. They conclude that regardless of the proportion of the product that is exported, not all of the tax burden accompanies the product; the proportion ranges from nearly no exporting (the tax burden falling on resource owners residing in the jurisdiction and labor) to nearly full exporting (the tax burden falling on nonresident owners of resources, and extractive firms, and on nonresident customers). Their work reveals that quantifying tax burdens depends on market conditions and multiple variables and so is both a complex and an uncertain task. The difficulties led McLure (1981) to conclude that the uncertainties are so great that the degree of tax exporting should not be a criterion for determining the constitutionality of a resource tax base or its rate.

Research on the economic costs of pollution, energy-related growth problems and financing their public services in boom towns, and the economic benefits of resource development is extensive. However, the state of knowledge is not yet accurate or complete enough to make valid quantitative conclusions to a jurisdiction regarding the overall benefits and costs of resource development that it can use in judging the appropriateness of various tax rates designed to bring those costs and benefits into balance (Schulze et al. 1981). In order to determine if a state tax is appropriately structured to ensure that interstate commerce pays its own way on a strictly quantitative basis, the Court would be compelled to hear facts and judge both the degree of tax exporting to ascertain who pays the tax and the costs and benefits of the resource-extractive activities. Because of this complexity and uncertainty, the Court's decision not to conduct factual inquiry was a wise one consistent with its limited role in adjudicating other state taxes. For example, in a 1980 opinion, the Court rejected a constitutional challenge to Vermont's method of taxing an apportioned share of Mobil Oil's foreign-source dividend income under its corporate income tax provisions.

The four-pronged test used to define the commerce clause has been used to strike down taxes. The Texas gas-gathering tax of 1954 is one example. The tax was levied on gas shipped in interstate natural-gas pipelines. Although the primary reason for striking the tax down was the now-discredited theory that it imposed directly on interstate commerce, the Court also noted that the tax did not relate to the length of the Texas portion of the pipeline or to any other reasonable relationship to in-state activity and therefore failed under the fair-apportionment criterion. Consequently, the *Commonwealth Edison* v. *Montana* decision is a benchmark in defining the Court's interpretation of the commerce clause and the four-pronged test.

During the 1978–1980 period, producing states sought novel means to increase their natural-resource taxes and to capture economic rents that were going to consuming regions due to price controls. Louisiana's first-use tax on offshore natural gas was one of these. The state taxed oil at 12.5 percent of the wellhead price, but natural gas at only $0.07 per mcf. However, offshore gas beyond three miles (ten miles for Texas and Florida) belongs to the federal government, and no provisions exist for sharing federal royalties from this offshore production although Louisiana is awarded a $10 million coastal energy grant yearly. Congressman Billy Tauzin (1979) reported that 95 percent of all offshore gas production coming from two to two-hundred miles from the Louisiana coastline is exempt from the state's severance tax, and 98 percent of this is exported. The state supports associated onshore activities, and he stated that its fishing industry is threatened by the activity and that it should be compensated. The first-use tax assessed $0.07 per mcf (a 2.0 to 3.5 percent tax rate in 1979) on all gas not subject to a Louisiana or other state severance tax by the first user who processes it and transports it through the state. The tax was expected to raise $250 million per year. Further, it requires that the burden of the tax be passed on to consumers (an FERC requirement) although paid for by pipeline companies, so the tax effectively singles out offshore federally owned gas brought onshore ("used") in Louisiana. The first-use tax was allowed as a credit against the state severance tax so that the tax rate was equal for onshore and offshore gas.

Gas-producing states have incentives to increase severance taxes and invoke similar taxes particularly when FERC regulations allow state taxes to be added to the regulated price and passed through to consumers. Regulated gas prices are below the market value of gas, so consequently a higher price due to a state tax will be entirely borne by consumers. Tauzin justifies Louisiana's first-use tax on the basis that a ten-year property tax exemption is given to onshore plant and equipment (forty square miles of coastal land are used each year) and no sales taxes are levied on goods, equipment, and boats serving the offshore wells. Others did not agree, and eight northeastern states led by Maryland, fifteen interstate pipelines, the federal Department of Justice and FERC, and forty-two natural-gas distribution companies challenged the tax on several constitutional grounds ("Gas Tax Flight," *Wall Street Journal,* April 21, 1981). The U.S. Supreme Court struck down the tax in 1981, judging it to be discriminatory because the tax-credit provisions for state severance taxes paid favored in-state gas consumers. Thus the Court scrutinized the matter of discrimination between in-state and out-of-state users on the basis of the nominal effect of the tax statute itself rather than on the ultimate economic burden of the tax. The state was forced to refund the $500 million it had collected since 1979 from natural-gas consumers in thirty states.

Alaska's tax revenue from state land royalties (a 12.5 percent rate) and oil-based taxes (12.25 percent production tax and the state corporate-income tax) have become almost an embarrassment of riches ("Alaska Doles Out Oil Cash, But Largesse Worries Some," *Wall Street Journal,* August 29, 1980). The Prudhoe Bay discovery in 1968, the trans-Alaska pipeline in 1977, oil-price deregulation in 1980, and state ownership of resources have brought the bonanza to Alaska. A $3 billion state surplus was achieved by July 1981, and $53 billion in surpluses is expected over the remainder of the decade. The effect of oil deregulation alone is expected to yield $37.3 billion in state tax revenues from 1980 through 1990 (excluding production royalties from state and Indian lands). The *Anchorage Times* ran a regular feature in 1980, "Helping the Governor Spend a Billion," where readers' suggestions were printed. Creative legislators came up with $16 billion in appropriations bills for 1981, although the 1980 state operating budget was only $1.3 billion. Subsidized home loans, immediately paying off the state's obligation to Alaskan natives, a permanent fund that would be invested in government and corporate financial securities whose income will replace oil revenues (Prudhoe Bay production is expected to decline starting in 1987), subsidized loans for job-creating businesses, and cash grants to residents in lieu of tax reductions are some of the ways the state plans to spend its riches. In 1981 the state planned to spend $533 million on public-works projects, repeal the state income tax, and add $900 million to a permanent fund that will be drawn on to pay annual cash dividends to residents of $50 for every year beyond the third year of residency. (The residency requirements were successfully challenged in the courts.)

Mieszkowski and Toder (1981) performed some calculations that reveal how successful Alaska is in capturing resource revenues. They estimated the effect of the decontrol of oil prices for the period between May 1979 and January 1981 on tax and royalty income for Alaska and Texas based on 1981 production levels. They calculated the net effect of these changes after accounting for the fact that all state taxes and royalties are deductible under the federal corporate income tax and state severance taxes and royalties are deductible from the windfall-profits tax. Total oil revenues from Alaska production increased by $13.5 billion, with $3.9 billion or 28.6 percent going to the state, 60.5 percent to the federal government, and 10.9 percent to private producers. In contrast, total oil revenues in Texas increased by $21.5 billion, with $2.2 billion or 10.1 percent going to the state, 67.0 percent to the federal government, and 22.9 percent to private producers. The substantial differences between the states' share is attributable to the small portion of production from state lands in Texas (under 10 percent) and their lower royalty rate (10 percent versus 12.5 percent in Alaska). An additional reason for Alaska's success is its special tax treatment of income to oil and gas corporations, introduced in 1978. The significant change was to introduce provisions requiring separate accounting for Alaska operations rather than a formula to apportion multistate profits based on sales, employment, and property as used for other corporations and by most other states. The effect is to deny some deductions and to increase substantially income earned in Alaska. The threat of constitutional challenge and court review led the state to revise the law in 1981, adding a special apportionment formula and a graduated tax rate applicable only to oil and gas companies. These provisions may be constitutionally challenged under the fair-apportionment and discrimination provisions. The reversion from separate accounting to an apportionment formula makes the state's law conform more closely to recent opinions, but the question as to whether the formula introduces the possibility of multiple taxation remains.

Energy-consuming states have not ignored the possibility of extracting tax revenues from perceived energy windfalls, and their efforts have ended up in the courts. In June 1980 California voters defeated a 10 percent state windfall-profits tax (Proposition 11, which was expected to raise $300 million to $420 million in its first year) on oil companies operating in the state after companies spent $5.6 million to defeat it. Several other states, including Illinois, Kentucky, Louisiana, Massachusetts, Maryland, North Dakota, and Pennsylvania, have considered similar taxes.

The city of Philadelphia enacted a $0.10 per barrel tax in 1980 on oil refined in the city, which was expected to yield $12 million its first year. In perhaps one of the most far-reaching taxes, New York State levied a windfall-profits tax on profits of worldwide oil companies that carried out any business in the state. The existing corporate income tax in New York on oil companies yielded $20 million in 1978, $42 million in 1979, and an estimated $60 million in 1980. This tax was appealed to the U.S. Circuit Court and the U.S. Supreme Court.

The Connecticut oil excise tax was also found to be unconstitutional by lower federal courts because of provisions limiting the right of companies to pass the burden of the tax on to consumers in the state. The federal district courts sustained the oil companies' claims that the provisions were preempted by federal legislation relating to the pricing of petroleum products in that federal price control and energy policies were frustrated. Hellerstein (1981) analyzes state tax court cases in detail and calls this doctrine of federal preemption, which also was touched on in the Louisiana first-use decision, as one that distinguishes a true tax from a tax masquerading as a regulation.

Although specific taxes have been struck down by the courts, the efforts of consuming states to enact energy taxes that are designed to be shifted to resource owners and producers (labeled *backward tax shifting* by economists) most likely will continue. However, the Supreme Court, in upholding Vermont's unitary income concept in 1980 (*Mobil* v. *Vermont*), may have opened up avenues for further taxes by consuming states. The concept defines the taxable portion of corporate income to be the apportioned percentage of worldwide income. This definition, in effect taxes dividends paid to U.S. multinational companies operating in the state that are paid by foreign affiliates and subsidiaries and thereby increases taxable income. ASARCO and Woolworth sought exemptions and Alcan aluminum challenged California on its similar provisions (in 1981 Vermont, California, Alaska, Illinois, and Oregon employed the unitary definition) while multinationals threatened to cut back on investments in the state.

The economic effect of energy taxes enacted by consuming states is transparent. Energy suppliers operate in markets where they receive the greatest rate of return, and for marginal investments (when the investment decision was made) they receive roughly the same returns net of taxes at all locations. A tax on energy refining, distribution, or consumption will, in effect, increase the cost of energy no matter who remits the tax payments to the state. If the net return to energy companies is diminished by the tax, they will curtail activities or cease operations entirely until the anticipated rate of return, net of taxes, is the same as in other locations. This implies that all or virtually all of the tax will be shifted to consumers. If this pass-through were prohibited, the energy companies would conceal it in the form of quality changes and other devices (such as special charge or fees) or shut down operations, although this would not happen instantaneously. Furthermore, higher energy costs would reduce the quantity of energy consumed and make the state less attractive to industry and to other economic activities.

Regardless of the outcomes of future court challenges, state taxation of energy and other natural resources produces enormous revenues to jurisdictions blessed with such resources. Moreover, Carter's National Energy Plan and the avowed Reagan administration policies of reducing the federal role in resource ownership, management, and control have benefited these states. For example, the U.S. Treasury estimates that the combined effects of oil-price deregulation and the windfall-profits tax wherein state royalties are untaxed and these and state severance taxes are deductible will increase oil-producing states' tax revenues by $128 billion from 1980 to 1990. Of that amount $106 billion was forecast as going to Alaska, Texas, California, and Louisiana. The Advisory Commission on Intergovernmental Relations has produced more-detailed estimates (Cuciti and Galper 1981) of recent state energy tax collections. They point out that states collected $4.2 billion in severance tax revenues in fiscal 1980, which was 46 percent more than in fiscal 1979 and 508 percent more than in fiscal 1972 although this amounts to only about 3 percent of total state tax collections. This growth is due to changes in production (increases primarily for coal), increased prices, and changes in tax structures. They also estimate the revenues from excise, sales, property, and personal and corporate income taxes and derive an average state tax structure based on the actual state tax collections, called the *representative tax system*. This is augmented by energy-lease revenues and when compared to revenues actually collected by each state, it is used as a measure of tax effort. For example, if a state collects the same total revenue as under the augmented representative tax system, its tax-effort index would be 100.0 because its tax structure is similar to that for the average of all states. In other words, its overall average effective state tax rate is equal to the average for all states. Next, they identified the eleven net energy-exporting states and calculated the actual tax effort for these and the energy-importing states and the required tax effort to achieve 1979 revenues if energy-related tax and royalty revenues were removed from each state's tax structure. Their results are displayed in table 2–5. The first column shows total state per-capita revenue in 1979, the second gives energy tax capacity or collections under the augmented representative tax system, the third shows the actual tax-effort index in 1979, the fourth gives the required tax effort index if energy revenues, including lease royalties, were removed, and the final column gives the percentage change in tax effort that would be required if energy tax revenues were not available but the state were to maintain total tax collections. Energy-exporting states have an actual average tax effort index of 74.7, which is 29 percent below the average for all other states. This would have to rise to 94.8 if energy revenues were not available or by 26.8 percent on average compared to a 2.2 percent increase for other states. The implication is that states fortunate enough to possess energy resources within their borders enjoy a fiscal advantage. However, the analysis is not intended to nor does it reveal the degree to which energy tax burdens may be exported. Furthermore, rapid changes in prices, production, and tax structures and the pending exhaustion of reserves in some areas reduce the significance of these outcomes. For example, total state severance tax revenues increased by 50 percent in 1980, and Mieszkowski and Toder (1981) estimate that energy revenues in Alaska in 1981 will be approximately $10,000 per capita. However, production from Alaska's Prudhoe Bay reserves is expected to slow down starting in 1987 and end in the 1990s.

Kresge (1980) has analyzed the effects of the proposed offshore leasing, where additional production will come from, on public and private incomes, employment, and population in Alaska for the period through the 1990. He concluded that a boom-bust cycle would occur because of high employment and activity during the construction phase and estimated that

**Table 2-5**
**Actual and Required State Tax Effort**

| | Total State Per-Capita Collections | Energy Tax Capacity Per-Capita under Representative Tax Structure | Actual Tax Effort Index | Required Tax Effort Index | Percentage Change in Tax Effort |
|---|---|---|---|---|---|
| Net energy-exporting states | | | | | |
| Alaska | $ 2,919 | $ 1,339 | 120.8 | 271.2 | 124.5 |
| Kansas | 818 | 88 | 86.5 | 95.4 | 10.3 |
| Kentucky | 659 | 67 | 86.4 | 94.7 | 9.6 |
| Louisiana | 829 | 282 | 80.6 | 111.1 | 37.8 |
| Montana | 885 | 103 | 87.9 | 97.0 | 11.3 |
| New Mexico | 936 | 322 | 86.4 | 123.0 | 42.4 |
| North Dakota | 766 | 119 | 78.3 | 89.1 | 13.8 |
| Oklahoma | 720 | 231 | 71.4 | 92.6 | 29.7 |
| Texas | 702 | 228 | 63.8 | 80.4 | 26.2 |
| West Virginia | 679 | 132 | 80.9 | 130.3 | 60.3 |
| Wyoming | 1,441 | 666 | 81.3 | 130.3 | 60.3 |
| Subtotal | 776 | — | 74.7 | 94.8 | 26.8 |
| Other states | | | | | |
| Alabama | $ 580 | $ 23 | 86.6 | 89.7 | 3.6 |
| Arizona | 974 | 10 | 115.7 | 117.1 | 1.2 |
| Arkansas | 569 | 25 | 82.2 | 85.2 | 3.7 |
| California | 978 | 38 | 95.1 | 98.7 | 3.8 |
| Colorado | 957 | 73 | 95.8 | 103.4 | 7.9 |
| Connecticut | 957 | 6 | 102.5 | 103.1 | 0.7 |
| Delaware | 932 | 23 | 95.1 | 97.4 | 2.4 |
| District of Columbia | 1,259 | 7 | 132.8 | 133.8 | 0.7 |
| Florida | 724 | 8 | 78.8 | 79.5 | 0.9 |
| Georgia | 710 | 5 | 96.7 | 97.4 | 0.7 |
| Hawaii | 1,195 | 11 | 128.2 | 129.7 | 1.2 |
| Idaho | 745 | 7 | 92.3 | 93.1 | 0.9 |

| Illinois | 974 | 28 | 98.8 | 101.8 | 3.0 |
|---|---|---|---|---|---|
| Indiana | 725 | 18 | 84.2 | 86.0 | 2.1 |
| Iowa | 878 | 3 | 93.4 | 93.7 | 0.4 |
| Maine | 781 | 3 | 110.7 | 111.2 | 0.4 |
| Maryland | 953 | 5 | 110.0 | 110.6 | 0.5 |
| Massachusetts | 1,165 | 5 | 145.3 | 146.1 | 0.6 |
| Michigan | 1,027 | 14 | 113.8 | 115.5 | 1.6 |
| Minnesota | 1,048 | 8 | 116.5 | 117.5 | 0.9 |
| Mississippi | 605 | 41 | 96.3 | 103.0 | 7.0 |
| Missouri | 695 | 7 | 82.9 | 83.6 | 0.9 |
| Nebraska | 838 | 10 | 98.4 | 99.6 | 1.2 |
| Nevada | 953 | 20 | 65.5 | 66.4 | 1.4 |
| New Hampshire | 672 | 2 | 78.3 | 78.5 | 0.3 |
| New Jersey | 1,049 | 19 | 117.4 | 119.9 | 2.1 |
| New York | 1,319 | 14 | 171.6 | 174.7 | 1.8 |
| North Carolina | 667 | 3 | 92.3 | 92.7 | 0.4 |
| Ohio | 757 | 24 | 86.3 | 88.7 | 2.8 |
| Oregon | 872 | 6 | 94.1 | 94.7 | 0.6 |
| Pennsylvania | 861 | 32 | 105.2 | 109.5 | 4.1 |
| Rhode Island | 907 | 2 | 122.8 | 123.2 | 0.4 |
| South Carolina | 632 | 3 | 92.3 | 92.8 | 0.5 |
| South Dakota | 693 | 9 | 84.5 | 85.4 | 1.0 |
| Tennessee | 630 | 7 | 87.4 | 88.2 | 0.9 |
| Utah | 788 | 62 | 99.0 | 107.5 | 8.5 |
| Vermont | 832 | 2 | 109.9 | 110.2 | 0.3 |
| Virginia | 727 | 15 | 88.8 | 90.4 | 1.9 |
| Washington | 884 | 10 | 97.3 | 98.4 | 1.2 |
| Wisconsin | 1,007 | 3 | 118.8 | 119.3 | 0.4 |
| Subtotal | 910 | — | 105.1 | 107.4 | 2.2 |

Source: Cuciti and Galper (1981).

the state would run fiscal deficits because of required expenditures on public facilities and services. Because of these disruptive booms associated with the resource development and exhaustion cycle, the funding of public natural-resource revenue permanent funds to replace tax revenues from depleted resources in Alaska, Montana, Wyoming, New Mexico, and other states is understandable. This possible overreliance on short-lived energy revenues led the U.S. General Accounting Office (1980a) to issue an evaluative report and to warn Oklahoma and Texas that they might be facing a future fiscal dilemma because of their dependence on tax revenues associated with rapidly depleting gas and oil.

## The Coal Saga

Until 1973, coal in the United States was a declining industry. In 1898 coal surpassed wood as the nation's primary energy source, and in 1910 it supplied 95 percent of U.S. energy. Its share of energy consumption had fallen to less than 20 percent by 1970 because oil and gas had become more-attractive energy sources. Several influential reports and publications that predicted exhaustion of many nonrenewable resources, severe degradation of the air and water, and food shortages, all of which were forecast to have catastrophic effects on the world's population (see, for example, Meadows et al. 1972; Forrester 1971), arrived coincidentally with the dramatic OPEC-inspired oil-price increases of 1973–1974 and the Russian-U.S. wheat debacle. These events upset many expectations about the future viability of consumer-oriented societies and caused investors and businesses to revise expectations about the future prices of natural resources. The price for current delivery (called the *spot price*) of virtually all natural resources rose dramatically during that period, and since the United States possesses one-fourth of the world's coal reserves, the DOE forecast that coal would become the primary energy source by the mid-1990s. Coal prices rose along with those of the other resources but then sagged badly in the worldwide recession of 1974–1975. Its anticipated growth has not been forthcoming. However, the structure of the coal industry has changed significantly as production and consumption of coal and investment in the industry have shifted from east to west.

The majority of coal is not sold on the spot market but is transacted based on long-term contracts. Before an electric utility builds a new coal-fired power plant, it assures itself of a reliable supply of fuel by signing a long-term contract with a coal-mining firm. Coal-mining firms, for their part, do not invest tens of millions of dollars required to develop a new mine unless sales are assured. Furthermore, investment bankers require secured long-term contracts before they are willing to lend to the electric utility or to a mining company. The contracts normally specify how much coal is to be delivered, its quality (the most important characteristics being heat content in British thermal units, sulfur, moisture and ash content, and the basic mine-mouth price, and provisions for future price increases based on changes in taxes and labor costs). Although coal mining is a competitive industry and although the major oil companies began acquiring mining firms in the late 1970s, the remainder of the major coal-related industries are regulated monopolies. Railroads are regulated by the Interstate Commerce Commision, and electric utilities, the primary coal consumers, are regulated by federal and state agencies. Since most of these regulatory bodies allow for the automatic pass-through of cost increases, the coal industry is uniquely able to shift taxes forward onto consumers (Church 1978). Because of these long-term contracts, the 1973–1975 events had relatively little effect on the coal industry aside from creating optimism with respect to its future role in energy production and to compel signatories of new long-term contracts to provide for the pass-through of additional increases in costs and factors reflecting the changing price of alternative energy resources.

From this period on, energy planners remained optimistic about the future role for coal. They had only to look at the immense U.S. coal reserves (4 trillion tons in place, 200 billion to 300 billion tons of economically recoverable coal, and an annual production of only 660 million tons in 1978, with excess capacity at that time) and the anticipated costs of alternative fuel sources to conclude that coal would play an increasingly important role. Coal is hoped to support an orderly thirty- to fifty-year transition from a petroleum-based energy system to one based on renewable energy sources.

The *National Energy Plan II* (U.S. Department of Energy 1979a) highlighted the importance of coal from 1980 through the beginning of the twenty-first century both in its direct use in electric power plants and for industrial boiler fuel but also in its use after synfuel processing (liquefaction, gasification, and solvent refining). The Massachusetts Institute of Technology–led world coal study (Wilson 1980) saw a similar role for coal in the world at large. It estimated that coal provided 25 percent of the world's energy at that time and that coal will have to supply one-half or more of total energy during the following twenty years. This would require that coal production increase by a factor of 2.5 to 3.0 and that world trade in coal increase by 10 to 15 times its 1979 levels. Furthermore, the study concluded that coal could be mined, moved, and used in ways that would be safe and would protect health and the environment (they discounted fears of increasing concentrations of sulfur dioxide and other pollutants, as well as carbon dioxide and its effect on warming the atmosphere). They also stated that technological advances in coal use would occur in the 1990s. A study by the International Energy Agency confirmed that a doubling of coal output by 1990 was a reasonable goal, and investments in new mines and transport facilities would require $1 trillion by 2000. These goals would require that output increase initially at 8 to 9 percent per year and accelerate later. Thus, the 1978 output of 885 million metric tons by the twenty-one Organization for Economic Cooperation and Development (OECD) countries plus Finland, France, and West Germany (970 million tons consumed in 1977) would have to increase to 1.7 billion by 1990 and to 2.4 billion tons by 2000 ("Coal: The Global Market Boom Forced by OPEC," *Business Week,* August 20, 1979). These projections would require large exports to Western Europe and Japan where South African and Australian exports (whose coal is 20 to 25 percent less expensive than U.S. coal) would have the largest share of the gains.

The U.S. coal production and use targets were not on track, for the expected 8 to 10 percent annual growth in domestic production did not take place, and excess capacity sat idle in 1980–1981. The reasons for this poor response can be traced to federal and state government energy and pollution policies, recession, and labor. National strikes in 1978 and 1981 interspaced with numerous wildcat shutdowns and other labor disputes made some apprehensive about becoming dependent on an uncertain supply and fearful of the recent history of coal operators' conceding to inflationary wage settlements, coupled with declining productivity. Government health, safety, and environmental regulations caused most of the productivity decreases. Uncertainty about the future of environmental regulations concerning smokestack emissions, problems with acid rain in the Northeast, and equivocation over rules mandating that power plants and industrial users of fuel oil convert to coal created uncertainties and made business unwilling to invest in plant and equipment using coal. Increases in coal-based taxes by the western states, an unexpected slowdown in the growth of electricity demand, and increased costs reduced the demand for coal. A major reason for these regulations, tax and cost increases, and uncertainty arose because of the increasingly aggressive competition over economic rents expected to accompany expanding coal production and ore. These conflicts are examined at the federal, state, and local levels.

The policies of the federal government affecting coal reviewed here are taxation, regulation, and the government's role in the competition between coal and nuclear power. The federal government levies output-based taxes on coal, as well as the corporate income tax on mining firms. There is a federal coal excise tax of $0.25 per ton on surface-mined coal and $0.50 per ton on underground coal and a reclamation tax (Surface Mining Control and Reclamation Act of 1977) of $0.35 per ton on surface-mined coal, $0.10 on lignite (low-BTU "brown," coal), and $0.15 per ton on underground coal. The black-lung benefit tax is levied on coal output at $0.50 per ton for surface-mined and $0.25 per ton for underground. The federal leasing provisions were detailed in table 2-4. Federal corporate tax preferences apply to coal as well as to oil and gas. The 10 percent depletion rate on coal remains in effect, and coal firms are estimated as paying one of the lowest effective income tax rates (refer to table 2-1). A National Academy of Sciences report (1980) indicates that total estimated tax benefits to eastern underground coal are equivalent to $1.54 per ton and are $0.50 per ton for western surface-mined coal.

Extensive coal acreage on federal lands has been leased in the western states (Church 1981). By 1971 mining and development had not taken place on most tracts, and concerns were expressed that large coal companies were tying up coal reserves in order to exert market power and to preclude the entry of competitors and that future mining might be environmentally harmful. Furthermore, one of the requirements for federal leasing is diligent development, and most lessees had not taken steps to begin development. Thus, a ten-year moratorium on coal leasing was put into effect in 1971. In 1976 the Coal Leasing Amendments and the Federal Lands Policy and Management Act of 1976 implied that the diligence requirement would be enforced in the future. With a high growth rate envisioned for coal in the National Energy Plan II and after studies undertaken by various government agencies, coal leasing was again initiated in 1981 in checkerboard (interspaced private and public lands) areas. Under the new leasing provisions, a 2.5 percent royalty rate is applied to surface mining and 8.0 percent for underground mining.

Federal regulations affecting coal are numerous and in the past decade have adversely affected labor productivity, especially in underground mines. The Federal Mineral Leasing Act and the 1976 changes to it have been referred to previously, as has the Surface Mining Control and Reclamation Act of 1977. Safety and health regulations are contained in the Coal Health and Safety Act of 1969. Although the requirement that utilities and industrial users substitute coal for petroleum fuels in the Power Plant and Industrial Fuel Act of 1978 would appear to bode well for coal demand, this has not been the case. One reason is that industries delayed conversion, and some expected the act to be modified. The Clean Air Act of 1970 and various amendments to it have had a critical effect on the coal industry (Bruce Horovitz, "Coal's Soiled Promise," *Industry Week,* April 6, 1981), and the revised clean air amendments have altered coal-development plans.

Another factor affecting the consumption of coal has been its competition with nuclear technology in new electric power plants. Although the Three Mile Island accident dimmed the future of nuclear power, it has enjoyed perhaps greater subsidies and tax preferences than other technologies. The *Wall Street Journal* (December 15, 1980) referred to a DOE draft report estimating that commercial nuclear power had been granted $37 bil-

billion in federal subsidies over the past thirty years. The benefits range from government-funded applied and basic research and disposal of waste to subsidized enriched fuel. The net result is that nuclear power was estimated to be 1.66 to 2.50 cents per kilowatt hour cheaper than it would otherwise be. This report apparently does not take the Price-Anderson Act into its calculations. The liability of private utilities is limited to $560 million for any single accident, and the federal government pays 80 percent of that.

Zimmerman and Randall (1980) analyze why the mid-1970s saw the cancellation of most nuclear power plants then currently on the drawing boards. The effect of far longer construction time (as interest rates rose) and cost overruns interacting with longer licensing reviews kept those plants under construction from going on line according to plans. The overall effect on costs were devastating. By 1980 the average length of time to order, build, and receive licensing approval increased to fourteen years. Zimmerman and Randall also analyzed the power plant investment decision in an economic model and concluded that the probability of selecting nuclear technology over the alternatives of coal and residual fuel oil achieved a high in 1975 or 0.95 and by 1978 the probability had declined to 0.28.

While the federal government has subsidized the commercial nuclear industry, the suppliers of uranium have sought to extract economic rents. New Mexico produces half of the U.S. and 18 percent of the world's uranium supply. When rising uranium taxes in 1977, the Three Mile Island accident, and increasing world competition decreased demand (the spot price fell from $40 per pound of yellowcake in March to $31 in August 1980), lobbyists made effective use of New Mexico's uranium mine unemployment to secure a tax reduction in 1981. The Grants Mineral Belt area is accustomed to this boom-bust uranium cycle after similar experiences in the 1950s and 1960s. New Mexico residents have become accustomed to some of the negative aspects as well. The mine tailings are radioactive (low levels) and a tailing-pond dam break in 1979 at United Nuclear, which flowed thirty miles down the Rio Puerco, has made New Mexicans more concerned about their health. Some of the dry-tailings piles are one-hundred feet tall, and 6 million tons per year are added to them ( *Wall Street Journal,* August 25, 1980).

Wyoming is the other major domestic supplier of yellowcake. In the late 1970s, the Tennessee Valley Authority (TVA) purchased rights to uranium in that state for its nuclear power plants. However, the U.S. Constitution prohibits units of government from taxing the federal government and TVA is government owned. Consequently it did not have to pay Wyoming severance taxes. As a negotiating weapon, the state denied operating permits for TVA mines and mills. In 1980 the state and TVA reached an accord whereby title to the mineral rights was turned over to a nongovernment trustee. This entity pays the state taxes and then transfers uranium ownership back to the TVA in order to circumvent the prohibition. (For an interesting comparison of state and federal coal and uranium taxes, see Gillis 1979.) The activity of state legislatures in coal-producing states and the response of coal-consuming regions has forced the federal government into negotiating their conflicts over rents.

Initial coal development took place in the eastern states and the Appalachian region at a time when this economic development was welcomed, despite how dirty and dangerous the jobs that accompanied it were. In the 1930s and 1940s coal was almost universally unionized, and the United Mine Workers were in the front of the aggressive unions successful in securing economic advances. After World War II, as technology changed and productivity-increasing mechanization took place, the union went along with the changes. However, as petroleum products became cheaper to use than coal, the industry went into decline, as did the living standards in these regions. Because of this history, state taxation and regulation of coal mining in these areas has been modest.

In the 1970s the market for eastern coal was adversely affected by environmental quality standards that identified the coal-burning by-product of sulfur oxides as damaging and requiring strict controls. Eastern and midwestern coal for the most part has high sulfur content, which makes it expensive to clean up. Vast reserves of strip-mining coal in the West, although lower in Btu content, are low in sulfur and can be mined with giant earth-moving machinery (some seam thicknesses are over fifty feet) more cheaply than underground mining. In 1972, 80 percent of low-sulfur production came from western states. The western coal industry is mostly non-union and highly productive. (For a good description of coal-mining technology and economics, see Zimmerman 1980).

A 1981 report produced by the DOE concerning the long-run prospects for domestic coal concludes that by the mid-1980s, 70 to 80 percent of U.S. production will come from western states, and western coal will be exported to some eastern states. Their forecast is based on surveys of coal-fired plants under construction and in planning, as well as long-term coal contracts.

This history and these conditions led eastern- and western-producing states to tax and regulate differently. In 1979, fifteen states levied severance taxes on coal production ranging from two cents to sixty-five cents per ton for specific taxes and 4.5 to 30 percent for ad valorem taxes, freight on board at mine mouth. In six states an excise tax, ranging from 2.5 to 4.75 percent, is also levied, and in two states coal that is used in-state as an intermediate good is exempted. Furthermore, taxes are levied in some areas as a property tax based on coal output. (For a detailed examination of state and local taxes, see Church 1981 and Morgan and Olson 1979.) Most states have a corporate income tax, which uses the federal tax base or some modification of it.

The relatively recent development of western coal, its low-cost (high labor productivity) and sulfur-content advantages, and growing concern over environmental impacts associated with strip mining induced the western states to tax coal aggressively. The northern Great Plains, with its Powder River basin (Montana and Wyoming, where 68 percent of the low sulfur reserves lie), is perhaps the area where those advantages are greatest, and both states increased taxes significantly (Church 1978). Most notable among these increases is Montana's coal severance tax enacted in 1975, with rates ranging from 20 to 30 percent depending on the characteristics of the coal. This tax, coupled with Montana's mineral mining tax, property tax, and corporate income tax, is estimated (Church 1981) to reach an effective rate of 46 percent of the mine-mouth price. While Wyoming has not achieved those levels, Church (1981) estimates it taxes to total an effective rate of 19.9 percent as of 1977, and it has since increased its severance tax to 17 percent (the legislature considered but rejected a 25 percent rate).

These tax rates do not reveal the total impact on state and local revenues. Extraction, processing, and transporting the resource is an economic activity with secondary and tertiary effects as the income flows to labor and owners of land and the extractive firms filter through the economy. Sales, personal, and corporate income and property taxes are collected from these economic activities. Krutilla and Fisher (1978) carried out a detailed analysis of the total impact of coal development in the northern plains on all tax revenues and expenditures by state and local government to estimate the net effect on state and local government. They concluded that no net fiscal deficit occurred.

Coal taxes were increased by Montana, Wyoming, New Mexico, and North Dakota in the 1970s. A 1976 Rand Corporation report was prophetic in stating, "The emerging pattern of state coal tax policy in the northern Great Plains is one of OPEC-like revenue maximization" (Nehrig and Zycher 1976, p. 148). Church (1978) had described the phenomenon as "tax leadership," and Gillis (1979) calls it the fiscal demonstration effect, citing resource tax increases in Canada as well. Multiple reasons for these increases may be found; for example, state policymakers have cited the fiscal and environmental burdens on numerous occasions (see Link 1978). However, the movement was not unidirectional. In 1981 a proposed coal severance tax was defeated in Utah, where there had been none previously. The reason for the defeat is that Utah coal is not competitive, and the tax would have affected the industry adversely.

The premise behind the justification for increasing coal-based taxes is that the environmental costs and required expenditures for upgrading highways and supplying services to rapidly expanding boom towns, often located in isolated areas, require additional revenues. The factual evidence of a fiscal burden is mixed (see Krutilla and Fisher 1978 and Murdock and Leistritz, 1979) but the rhetoric is strong. For example, U.S. Congressman Tauzin (1979) of Louisiana cites the Butte Montana copper mining area where extraction took place from 1910 through 1975, when the mine was closed. The population rose to 100,000 in the early part of the boom and fell to less than 25,000 in 1979. Its glory faded as in the case of many boom towns, to "a battered town, an unloved town . . . where everything was exploited."

Numerous authors have discussed the potential for exporting tax burdens in order to capture economic rents (Church 1978, 1980, 1981; Gillis and McLure 1975; Gillis 1979; McLure 1978; Shelton and Morgan 1977; Burness 1976). Church (1981) tested the hypothesis that states weigh two conflicting policy goals—maximizing tax revenues versus maximizing the development of the coal resource (as measured by the wage bill paid to miners)—and tested this hypothesis for the sixteen coal-producing states in 1978. The relative importance of each conflicting goal is revealed by state tax policy and the prevailing production cost and demand (market) conditions. The estimated policy weights indicate that western states place a high weight on tax revenues, whereas midwestern and eastern states weight the wage bill more heavily.

Another aspect that has unsettled consuming states is that the western coal states are investing severance tax proceeds in order to provide future revenues, as well as spending them and cutting state taxes, which makes them more-attractive locations for industry. Griffin and Shelton (1978) report that Montana and Wyoming place about 25 percent of coal severance tax receipts in mineral trust funds and allocate about 19 percent to local communities affected by resource development. Montana increased the trust fund contribution to 50 percent in 1980, whose principal "must forever remain inviolate" unless appropriated by a vote of three-fourths of the members of each house of the legislature. In 1981 the New Mexico legislature required that severance-tax trust funds be invested and used to retire outstanding bonded indebtedness to ensure that assets would grow and be available in the future.

Other ways exist to capture economic rent from coal. Extensive low-sulfur coal reserves in New Mexico and lenient environmental quality regulations relative to those in southern California have led utilities to locate coal-fired power plants there. The Public Service Company of New Mexico was the most profitable electric utility in the country in the late 1970s, and 85 percent of its fuel comes from coal. The Four Corners plant, the world's largest, is jointly owned by five utilities, and most of the power is exported to Arizona and southern California. In 1975, the New Mexico legislature enacted a tax on electric power generation in which locally consumed power was exempted by means of crediting the gross-receipts tax that was already in effect (Chung, Church, and Kury 1980). The out-of-state utility owners and power purchasers challenged the act unsuccessfully in the New Mexico courts and successfully in the U.S. Supreme Court. Section 2121(a) of the Tax Reform Act of 1976, inserted as a result of utility lobbying efforts, was written in such a way as to apply exclusively to the tax, and it was on this provision and the discrimination test under the commerce clause of the Constitution that the U.S. Supreme Court struck the tax down. Chung, Church, and Kury point out that the plant was built in New Mexico because of cost advantages and therefore earns economic rents; however, the tax was an inefficient mechanism to capture those rents. This episode illustrates the use of indirect means in competing for economic rent associated with coal extraction.

A related episode comes from the Northwest power bill. The impetus for the bill comes from the transition from a renewable natural resource that previously had not been used to capacity to a situation in which its capacity had become fully utilized. The resource is electricity produced from federally funded dams and hydroelectric projects, and the competition is over economic rents. Originally the bauxite-aluminum refining industry was built in the Northwest states in response to cheap hydropower (this technology is a heavy user of electricity), which was offered as an incentive for locating there when a large, unused capacity was foreseen. However, other industries located there for the same reason, and population growth increased demand, which outstripped capacity by the late 1970s. The situation was accentuated by drought conditions during the period. Conflicts arose among the aluminum industry, whose existence depended on this natural resource, other industries, farmers in electrical cooperatives that purchased hydropower, and residential users. New capacity from a number of nuclear power plants under construction and planned coal-fired plants would cost several times the prevailing hydro rate, and the differential created economic rents that each segment was willing to fight for.

The solution was arrived at politically because the dams are federally owned and electric power production is an industry regulated by individual state commissions. The Northwest power bill provides for the pooling of various power sources and a formula for distributing the low-cost existing hydro capacity and the high-cost nuclear and coal power among the competing groups. The solution is advantageous to residential customers because they represent more political votes than do any of the other contenders. However, the impetus for the bill came from the aluminum producers, which were fearful that if the conflict remained unresolved for long, they would end up with no share of cheap energy and would be forced to shut down, with a resultant loss of jobs and economic base for the area.

The rapid rise of western coal, its accompanying rent, and the recent tax increases by western states stimulated two reactions. Consuming states sought to constrain these increases by invoking air-pollution regulations, by challenging Montana's 30 percent tax in court, and by supporting federal legislation to place a cap on severance tax rates. Railways sought to transfer rents by exercising monopoly power over moving coal and in so doing competed with producing-state governments and consuming regions.

Regulation has been used by midwestern coal-producing states as a device to create economic rents. The Clean Air Act of 1970 gave low-sulfur coal a significant competitive edge because utilities using it would not have to install scrubbers to achieve clean air standards. By the mid-1970s a coal-fired power plant with scrubbers and filters was estimated to cost virtually the same as a nuclear power plant, and elimination of these by using low-sulfur coal created enormous cost savings (Zimmerman 1980).

Ohio legislators had sought to impose a tax on consumption with a high rate on low-sulfur coal and a low rate on high-sulfur coal in order to benefit its in-state high-sulfur coal producers. The tax was struck down by the courts as being discriminatory. An alternative was for the midwestern and eastern states to lobby for enactment of stiffer air pollution requirements, which would favor high-sulfur coal. The perverse manipulation of environmental regulations to create economic rent for high-sulfur midwestern and eastern coal and diminish demand and economic rent for low-sulfur western coal was brought about by an unlikely political alliance of environmental activists (the Sierra Club and the Natural Resources Defense Council), the owners of high-sulfur coal, and the United Mine Workers, which represents midwestern and eastern workers but not western strip miners. The commonalities of interests is obvious. The environmentalists prefer cleaner air and usually ignore economic costs of achieving it; the industry wanted to create markets; the unions wanted development and jobs in the stagnant industry; and the states wanted tax revenues (see Ackerman and Hassler 1981).

The Clean Air Act of 1970 made a distinction between existing pollution sources and new sources built after the act. Old sources were to be controlled by states (state implementation plans) and monitored by the Environmental Protection Agency (EPA). New sources fell under EPA regulation. Congress and EPA later mandated that "best available control technology" (BACT) be implemented with minimal consideration to cost. In 1976 Congress enacted new-source emission standards, and eastern and midwestern coal interests realized the opportunity to manipulate the standards. They were successful in having Congress and EPA require that all new sources install scrubbers on plants built after 1979 regardless of the stack emissions that could have been achieved with low-sulfur (western) coal and no sulfur scrubbing.

The DOE and President Carter's Regulatory Analysis Review Group pressured EPA to change the wasteful decision. Scrubbers make coal-fueled plants nearly as expensive to build as nuclear plants (the standard would cost billions), reduce the efficiency of energy use, require vast amounts of water, result in sulfurous sludge in large quantities and sulfuric acid, and, ironically, require minimum sulfur to work so that in certain cases sulfur would have been added to coal. However, the alliance protected its newly won rents with the minor concession of allowing the lower-cost dry scrubbing, an untried technology. This use of regulation is yet another episode in the ongoing competition over natural-resource revenues and rents.

The Powder River basin of Wyoming and Montana dominates the low-sulfur coal market from the Midwest in a southerly arc through Texas. Fourteen midwestern coal-consuming utilities and, somewhat ironically because of the city-owned utility, Austin, Texas (with ex-Secretary of State William P. Rogers as counsel), challenged Montana's 30 percent severance tax on a number of constitutional grounds. In 1981 a coalition of Midwest and Northwest congressional representatives filed a brief in support of the plaintiffs estimating that the tax would cost their consumers $11.3 billion over the next twenty-five years. In 1980 the coal-severance tax produced $81 million for Wyoming and $71 million for Montana, nearly doubling their 1978 revenues. The uncertainty of the Montana court case and the concern over future electricity prices, and its federally mandated dependence on coal and nuclear energy, led to congressional action to limit state coal severance taxes. The National Coal Consumers Alliance, "a self-proclaimed movement to protect consumers from impacts of unfair taxes on energy" ("Limit on State Severance Taxes on Coal Recommended," *Public Utilities* 105, April 1980), made up of private and public utilities, actively lobbied for a bill to limit severance taxes on coal to 12.5 percent in 1980 and 1981. Apparently this rate was chosen because it equals the portion of federal royalties previously granted to the states in which the mineral was extracted. They pointed out that Montana had increased its coal tax rate five times since 1973 and that a cap on Montana's 30 percent tax and Wyoming's 17 percent would have saved consumers $41 million in 1978. The 1980 bill had forty cosponsors in the House of Representatives.

Montana's representative, Ron Marlenee, led the opposition to the bill, citing that sales taxes on electricity and the revenues of taxes on oil and gas to Texas, Louisiana, Oklahoma, and Alaska far exceed those to Montana or Wyoming. One Montana legislator said the bill could ignite an economic war among states that would "make the Sagebrush Rebellion look like a garden party." In congressional hearings Ed Herschler, governor of Wyoming, maintained that the federal government's taxes, royalties, and regulations accounted for over 50 percent of the cost of their coal, whereas Wyoming's severance tax accounts for 2.5 percent of the delivered per ton price ($25.55) of coal in San Antonio when utilities have purchased their own railway cars. The Congressional Research Service estimated that the Wyoming severance tax adds from 0.8 to 1.5 percent on to the end-use cost of electricity, while the Louisiana oil severance tax adds 7.2 percent. These points are emphasized by comparing the effect of severance taxes on the price of energy for gasoline, home heating oil, natural gas, and electricity produced from natural gas, oil, and coal in table 2–6.

**Table 2-6**
**Severance-Tax Impact on the End Product**

| End Product | Price at Point of Taxation | Amount of Severance Tax | End-Use Cost | Percentage of End-Use Cost as Tax |
|---|---|---|---|---|
| Oil-fired power plant (electric) | $17.00/bbl | $2.125/bbl | $.07/kw | 6.3 |
| Home heating | 17.00/bbl | 2.125/bbl | .86/gal. | 6.3 |
| Gasoline | 17.00/bbl | 2.125/bbl | 1.20/gal. | 4.1 |
| Residential gas | 1.30/mcf | 0.13/mcf | 3.50/mcf | 3.8 |
| Coal-fired power plant (electric) | 12.00/ton (MT-9300 btu/lb.) | 2.64/ton | .045/kw | 3.6 |
| Gas fired (electric) | 1.30/mcf | 0.13/mcf | .045/kw | 3.4 |

Source: Larry Parker, "Energy: Limiting State Coal Severance Taxes," Issue Brief Number 1B80060, Environment and Natural Resources Policy Division, The Library of Congress, Congressional Resource Research Service, Major Issues System, November 4, 1980.
Note: Assumes highest state tax rate in effect: 12.5 percent on crude oil (Louisiana), 10 percent on natural gas (Alaska), and 30 percent on coal (Montana).

The arguments surrounding the coal tax limitation bill go back to negotiations over the windfall-profits tax in 1979. Legislators were aware of the potential magnitude of the tax on state tax and royalty income in producing states. Senator Robert Danforth of Missouri made an unsuccessful bid to make state oil royalties subject to the tax instead of exempting them because it would enable states to "conduct what amounts to economic warfare on the rest of the country. . . . They will begin doing what the OPEC countries are doing, building up their economic base at the expense of the rest of the country" ("Economic War over Oil Looms at the State Level," *National Journal,* December 22, 1979). Further, he expressed concerns that these revenues would be used to attract nonenergy business and industry and allow what economists term cross-subsidization. However, Danforth was turned down because his proposal could alter concepts of federalism. Another amendment proposed and turned down would have removed energy tax revenues from the calculation of tax effort, which is used as a factor in federal general revenue-sharing formulas to state and local governments. If the federal government began taxing state oil and gas revenues, it would open the way to taxing other state activities. This is a states' rights issue and as Justice Thurgood Marshall stated in the Montana coal tax decision, the states' "power of taxation is indispensable to their existence," and thus any efforts to limit this power would have to be considered most carefully. There is no question that Congress can limit the taxing power of states, and the question of Louisiana's first-use tax preempting federal energy legislation was one reason why it was struck down in part because it took on the guise of regulation that conflicted with congressional intent (Hellerstein 1981).

Discussions over the significance of energy taxes on national energy policy and the regional distribution of income continued. In the 1980 presidential campaign, candidate John B. Anderson called for Congress to limit the revenue that states could raise from taxes on coal, oil, and natural gas and to act to redistribute benefits throughout the country. Because of election activity, the severance tax limitation bills failed to be acted on in 1980, although the House Interstate and Commerce Committee approved the tax-limit bill. Minnesota Senator David F. Durenberg introduced a 12.5 percent limitation bill on coal mined on federal lands (most of the Powder River basin coal is on such lands), and former Massachusetts Senator Edward B. Brooke lobbied on behalf of the Coal Consumers Alliance for it in 1981 ("Western Coal Sparks a Test of States' Rights," *Business Week,* February 16, 1981). In a reply to an editorial in the *Wall Street Journal* decrying the tendency of increasing severance taxes to balkanize America, Wyoming Senator Malcolm Wallop ( *Wall Street Journal,* June 16, 1980) stated, "Such efforts trample on the very concept of 'republic!' Why shouldn't Congress limit state corporate income taxes, sales taxes, or any other measure local and state governments use to raise revenues? After the first victim is strung up, the rest will come easy."

The likelihood of such a bill's being enacted and its effect is problematical. New political coalitions on the national level are difficult to form and are more frequently than not easier to speculate about than construct, and once constructed tend to be unstable. Uncertainties as to changes in natural-gas price regulations, future coal exporting from eastern states, national energy policy, and the far larger state revenues to producing states from oil and gas extraction make a coalition supporting coal tax limitation difficult to form because of existing differences and potential conflicts and competition among coal-importing states. Furthermore, state-level policymakers are resourceful, and state tax structures are diverse and protean in their character. If a limit on severance taxes were introduced, then states could shift to special excise, occupation, and privilege taxes, property taxes (many of which in effect currently are based on physical output or its value), and corporate income taxes designed to single out coal or other energy producers.

Efforts to limit states' ability to levy severance taxes brings forth the fiscal federalism issue. Such a move would fundamentally alter this delicate structure. Any immobile and unique resource or natural advantage that draws visitors and business or whose product is exported creates economic rent and the potential for creating monopoly rents, part or all of the burden of which may be exported. If Congress targeted coal revenues, then all sources of tax revenue based on natural resources, or other unique and immobile attributes, would be fair game and from an equity standpoint should be considered. Thus, Nevada's and New Jersey's gambling taxes,

New York's stock transfer charges, and California's taxes on wine should be treated similarly.

Although altering the distribution of income among persons and geographic regions may become a politically attractive reason for the federal government to interfere with state tax and regulatory policies, intervention to ensure that natural resources are extracted and consumed efficiently are yet a more compelling reason. As noted in chapter 1 and detailed in chapter 3, taxes and regulation produce two effects, which economists are adamant about keeping distinct on both the theoretic and empirical levels. The first is who bears the burden and benefits of government policies and thus how they alter the distribution of private incomes and wealth. The second is how these policies alter the production and consumption of natural and man-made resources. Policies that distort the allocation of scarce resources away from their highest and best use or most-efficient use create economic losses that exceed the amount of redistributed income. Economists are able to measure these net economic losses and call them *excess burden* (for a tax this is the loss in excess of the tax revenues received) or welfare losses, for if the distortion were removed, aggregate welfare would rise. Only those regulations and taxes that result in no alterations in consumption and production activities are free of distortions and excess burdens. These policies serve only to redistribute income and wealth. However once sufficient time passes so that people may respond, virtually all tax and regulatory policies alter when, how, or how much of a scarce commodity is produced or consumed and thus produces an efficiency or welfare loss. In discussing natural resources, the potential distortions may be placed into three classifications, which relate to how rapidly the distortion occurs.

Over relatively short time periods—approximately five to ten years for nonrenewable resources—production and consumption are determined primarily by identified and developed reserves. The decision of the extracting firm management centers on how much to remove in each period of time (the rate of extraction) and the quality of the resource that is extracted (ore cutoff grade), although this latter decision is not a factor in oil and gas production. Clearly the two decisions taken together and over time determine the total amount of resource extracted (total recovery). It has been demonstrated that taxes and regulations affect both decisions and thus introduce distortions in resource production and, ultimately, in consumption. The decision to explore for and develop natural resources is an investment decision, which is a long-range management function, that determines how rapidly resources are increased. Tax and regulatory policies may interfere with that decision. This is particularly true when policies vary among jurisdictions because investment will be shifted until the net rate of return on investment after accounting for taxes and regulatory costs is equal in each activity and in each region. In the process capital is said to be mobile, and distortions are likely to result in the same time frame as development decisions are made. This is usually a ten- to thirty-year span. When states tax natural-resource development, distortions depend on how the taxes affect investment and exiting operations and how the tax revenue is spent. If it is used to reduce other tax rates, distribute tax revenue directly to residents as Alaska has attempted, or spend them on publicly supplied services and other programs that encourage the migration of industry, employment, and people, distortions will result. It is the cumulative effects of these distortions of extraction, recovery, investment, and development decisions, and their interference with national energy policy that is perhaps the most valid reason why the federal government should intervene and preempt state authority. However, few legislators understand the effects of these tax and regulatory-induced distortions, and perhaps the largest distortions are created at the federal level.

The third distortion occurs over roughly the same time frame as the one just described, but its scope is greater. States in which investment in natural-resource production takes place receive direct and indirect economic benefits. The industry payrolls and induced economic activity stimulate economic growth. This activity creates indirect demand as private incomes are spent, and the multiplier process takes place. Taxes are paid by resource firms, their employees, and all the economic activity that is directly and indirectly induced by resource development. When the public tax revenue share is used to attract industry and either directly or indirectly to subsidize any other activities such as providing mortgage loans to state residents at below-market rates, distortions arise. The potential for resource-rich areas to cross-subsidize activities that attract industry and jobs has been alluded to by media commentators, elected officials, and numerous public and private sector spokespersons. However, accurate measures of the actual extent and future potential for these migratory distortions on capital and people are unknown.

There is evidence that the demonstration effect of increases in energy taxes has spilled over into other states and other minerals. Wisconsin enacted a tax on net proceeds in 1979 from mining with a 20 percent marginal rate after the discovery and planned development of extensive copper sulfide ores in the state (Cherry 1979). The Montana legislature introduced a 30 percent surface and 15 percent underground severance tax for all hard-rock mining in 1981 up from the previous 1.4 percent tax. The target is two proposed platinum mines ("Taking Platinum Back into the Ground," *Business Week,* March 2, 1981). The tax base allows for the deduction of other taxes, which reduces the effective rate to 22 percent from surface and 11 percent from underground production. Mines producing before 1980 would be exempted, thus freeing Anaconda's large copper mine in Butte, but it would affect Asarco's copper-silver mine at Troy (*Metals*

Week, February 9, 1981). South Dakota imposed a severance tax on gold in 1981, which is expected to raise about $7.5 million annually.

The railroads utilize the monopoly powers granted to them by the Interstate Commerce Commission (ICC) in order to compete for their share of economic rents from coal. Zimmerman (in Church 1981) used his model of the Montana-Wyoming cartel maximizing the present value of coal severance taxes to estimate an equivalent rail haulage rate. The optimum severance tax rate was estimated to be 62.5 percent or about $4 per ton in 1980 (net of federal and state taxes and fees). In 1977 the Wyoming severance tax rate made up approximately $1 of that, and the $3 difference represents 16 to 24 percent of transportation costs to Chicago. Rail rate increases during the years accounted for approximately this amount.

The exclusive rail hauler to the area is the Burlington Northern (BN), which from 1977 to 1979 spent $600 million upgrading track and running a new 116-mile railroad line to the Wyoming coal fields. It planned on spending $2 billion by 1985 (*Business Week,* August 20, 1979). So that BN could recoup its capital investment, the ICC allowed a series of rate increases and, more important, differential rates on the enormous 100-plus car unit coal trains. The San Antonio city public utility's appeal on those rate increases failed in part because financial analysts maintained that a 75 percent rate increase was necessary to justify investments (*Business Week,* June 30, 1980). The rates for the San Antonio utility increased over 60 percent in the three years after converting its natural-gas plants to coal (from the 1970s to 1980 the rate increased from $8 to $18 per ton). The ICC formula allows the railroad to recover its cost of moving coal and a fair return on its investment plus 7 percent of the sum of these two amounts. The city called the 7 percent arbitrary and lost its appeal, nevertheless, the courts held the ICC must justify this amount or come up with an alternative. As of June 1980, the ICC had thirty-three filings for rate increases, so it has recommended a formula approach tied into long-term contracts. These increases imply that the BN is capturing rent and in the process may be using the coal revenues to cross-subsidize other rail operations ("The Railroad Blackmail," *Wall Street Journal*, July 1, 1980). The success of the BN has been duly noted by the investors. The *Wall Street Journal* (September 15, 1980) noted that railroads are benefiting from rate increases, deregulation, and mergers. This was reflected in the transportation stock average increasing 28.6 percent (36.0 percent for the eleven railroads) in the first three quarters of 1980 versus a 13.6 percent increase for industrials. The paper attributed much of this to the role rail is playing in energy, particularly coal.

Three factors infringe on the BN's success: deregulation of railroads, proposals for a competing coal slurry pipeline system, and entry of a railroad competitor. The House of Representatives passed the railroad deregulation bill in September 1980. While it will aid some railroads by allowing mergers and rate increases, BN might be hurt (*Business Week,* September 22, 1980) because it may lose its monopoly position.

Recent advances in technology and increasing energy costs have made it possible to transport coal by pipeline. The coal is pulverized, mixed with water, pumped through a pipeline, and separated and dried at the point of consumption. Several proposals for systems from the Powder River basin to the Midwest have been made, but two problems have prevented their realization. The water requirement concerns Montana and Wyoming residents, and there has been much opposition from these groups. The second is that the pipelines must secure rights of way and lack the power to condemn (eminent domain). They would have to cross railroad rights of way, and those companies have refused to grant the privilege, thus blocking the proposals. Project developers have approached the U.S. Congress in order to secure the right of eminent domain, without success.

Another source of competition for rent going to the BN, the nation's largest, is the Chicago and Northwestern (C&NW) proposed route from Lusk, Wyoming, to Joyce, Nebraska, or Cheyenne, Wyoming, where it would connect with the Union Pacific system, one of the richest rails in the nation. The rail deregulation bill contains a provision for federal financial aid, which would permit the ailing C&NW to build the link (*Wall Street Journal,* September 23, 1980). The BN's first tactic was to fight the proposal, but under deregulation, its power to halt competition would be stymied. The BN has offered an alternative to C&NW of hauling its coal at cost east to Iowa where connections onto their own and not UP's road would occur.

Railroads are also potential beneficiaries of the growth in U.S. coal exports, for their rail links are critical and competition is minimal. In some cases, they own dockside facilities, which give them additional bargaining power. The major coal exporters are South Africa and Australia. Analysts expect the United States (1980 exports of $3.7 billion) to join the ranks of top exporters to Western Europe and Japan (MIT researchers predict U.S. exports may triple by 2000), and there is a potential for exporters to form a cartel in order to create and capture economic rents ("Coal's Sudden Importance Suggests Exporters Could Form Cartel," *Wall Street Journal,* December 2, 1980). However, railroads and ports are constraints on U.S. exporting. For example, in 1981 ships waited as long as sixty days in Maryland and Virginia to load ("Shaping Up to Ship Out," *Forbes,* February 16, 1981).

These examples of competition for natural-resource income by consumers, owners of resources, and capital show that ownership rights can be captured and transferred, and the competing authority of federal, state, and local governments can be employed by each group in that struggle. The complex legal, political, constitutional, and social institutions that are subject to change in the competitive process means that rents may end up being dissipated. Furthermore, the struggle impinges on other natural resources and the entire company. For example, competition over energy affects the renewable resources of water and agricultural land. Processing nonrenewable resources involves enormous amounts of water, which may be made unfit for any other use. Dewatering of mines contaminates surface waters and groundwater and lowers underground watertables. Such acid contamination of eastern surface streams near coal mines is well documented, and the collapse of a uranium mine-tailings dam in New Mexico and the resulting contamination is a reminder of this potential. Coal-slurry pipelines would require enormous quantities of water from the arid West. Oil-shale processing would contaminate far greater quantities of water than any projects previously undertaken in the West. Boom towns, housing construction, workers, and operations personnel in remote areas would place additional demands on scarce water supplies. This water would have to come from either current users, primarily agriculture, or underground water aquifer would be mined, thus treating water like an exhaustible resource. The impending conflicts between energy development, water use, and agriculture are only beginning to be felt and will become yet another factor in competition for rents.

Modern agriculture depends on petroleum for mechanization, irrigation, fertilizers, insecticides, herbicides, and transportation. These resources are energy dependent, which explains one reason why food prices have been components leading inflation along with energy. Some predict that food in the future will "become in the 1980s what oil became in the 1970s—scarce and expensive" ("World Demand for U.S. Grain—Reserves Depleting," *Wall Street Journal,* November 25, 1980). In 1980 the United States supplied 60 percent of the work grain trade.

In several western states, water rights are owned and are transferable property rights. Called *appropriative water rights,* they are awarded to the first beneficial user. The courts, legislators, and bureaucracies that define and enforce these rights have become ever-more important institutions. For example, the state water engineer of New Mexico, Stephen R. Reynolds, is powerful because his office supervises the system of water rights. There are twenty-six declared water basins, over 60 percent of the state, which he regulates, and market values of up to $12,000 per acre-foot prevail (*Wall Street Journal,* May 1, 1980).

The history of western conflicts over water rights is long and bitter. Montana has implied that coal-slurry pipelines may not be considered a beneficial use. Colorado forbids exporting of its water, and its public-utility regulations require building facilities only for the benefit of in-state users. One battle yet to be resolved is the precise ownership to be granted to Indians and the federal government under the concept of prior rights and reserved federal rights. Since all water rights have been assigned in New Mexico, the center for the struggle, granting Indians and the federal government rights means taking someone else's away. New Mexico also became enmeshed (1981) in a battle with El Paso, Texas, over groundwater. New Mexico law forbids exporting water, and the Texas city took the matter to the courts.

To the east of the Rockies, riparian rights means those with access to the water can use it. The effect in drier areas has been devastating. Some Texas panhandle cities are seeing their wells drying up, for the Ogallala aquifer running from South Dakota to Texas is receding. Farmers have been unable to afford to pump from deeper wells, and huge areas may have to convert from irrigated to dryland farming (*Wall Street Journal,* August 6, 1980).

In the western states where the federal government owns from one-half to two-thirds of the land, concern over the more-populous eastern states controlling those lands and resources has fostered the "sagebrush rebellion," a loose organization led by Nevada that claims that transfer of ownership to state governments would create more-timely and efficient use of these lands. Although this particular movement does not appear to be successful, regional organizations have formed in order to act collectively with greater power on the national political scene. One such group is the Southern Growth Policies Board, formed in 1980 and made up of fourteen southern states and Puerto Rico. Their concerns are federal energy policy and its effect on the region ("Commission on South's Future Grapples with Conflicting Goals," *Wall Street Journal,* December 23, 1980). Colorado, Utah, and Wyoming formed the Tri-State Consortium in 1980 to work toward regional policy concerning industrial development and energy impacts on labor. The Western Governors' Policy Office, formed in 1975, has been active in energy and resource issues affecting its ten state members (Hayes 1980). In 1981, the Sun Belt Council, made up of ninety House members from seventeen southern and southwestern states, was formed to protect their interests against the Northeast-Midwest Coalition formed in 1976 and its research arm, the Northeast-Midwest Institute ("Sun Belt Legislators Form Caucus," *Boston Globe,* April 22, 1981).

The popular press and some political leaders have begun to refer to the various movements in the United States as balkanization. *U.S. News and World Report* published a long article on the subject on June 16, 1980: "New War between the States—Our States—over Energy." The *Chicago Sun-Times* ran an editorial (June 22, 1980) decrying the ability of energy-rich states to cut or eliminate corporate income taxes and employ other incentives to lure industry as "intolerable" and opined that the next civil war would not be fought with bullets but with lawsuits and legislation. The *Wall Street Journal* reported on October 21, 1980, on "State Taxes on Resource

Exports Threaten New National Conflicts,'' and stated that the conflict is East versus West rather than the North-South conflict of the Civil War. However, its editors questioned the depth of the sunbelt/frostbelt conflict and noted the strong relative economic growth of the Northeast in 1980 (February 17, 1981).

## The Canadian Case

Competition over natural-resource income and wealth by means of taxation and regulation in Canada, while equally or perhaps even more heated than in the United States, has followed a considerably different path because of Canada's economic, social, and political-historial development. The size of the resource base, its time path of development, and the character of demographic development has led to four major differences in Canada's economic and political framework.

Canada is governed under the parliamentary system, and as such the governing party and its prime minister enjoy great power. Because of the historical development of Canada and its slower westward movement, its population is concentrated in Ontario (roughly 40 percent of the population), and thus this province dominates national politics. Furthermore, the British North America Act (BNA) of 1867 acted as the country's constitution until 1982. Given Canada's commonwealth status, concerted independence efforts began in 1978 to "bring the constitution home" and in the process redraft it. The call for a Canadian constitution has created political and institutional instability, for although the new constitution must be approved by Westminster, its formulation is a Canadian affair, and there has been some uncertainty as to whether unanimity among the provincial governments is required. Under the BNA, the provinces are granted wide discretionary powers, and section 109 conveys ownership of mineral rights to the provincial governments. The populated coastal and eastern provinces, with the exception of hydroelectric development, long ago alienated those rights and conveyed them to private hands. However, the prairie provinces of Alberta, Saskatchewan, and Manitoba entered the federation at a late date, and their ability to alienate was not granted until 1930 because their status had been one of an agricultural frontier.

Because of this quirk of history, these provinces had a delayed start, and Alberta in particular has retained mineral rights, conveying only a minority to freehold private ownership. As of 1981, approximately 90 percent of Canada's oil production took place in Alberta, and oil and gas reserves are concentrated there, as well as in Sasketchewan and British Columbia. Potentially rich hydrocarbon discoveries have been made of the outer continental shelf of the maritime provinces and in the arctic regions, all of them owned by the federal government. The prairie provinces and British Columbia also contain the majority of other resources, including enormous oil reserves contained in tar sands and oil shale, potash, and other hard-rock minerals. Furthermore, provinces are granted wide tax and regulatory authority, and because of past socialist governments in the prairie provinces, government corporations exist and expropriation of natural resources is not unknown. Section 125 of the BNA states that the crown is prohibited from taxing the crown so that absolute intergovernmental tax immunity exists, and this may extend to government-owned enterprises.

The second institution that distinguishes the Canadian situation from the U.S. one is the post-World War II growth of intergovernmental grants. The purpose of these grants is to equalize tax revenues (capacity) among the provinces; these allow the poorer provinces, the maritimes and Quebec, to run deficits equal to 25 percent of their intraprovincial gross domestic product, and government activity has become nearly equal to income produced in the private sector. By 1981 the Provincial Equalization Program equalized tax capacity based on twenty-nine separate taxes, although the formula underrepresents natural-resource revenues by approximately 30 percent relative to other tax bases. Although the system has been labeled the "fiscal wonder of the world," the burgeoning energy-resource revenues in the western provinces and their increasing combativeness, coupled with the scheduled 1982 termination and thus renegotiation of the fiscal program, makes this an additional situation fostering uncertainty and instability (Boadway and Flatters 1981; Whyte 1981).

The third institution affecting competition over natural-resource revenues is the inauguration and continuation of federal price controls on oil and natural gas. Instituted in 1973 after the worldwide oil-price increases, these controls remained in effect into the 1980s and became a source of bitter controversy between producing and consuming provinces. The eastern provinces import oil from world markets, and the federal government subsidizes these imports so that net price equals the regulated price. Thus producing provinces are subsidizing consumers by regulated oil and by direct fiscal subsidies, which end up going to oil-exporting countries. The steps and speed of price deregulation have made for bitter controversy in Canada, which reached a climax when the producing provinces initiated talk of secession.

The final institution that distinguishes the Canadian case is its perceived status as an economic colony. In part because of growing feelings of separatism and controversies over energy revenues, Prime Minister Trudeau announced the goal of Canadianizing energy companies. The means were incentives in the form of exploration and development subsidies to Canadian-owned companies only, reductions in income-tax deductions for non-

Canadian companies, expropriation of portions of oil leases on federal lands, and government-owned enterprise acquisition of foreign-owned energy companies. One reason for this move, initiated in 1980, was to enhance the prime minister's power in the negotiations over fiscal sharing, forming the Canadian constitution, and energy-price deregulation and the division of natural resource-revenues among the provinces and the federal government, where the ebb and flow of political power between the provinces and the federal authorities has been continuous since its founding.

### The Process of Conflict in Canada

Canada, from its early colonial period until relatively recently, has accepted its role as a supplier of raw and semiprocessed natural resources, first to England and Europe and later to the United States. Agricultural and nonrenewable natural resource riches were essential to its economic development. However, as the country grew and developed, nationalism and regionalism grew strong, and by the late 1960s, these issues gradually began to overshadow Canada's previous role as the compliant supplier. Growing foreign ownership and the surge of U.S. investment in the 1950s gave impetus to these concerns. OPEC and the mideast oil cutoff shocks of 1973 laid the groundwork for the most-significant changes in Canada's natural-resource policies ever, and the resulting conflicts parallel and even presage events in the United States.

Canada shed both its legal and economic colonial status more slowly than the United States and remains a member of the commonwealth. Its renewable and nonrenewable resource wealth—first the fur trade and then precious metals—served as the major initial attraction. Next came the discovery of base metals and the development of the rich western plains for agriculture. Prior to World War I, gold and silver were the primary nonrenewable resources of interest. Only the highest grades were exploited due to the prices of those metals and the prevailing technology, so mine life was short and the boom-town phenomenon prevailed. Subsequent improvements in technology permitted lower-quality ores to be economically exploitable, and the base metals exports of zinc, lead, nickel, and copper became important to the economy. During World War II and thereafter, U.S. markets and their investment capital became increasingly important. During this period, there was a tacit agreement between the federal government and the provinces that the exploitation of resources and settlement of land should be encouraged in order to accelerate the development of the country. The railroads were instrumental in this process. In the 1920s they opened up the continent to exploration and development. Later resource discoveries dictated where new railroads would go.

This attitude led to the favorable tax status for natural resources, which was codified in the 1955 federal budget when the concessions were made permanent. These included low royalties, transfer of ownership to private hands and tax discrimination created by favorable depletion (a 33⅓ percent rate to firms and 10 to 20 percent to shareholders) and depreciation allowances, the expensing of exploration and development costs, including special exemptions to prospector's and grubstakers' exploration, and a three-year tax holiday for new mines (Burns 1976). Provincial concessions included tax holidays or reductions for new mines, allowances for writing off preproduction expenses, and eventually concessions for further processing. The 1967 Carter Commission estimated that the total forgone revenue from these concessions in 1961 exceeded $150 million. In the United States, the Paley Commission Report released in 1952 raised the issues of exhaustibility of domestic natural resources as the United States saw itself becoming a net importer of certain materials. One result was the acceleration of Canadian investments by U.S. firms. This led to fears of foreign domination and a realization that dependence on the rapid exploitation of natural resources increased risk, promoted dependence on few industries, and made the economy unstable.

The provinces continued to promote actively exploration and development of nonrenewable resources well into the 1960s. The Canadian Constitution, the British North American Act (BNA), clearly assigns resource ownership to the provinces, as well as the management and sale of public lands, but reserves certain controls for the federal government. Section 109 of the BNA explicitly granted ownership of "Lands, Mines, Minerals, or Royalties" to the provinces of Ontario, Quebec, Nova Scotia, and New Brunswick. British Columbia, Prince Edward Island, and Newfoundland were granted similar powers upon their entry to the dominion, and the three western prairie provinces of Saskatchewan, Manitoba, and Alberta were granted full ownership in 1930 (Burns 1976, p. 16). Section 92 grants the provinces the right to make laws in relation to those minerals. Thus provincial policy is dominant.

The Provincial Mines Ministers' Conference (1945) and the Canadian Ministerial Conference on Mineral Policies were established during this period. These groups advocated coordinating policies and expanding the powers of those bodies into finance and the environment in order to effect long-term solutions and make resource extraction a stable component of the economy. Although resource-management, ownership, and investment policies are interdependent, they are complex, and regional and parochial interests began to emerge. As Kenneth Eaton, the author of much of the Canadian tax legislation during the period, said of the making of the tax policy:

to know the range of problems in governments as it inexorably extends its influence into the private economy, must always depend for a fair solution on the good sense and integrity of the lonely few who know what they are all about. The official Opposition and least of all the general public, can never intelligently probe the depths of their intricate significance. [Burns 1976]

Section 125 of the BNA, the taxation-immunity clause, exempts royalty payments to the provincial governments from taxation by other units of government (Campbell, Gainer, and Scott 1976). This has been labeled the "incest clause" for it prohibits other family members, units of government, from "doing it to each other." For example, the provincially owned British Columbia Petroleum Corporation makes voluntary in-lieu payments based on the income tax structure.

The provinces had relinquished most independent sources of tax revenue at the confederation, and ownership of resources was perhaps a concession to their independent self-government and as an extension of control of property and civil rights, a provincial matter. Section 92 of the BNA also grants provinces the power to employ direct taxation. The courts have applied the commerce clause to interprovincial and international trade flows, but the application is more limited than the courts liberal interpretation of the comparable U.S. Constitution's commerce clause. The BNA gives the federal government authority to regulate trade, exploration, and development by the powers to regulate communications, transportation, and commerce.

The antecedents for change in the provincial-federal relationships, especially with respect to sharing in and redistributing resource-based revenues, date from the late 1930s, resurfaced in the mid-1960s, and grew to full-fledged economic war in the 1970s. During the Royal Commission on Dominion-Provincial Relations in 1931, Ontario and British Columbia defended the special tax status of mining income because of its exhaustibility. The commission recommended a special rebate to each province of 10 percent of mining and oil industry federal tax revenues, as well as from smelters and refiners of domestic ores. With the advent of international conflict and the Wartime Tax Agreement Act of 1941, the provinces relinquished income tax policy to the hands of the federal government. The postwar era brought about needs for reconstruction supported by federal revenues. Efforts were made to negotiate agreements with the provinces to "rent" their tax powers, and these were signed separately except with Ontario and Quebec. The profits from mining but not from further processing of the resource were subject to provincial income taxation, with maximum deductions limited to 65 percent of net profits; these taxes were deductible from the federal income tax base. The 1947 tax act also explicitly recognized that royalties were to compensate the province for the "severance taking, extraction or removal" of the resource.

The federal income tax rates gradually increased from approximately 33 percent to 47 percent by 1967, while provincial mining taxes, although variable, generally remained below the 15 percent maximum rate previously agreed to. Provincial royalties, at 36 percent, were a significant source of revenues since 80 percent of all mineral rights were on leaseholds owned by the provinces (Martin 1978). The deductibility of provincial royalty payments and income taxes reduced their burden by nearly one-half and was in effect a method of transferring revenue from the federal government to the provincial treasury. The special tax incentives remained in effect throughout the period. The Carter Commission *Report* (Carter 1967) and in particular the contributions of Bucovetsky and Timbrell to that report changed much of this thinking. While their arguments for tax changes rested on economic analysis, the political basis for the recommendations stemmed from concerns over foreign ownership and control and over exhaustion of nonrenewable resources.

The premise on which the *Report* was based was that Canadian tax policy lacked a consistent focus and caused "confusion, uncertainty, and incomprehensible tax burdens." The major slogan was that a "buck is a buck is a buck," and thus income from whatever source should be treated equivalently. Economists defined a tax structure as neutral when it does not distort consumption, investment, and other economic decisions away from what would occur without the tax or alters all prices by the same percentage so no resource distortions occur. The Carter Commisson advocated across-the-board tax neutrality. It reviewed arguments for the special tax status of the mineral industries and concluded that most of them were unfounded. It decided that most tax concessions were unjustified and led to the inefficient use of resources; the only tax advantage that could be justified was the expensing of exploration and development costs. While acknowledging that extractive industry investments in separate ventures are risky, the council also pointed out that large concerns are able to diversify and spread risks over many projects; thus nonneutral tax treatment was ill suited to remedy any remaining differentials. It did however, concede that direct subsidies might be justified under certain circumstances. The result was that the Carter Commission recommended the following changes to achieve tax neutrality: elimination of tax holidays (to be replaced by rapid write-off of exploration and development expenses), elimination of all depletion allowances, elimination of prospectors' and grubstakers' exemption from income taxation, and separate treatment of exploration (100 percent deduction) and development (10 to 20 percent deduction) capital costs. It suggested that the deductibility of provincial royalties, leases, and tax payments remain.

The proposals were heavily modified and appeared in the government's *Benson White Paper* in 1969. The major difference was a recommended "earned" depletion to account for exhaustion when substituted for the existing depletion arrangement; the other modifications ended up as no net changes. At this point the provinces began to complain. Charles McNaughton, Ontario's treasurer (Ontario 1970), criticized the federal proposals and advocated continuing the tax concessions. The minister of finance offered a compromise in a letter in the *Canadian Tax Journal,* (Brown 1970), which included an additional 15 percent abatement from the federal tax for mining firms as a quid pro quo for the eventual removal of the deductibility of provincial mining tax. Alberta and Saskatchewan voiced their concern also.

The Parliament reviewed the various recommendations and was disposed to the favorable treatment of the mineral resource industry. Tax reforms became law in 1972, and changes were gradually implemented until 1977. The 1972 act eliminated the three-year tax holiday and substituted rapid write-offs of capital expenditures for immediate expensing; eliminated prospectors' and grubstakers' income exclusions; made provincial mining taxes and royalties for oil and natural gas temporarily deductible; and substituted an earned depletion deduction for percentage depletion (deduction) of $1 for every $3 spent in Canada on exploration and development with a 33⅓ percent of production maximum) (Carson 1978).

In the meantime, the provinces had not been inactive. British Columbia tried, unsuccessfully, to apply its mining tax to processing operations in 1968, for the original tax was found to be nondeductible from the federal income tax base. Quebec exemplified its independent course by signing an agreement with France for exploration and development of copper reserves. Plummeting potash prices (from $20 to $3 per ton in the late 1960s) prompted Saskatchewan to institute production quotas, a price floor, and a tax on reserves in order to restrict output and increase price. Since the province's one of the world's major suppliers and exports 99 percent of its output, these changes were thought to be a way to affect market equilibrium and to protect this source of royalty by exerting market power. The regulations were challenged in 1969, and the Supreme Court ruled in favor of the federal government by holding that quotas and prices were the purview of the federal government under the regulation of commerce provisions of the BNA (Chambers and Reid 1979), in effect granting the federal government powers over resource property right. The province responded by nationalizing the industry and establishing a crown corporation (potash corporation of Saskatchewan) which it interpreted as being exempt from federal taxation. The provincial attempt to regulate potash production and prices was struck down by the Supreme Court in 1978 because it interfered with the federal trade and commerce powers over products entering extraprovincial trade. This case continues to be important because of the role of state enterprise and regulation over oil and natural gas.

This move coincided with the election of socialist majorities in that province, British Columbia, and Manitoba, all of which initiated actions in the resource area. The Krerans report in Manitoba sought to resolve conflicts between the secretariat officer and the technocrats in the Mines Department over the role of the public and private sectors in development, for high profits in mineral industries in the 1960s whetted politicians' appetites for a bigger piece of the pie. Alberta's royalty rate on oil and gas was 22 percent and Saskatchewan's was 17 percent. Most western provinces derived a majority of their revenues from resource royalties based on value of output, income taxes applicable solely to mining firms, and, to a lesser degree, acreage taxes on surface lands owned or leased by extractive firms.

Changes in tax policies and a sharp fall in metal prices following a generally successful period occurred in the 1970s. The rate of return on investments in mining fell from 10.6 percent in 1970 to 3.3 percent in 1972, whereas the all-industry average was 6.8 percent. However, in 1973–1974, the OPEC embargo and subsequent natural-resource price increases and concern over imminent exhaustion of all nonrenewable resources resulted in frenzied buying. Petroleum and coal prices soared, as did those of copper, gold, lead, silver, and zinc. In 1973–1974 profits in Canadian mining companies grew by 52 percent (Burns 1976). Thus during the early 1970s, resource markets were highly unstable, and the OPEC-inspired price increases encouraged provinces to scramble for their share of economic rents.

The federal government imposed price controls on oil and natural gas in 1973 and thereafter maintained domestic prices below world prices. Export levies were imposed to bring these prices up to the world standard, and direct subsidies were made to eastern oil-importing provinces so that net prices equaled the regulated price. These actions made energy-rich western provinces realize that they were in effect subsidizing consumers in other provinces and losing their share of economic rents.

British Columbia's Mineral Land Tax Act of 1973 and Mineral Royalties Act of 1974 set the provincial pace with a base (5 percent of market price minus smelting, refining, marketing, and transportation costs), and incremental (50 percent of the amount by which the gross value of mineral production exceeds 120 percent of the basic value) royalty on thirteen minerals. The act also included punitive levies on certain windfall profits. Observers calculated the combined federal and provincial tax rates at approximately 71 percent (Burns 1976, p. 36), and in some cases incremental rates exceeded 100 percent (Church 1981). In late 1973, British Columbia, Saskatchewan, and Alberta increased oil and gas royalties (to an average of 36 percent) and introduced incremental systems, which would be more responsive to changes in prices (50 percent, nearly 100 percent, and 65 percent, respectively by province). The British Columbia Petroleum Corporation, and the Alberta Petroleum Marketing Commission were established to enable the provincial governments to retain exclusive rights to purchase oil and gas at below-market prices (Carson 1978), and British Columbia required that 50 percent of minerals be processed and refined in the province. Saskatchewan's 1974 Mineral Tax Act placed a tax on potash reserves, granted new regulatory powers to the cabinet, and inserted a provision to pay taxes with physical output, and the government planned to participate directly in exploration and development. Natural gas was required to be sold to the Saskatchewan Power Corporation at below-market prices. Saskatchewan's 1973 Oil and Gas Conservation, Stabilization, and Development Act expropriated mineral interest in all tracts over 1,280 acres and compensated owners at current regulated market prices with no provisions for future adjustments as prices escalated (about one-half of the 40 percent of the producing tracts held as freehold were expropriated) (Martin 1978). The mineral income-tax rate or royalty surcharge was boosted to 100 percent of the difference between the price received at the wellhead and the basic wellhead price established in the law. The effective burden, however, was less than 100 percent because there were deductions for increased production costs and extraordinary transportation costs, and these were deductible from the federal corporate income tax. Carson (1978) reports that the combined federal and provincial marginal tax rates on oil and gas in Alberta were 90 percent, and in Saskatchewan a rate over 100 percent was possible.

The Saskatchewan Court of Appeal upheld the tax, but it was reversed by the Supreme Court in 1977, which interpreted it as an indirect tax interfering with interprovincial trade (Whyte 1981, p. 9). The Court upheld the expropriation of freehold interests as constitutional but struck down the royalty scheme as an unacceptable tax. The Court held that the tax affected the regulated oil price and was therefore affecting the federal powers to regulate trade and commerce.

In 1974 the federal government, Alberta, and Saskatchewan reached an accord that allowed the regulated crude oil price to rise from $2.70 to $6.50 per barrel. However, escalating world prices and the growing gap between the domestic price and world price meant that the costs of compensation to the eastern provinces exceeded federal revenues. In July 1975 the federal government instituted a ten cent per gallon excise tax on gasoline not used for business purposes and increased the prices of crude oil and refined products closer to world prices (Martin 1978).

Manitoba's 1975 Metallic Minerals Royalty Act set at 15 percent rate on taxable profits, up to 18 percent of a company's investment base and 35 percent rate thereafter. Ontario enacted progressive income tax rates of up to 40 percent on mining. Quebec's 1975 budget included progressive rates to 30 percent on gross output and disallowed their deduction from the provincial corporate income tax base, replaced the 33⅓ percent depletion with earned depletion, and instituted a tax-payment averaging method. Manitoba, British Columbia, Ontario, and Quebec enacted tax concessions to firms that conducted further processing in the province. Newfoundland's Mining and 1975 Mineral Rights Tax Act increased the mining profits tax rate to 115 percent and instituted a 20 percent levy on royalties paid to landowners (Burns 1976). All provinces included special considerations for exploration and development, although the effect of these tax, royalty, and regulatory changes brought exploration nearly to a halt (Church 1981).

The federal government responded rapidly to these early assaults on resource revenues. In November 1974 the minister of finance disallowed deduction of all provincial royalties retained by the provinces (which had been allowed in the 1972 and previous legislation) because he considered the increased royalty rates merely to be disguised taxes. In presenting the 1974 budget, the minister of finance stated the federal position:

> In Canada our provinces have adjusted royalties, mining taxes and other arrangments to derive what they perceive to be a fair share for the benefit of their people. However a provincial resource is also a national resource, and the federal government has a responsibility to see that a reasonable portion of the gain is shared by all Canadians. In these circumstances, the federal government has had to assess its over-all taxation policy with respect to this key sector of the economy. . . .
>
> . . . I am saying these developments are making it almost impossible to arrive at a meaningful distinction between mining taxes and the varying types of royalties and arrangements which have similar effects in terms of what is or is not allowed as deductions for corporate income tax purposes. [Burns 1976, pp. 37–38]

This disallowance resulted in marginal royalty and tax rates in excess of 100 percent. For example, in Saskatchewan the incremental rate of 100 percent became an effective rate, and the federal rate added another 42 percent to this.

The 1974 budget proposed to remove the deductibility of all provincial royalties; to tax sales to provinces as if they were held at market prices; to withdraw the 15 percent abatement that had been allowed to the provinces; to reduce the federal tax rate on production profits for oil and gas from 30 percent to 25 percent (it was estimated that the prevailing effective federal rate was 36 percent after royalty deductions); to terminate the earned-depletion deduction of 25 percent in 1974 instead of at the end of 1976; and to allow a 100 percent expensing of exploration expenses and a maximum deduction of 30 percent per year for development expenses in Canada the first year and to decline thereafter.

After reflection on other changes and the uncertainty, to say nothing of the financial burdens these changes invoked, the provinces settled down a bit. Alberta, British Columbia, and Saskatchewan provided for refunding of the disallowed portion of royalties from federal income taxes to producers. Alberta introduced a drilling-incentive program and dropped its incremental royalty rate on price increases from 65 to 50 percent. Exploration had fallen to nearly zero in the western provinces.

The federal finance minister, John Turner, also revised net corporate income tax rates in the 1975 budget to be the same for all corporations and dropped it from 50 to 46 percent, effective in 1976. A resource allowance of 25 percent of profits before deductions for interest, earned depletion, development, and exploration expenses was proposed. The 1976 budget saw the introduction of full deductibility for Canadian exploration and development expenses, and the 1977 budget saw extra depletion for exploratory drilling costing over $5 million and a special 5 percent tax credit for research and development costs. In 1978 the federal budget allowed for an additional 50 percent deduction for incremental research and development costs for ten years. That budget included incentives for nonconventional oil sources of a 50 percent depletion for enhanced recovery, a maximum 25 percent income tax rate on bituminous oil sands recovery projects, and lower rates for upgrading of refineries to process this oil.

In 1975 Canada became a net importer of oil, and by 1977 the regulated domestic price of oil was $10.75 per barrel of oil, so the federal government had to continue subsidizing imports.

Between 1970–1971 and 1975–1976, provincial tax revenues rose 460 percent and federal and state mining-related revenues increased 650 percent, while after-tax profits for those firms increased 126 percent (Fowler 1979). The effect of taxes and royalties gave 45 percent of any price increases allowed under price regulation to the provincial government, 10 percent to the federal government, and 45 percent to the producer. The energy-producing provincial governments were not pleased with the arrangement because price regulation deprived them of between $7 and $9 per barrel in potential revenues, had an equally negative effect on gross revenues to producers and thereby discouraged exploration, development, and production, and in effect shifted these resource rents to consumers throughout the country. The more heavily populated eastern provinces enjoyed most of the benefits.

After the Canadian Supreme Court ruled in 1977 that Saskatchewan's royalty was an indirect tax and was unconstitutional because indirect taxes are reserved for the federal government, the province responded by making an oil-well income tax retroactive to 1974, which exactly offset the potential repayment of $500 million in royalty revenues. By the summer of 1980, the regulated price of oil was at a $12.82 per barrel interprovincial price set by the federal government (whereas the world price was about $30) and natural gas was regulated at $2.17 per thousand cubic feet (mcf).

The negotiating process over the formulation of the new constitution and the regulation of natural-resource prices and competition over revenues become intermingled in the 1978-1980 period. At the first Ministers' Conference in September 1980, the eleven-sided negotiations over the BNA broke down, and the federal government decided to pursue a unilateral course and formulate a constitutional bill. The federal New Democratic party (Labour Socialist) sided with the western provinces on resource taxation and the ownership of hydroelectric facilities in Ontario and proposed ones in Quebec. The likelihood that the United Kingdom Parliament would enact a constitutional bill without support by the provinces was unlikely. Thus the continued uncertainty over Canada's constitution created legal, political, and economic instabilities.

In 1980 the Trudeau government committed itself to continuing price regulation and promised to allow the regulated price of oil to increase a maximum of $4 per barrel despite the enormous increases in world prices in 1979. Trudeau also proposed an export tax on natural gas of $2.50 per mcf and on oil, which would bring export prices to the world level and usurp virtually all incremental economic rents on exports for the federal government.

The provinces were ready to defend their independence. They believed they had been exploited and treated as mere colonials to Ontario and the eastern-populated provinces for a number of years. During the 1979-1980 period, calls for secession were heard from the Quebecois as the referendum issue over moving to independence was defeated and new protests fromt he heartland energy-rich provinces arose. The western provinces felt that the election of the Parti Quebecois separatists in 1976 threatened their position. The policies complained about most were the price regulation of fuels and railroad rates. The government rail monopoly discriminated against the western provinces from developing a diversified industrial base (costs of shipping manufactured products east were twice the rates for raw materials). The effect of regulated oil and gas prices and the federal export taxes was to shift the economic benefits from resource reserves that traditionally had belonged to the provincial governments in Ottawa.

Furthermore, for years Canada had a revenue-sharing arrangement under which tax reveneus from the richer provinces, now in the west, were redistributed to the poorer provinces, primarily Quebec and the maritimes in the east (Scott 1976; Courchene 1976; Boadway and Flatters 1981). These transfers aimed at achieving interprovincial government revenue equality had been labeled by some as the ''second fiscal wonder of the world,'' and having the federal government usurp power over resource tax powers on top of these transfers caused talk of secession. The costs to British Columbia alone for these provisions approximated $2 billion per year.

Anthony Scott (1976), the respected resource economist, reviewed the transfer program in lieu of energy-related revenues and computed the effects of hypothetical outcomes under the redistribution program (also see Courchene 1976; Boadway and Flatters 1981). Scott points out that it would be unfair to provinces in which resources were just becoming exploitable to change the rules of the game suddenly. For example, British Columbia's mining and therefore tax-revenue boom had occurred primarily from 1900 through 1913, whereas Alberta's and Saskatchewan's resource revenues became significant starting in the 1950s and Quebec's resource-related revenues started in the 1970s. Disallowing provincial royalties and therefore effective ownership of virgin government lands would be discriminatory. Scott also defended the provinces' wish to affect their own resource policies and timing of resource development. To restrict these preferences would be discriminatory, he said, and would violate the traditional determining role of these units of government in property and civil rights. His views and those of a number of other Canadian economists were made at a 1975 conference on tax-revenue sharing. The significance of provincial revenue sharing came from the importance of resource revenues and policy in the light of the 1973 OPEC price rise, its likely impact on interprovincial redistribution, and, perhaps most important, the arising conflict among the provincial governments and with the national government.

The events of 1980–1981 brought these conflicts to a head when Trudeau regained his position after the Conservative government lost because of its commitment to move to parity pricing within Canada with world energy prices. Trudeau promised to maintain price controls, and on August 1, 1980, Alberta unilaterally increased oil by $2 per barrel to $16.75; the federal regulated price was then allowed to increase to this level as well, whereas the world price was $35 per barrel. This regulated price was estimated as costing Alberta $30 billion in total lost royalty payments and Saskatchewan as losing $1 billion per year (one-third of its budget). The National Energy Program introduced in the fall of 1980 proposed a $0.30 per mcf on natural gas and an 8 percent petroleum and gas revenue tax that would be levied against the provincial royalties. British Columbia and Saskatchewan challenged these taxes and refused to pay them for their crown-operated oil and gas production and distribution businesses. Alberta politicians were also willing to fight Trudeau's proposed $2.50 mcf natural-gas export tax and his inconsistency over a commitment made during his previous regime to allow tar sands syncrude oil to be sold at world prices. The Alberta Court of Appeal held in spring 1981 that the tax was unconstitutional on provincially owned gas exported to the United States, and the case went to the Supreme Court. Uncertainty over prices, taxes, and regulation threatened to scuttle further investment in the $36 billion tar sands project.

Alberta's prime minister called the natural-gas export levy a "revenue grab" and expropriation." Alberta blocked the sale of oil to an Ontario refiner, Petrosar Ltd., and introduced laws favoring provincial processors. At September unity talks held with the ten provincial leaders concerning changes in the BNA, basic conflicts over resource control and revenues were voiced. Some observers held that failure to reach an agreement would lead to the balkanization of Canada. Earlier Quebec Separatist Premier Rene Levesque had failed in his referendum to allow negotiation over sovereignty; new talk of secession by western provinces was in the air. Pat O'Callaghan, publisher of the *Edmonton Journal,* said, "The western provinces have always resented their secondary role as a colony, exploited by central Canada. They are united now in demanding a shift in the balance of power" (*U.S. News and World Report,* September 15, 1980).

Related concerns were developing over the movement of each province seeking to maximize benefits from economic growth by means of exploiting other provinces. The provinces that formerly were placed in near colonial status as economic dependents began to flex their muscles. New Brunswick, Quebec, and Nova Scotia all introduced measures granting preferences to in-province businesses for government purchases. Newfoundland regulations gave hiring preferences to local labor for offshore drilling, and Premier A. Brian Peckford challenged the federal government over ownership of the Heberina structure, which is estimated to hold 1 billion to 2 billion barrels of oil ("Balkanizing Canada—The Cost of Provincial Barriers," *Business Week,* September 15, 1980). Under the BNA, the federal government owns offshore resources, a position reaffirmed by the Supreme Court, but the province in effect controls the resource through regulation of onshore activities. Saskatchewan passed laws requiring that natural resources be processed within the province, and Alberta assumed veto power over oil and gas sales for use outside of the province. They exercised the veto in a sale to Petrosar and required that up to 50 percent of oil output be delivered to local refiners. With a domestic market of only 24 million people, these barriers to the movement of people and capital could introduce large-scale inefficiencies as each province seeks to maximize its benefits, frequently at the cost of economic rent and economic distortion to other provinces. Retaliatory moves result in further losses and dissipation of rents.

The next step in the battle was Premier Trudeau's move to Canadianize the resource industries (*Business Week,* October 6, 1980). There were growing concerns that oil and gas companies that were primarily subsidiaries of the large multinationals might control Canada's capital market. In 1979, 22 percent of $32 billion in cash flow realized by corporations went to the foreign-owned oil and gas companies. This realization stimulated moves beyond taking more of the economic rents most believed energy companies were earning to calls for nationalization and Canadianizing companies by required percentage ownership (50 percent was frequently suggested) and by government equity participation.

The 1976 and 1978 budgets included exploration and development deductions switching to government grants for exploration (only to Canadian firms) and a two-tier investment tax credit that explicitly benefited Canadian-owned resource companies. Trudeau announced plans in the 1981 budget to reduce the estimated 70 percent foreign ownership to 50 percent by 1990 as part of the government's national energy program. Companies were required to be at least 50 percent Canadian owned to participate in the promising Canada Lands (northwestern territories, Yukon territory, and offshore deposits) ("Canada Adds Fuel to a 'Resource War,'" *Business Week,* July 27, 1981). The Energy Security Act of 1981 would totally end depletion allowances and offer direct subsidies to Canadianized producers. Those concerns 65 percent Canadian owned (75 percent by 1985) were offered 80 percent grants toward exploration and development costs, while companies less than 50 percent Canadian owned (COR) were granted a 25 percent minimum. A number of stock transfer agents established services to verify Canadian ownership among individual shareholders, pension plan beneficiaries, and trusts ("Canadian Oil Firms Seeking Grants Are Discovering the COR of Problem," *Wall Street Journal,* July 7, 1981).

Total foreign investment was $25 billion in 1980 (*Wall Street Journal,* October 23, 1980). Since 1974, Canada's Foreign Investment Review Agency has imposed restrictions on investment and has required promises for future conversions to Canadian equity ownership.

Another means to achieve this end was to have Petro Canada, a government-owned concern with over $600 million in sales in 1979 and estimated to be $9 billion in 1983 and possessing a credit line of nearly $6 billion, to buy out foreign subsidiaries. The Belgian-controlled Petrofina Canada was bought as part of $5 billion in acquisitions, and the 49 percent government-owned Canada Development Corp. initiated new acquisitions as well. Petro Canada was also given the right to back into existing leases by buying 25 percent of ownership and a free right in private exploration leases on federal lands and offshore. Further, it would be entitled to an additional 25 percent interest in leases at renewal time, giving the government a 43 percent interest in all exploration activity. Foreign companies were concerned over financial losses because the leases might be valued by Petro Canada at below-market value on the purchase date, and many threatened to pull out their Canadian operations. Further uncertainty arose because of continuing negotiations over the revision of the BNA and over the future of promising Arctic and offshore regions, which were estimated to require $450 billion investment over the next twenty years. The Trudeau budget specified the 1980–1983 goals of increasing the federal share of oil and gas revenues from

10 to 24 percent, lowering the provincial share from 45 to 43 percent, and dropping industry's share from 45 to 33 percent. An additional proposed tax of 8 percent of net revenues to oil and gas producers and a thirty cent tax per mcf of natural gas increasing to forty-five cents by 1983 was estimated to yield $11.7 billion in revenue over 1980–1983.

As more information on the Trudeau budget and the national energy program appeared, the situation became more dismal for foreign operators and the provinces. The 1981 $60 billion budget was shackled with a $5 billion deficit, while the energy-rich provinces of Alberta, British Columbia, and Saskatchewan had no such problems, and this reduced their leverage somewhat in securing additional resource revenues. The energy plan called for a gradual increase in the regulated wellhead price of oil from $16.75 by $1 per month until the end of 1983. Thereafter the price would be increased $2.25 every six months until 1986, when $3 boosts would take effect until the domestic price hit 75 percent of the world price, although Trudeau retained the power to accelerate that rate and would use it in his negotiations with the energy-producing provinces.

The initial effect on Canadian oil and gas stocks was described by some as "black Wednesday" ("Canadian Oil Shares Drop Sharply on Fears of Government Takeover," *Wall Street Journal,* October 30, 1980). The longer-range effects were to discourage production, exploration, and investment in Canada and to place strains on the domestic capital markets. Companies rewrote investment plans, and exploration plans fell by $2 billion from a projected $6 billion level in 1981 (to 70 percent of the 1979 level). The Independent Petroleum Association of Canada estimated that $16 billion of the $32 billion planned capital spending from 1981 to 1984 would be curtailed. In 1979, $3.9 billion was raised in Canadian equity markets, of which 45 percent went to oil companies. The moves diminished chances of raising capital as had traditionally been done in the United States, Britain, and Germany. Most observers doubted the ability of Canadian capital markets to finance the necessary takeovers for Canadianization, much less the enormous investments in exploration and development that would be required in the future. The Alsands Consortium delayed an $8 billion oil-sand project, and some estimated 65 percent pf Canada's 500 drilling rigs moved south to the United States where drilling costs are one-third less, land is cheaper, and royalties are typically 12 percent versus 36 percent in Canada in 1980–1981 ("Canada's Oil Policy Is Starting to Hurt," *Business Week,* December 8, 1980). The price regulation that established a $18.25 barrel price for a Suncor $500 million syncrude plant in Alberta was devastating, whereas a consortium of Canadian companies was granted a $38 price, which allowed it to take over the project.

Trudeau's budget and Canadianization plan was designed to counter the actions of the provinces in displaying their independence and intent to accomplish a continental tilt by shifting power to the west. Negotiations with the western provincial ministers collapsed in late 1980. Trudeau's plan was to appeal to Canadian nationalism and concern over foreign ownership and investment in order to accomplish his ends. This explains Canadianization, which had national appeal, and his proposals for a new federal constitution to replace the BNA. However, gradual energy price deregulation and increasing the federal share of resource revenues was met with resistance by the western provinces. Furthermore, Canadian companies chose not to pursue acquisition of Canadian subsidiaries of energy multinationals, as the incentives in the federal energy plan had been designed. For example, Montreal-based Seagrams' offer of $2.6 billion for Conoco was indicative of the skepticism among Canadian companies and their shift to the American energy and resource companies. The Reagan administration also responded negatively to the Canadianization policy and threatened to invoke countervailing rules on leasing U.S. federal lands and international capital movements.

On December 20, 1980, the provincially owned gas company in British Columbia announced it would not pay $100 million in new federal natural gas taxes, and it withheld construction permits permanently on $20 billion in oil-sands projects. On March 1, 1981, Alberta began a 15 percent cutback on oil production (amounting to 10 percent of Canadian production) and refused to authorize construction of two oil-sands projects. It could do so because 85 percent of the province's oil rights are on government land, and the regulated price was diverting resource wealth to the federal government (the federal budget for 1981 succeeded in freezing provincial revenues but expanding its revenues by an estimated $7 billion) and to consumers and manufacturers in Ontario and Quebec (the budget projected a $2 billion increase in federal subsidies to make up the $20 per barrel difference in the regulated price versus the world price of imported oil) (*Business Week,* January 19, 1981, and "Canada: A Nation Turns against Itself and the U.S.," *Business Week,* March 16, 1981). Alberta's premier, Peter Lougheed, demanded that domestic oil prices be allowed to rise to 75 percent of the world level and implied that further cutbacks and court cases challenging the federal regulation and taxation would be sought, as well as stopping oil-sands development until an agreement could be reached ("Peter Lougheed and Canada's Oil Wealth," *Wall Street Journal,* April 9, 1981). Concerned about future resource exhaustion, Alberta deposits 30 percent of its oil and gas revenues in the heritage trust fund, which had accumulated $8 billion from 1976 to 1981 and is expected to total $20 billion by 1985.

In early September 1981, federal energy minister Marc LaLonde and Alberta premier Peter Lougheed reached an accord on oil prices: a dual price structure for new and old oil with a federal profits tax on windfalls from old oil of 50 percent of the difference between the higher price and the old regulated price. Prices would be gradually deregulated, with the maximum price reaching 75 percent of the world price. Also the federal government agreed to drop the levy on natural-gas exports. The price of new oil was allowed to rise immediately, and the price of old oil increased to $21.25 on October 1, 1981 (the world price in Canadian dollars was $42.40). Further, there would be increases by $4.50 per barrel in 1982 and $8 per barrel each year thereafter through 1986.

Trudeau's national energy policy, Canadianization, federal budgets, regulated oil prices, and the response of the provinces led to such uncertainty and international concern that Canada's dollar fell to a fifty-year low in 1981.

The case studies of Canada and the United States present clear evidence of the interjurisdictional competition over resource rents and the critical role that government tax and regulatory powers play. The techniques used are complex, and the success or failure is not always as clear-cut as special-interest groups would like nor does it go unchallenged or without retaliatory moves. This evidence also shows the toll extracted by the use of indirect and complex regulatory mechanisms and taxes that affect the location and technology of investment, reduce production and increase prices, or reduce them by regulation. Distorted resource allocation (away from maximum efficiency) as evidenced by prices that do not equal opportunity cost are obvious, and these induce changes in behavior and create distortions. Furthermore, the competition surely results in the dissipation of rents. Just how much is dissipated and how much is transferred without loss is difficult to estimate. However, the case studies imply that the fights absorb resources and that a large fraction of these resources are lost.

# 3
# Analyzing Competition over Resource Rents and the Role of the Public Sector

The case studies of taxation and regulation in the United States and Canada illustrate how regions and interest groups have competed for control and revenues from energy resources. The two cases reveal similarities and distinctions, but it would be difficult to discern a distinct pattern of behavior and to construct a model based on it for predicting how the competition will proceed in the future. The purpose of this chapter is to take steps toward developing analyses that can be used to understand the reasons for the competition and the issues that are involved.

## Why Abstractions Are Difficult to Draw from the Case Studies

The descriptions of energy regulation and taxation in the United States and Canada reveal that public policies and the direct and indirect role of government ownership are highly interdependent and dynamic. The analyst seeks to distinguish the effects that are initiated outside of the situation being studied (exogenous factors) and those that are internally determined by the system being observed. These endemic relationships and then the effects of exogenous variables on them are predictable (the exogenous variables determine the endogenous variables). The unpredictable world events occurring in 1973 and 1979—wars, supply disruptions, and embargoes—must be treated as exogenous for they were unpredictable. However, economic and political adjustments to these events display similarities in the United States and Canada, and these can be modeled, although not perhaps within the conventional confines of the separate disciplines of economics and political science. Those responses, particularly in public policy, which are incapable of being explained within models of individual and collective behavior, are called aberrations, accidents, prediction errors, and plain disorder. As the historian Crane Briton has said, disorder in some sense appears to be endemic to all societies.

The economic and public-policy responses described in chapter 2 are so wide-ranging in terms of the time period discussed, the various energy resources, and the interplay of various levels of government and their supporting constituencies that no single model would be capable of explaining the observed events. Therefore, the apparent regional and interest-group competition in which a series of actions and responses takes place over time must be narrowed in order to make it amenable to analysis.

The economic modeler normally assumes that the framework or institutions within which markets function are given and constant. Economic modelers concentrate on how people's preferences are expressed and how the endowment of natural resources and the initial level of man-made resources (capital stocks) are used to satisfy those preferences. In a market economy, these are resolved in voluntary exchanges and in production and consumption decisions. The key variables determined by these decisions are relative prices and real incomes, and these determine how resources are allocated within the technological constraints of the feasible alternatives.

Economic models, however, are erected over a foundation that assumes that legal and social institutions are predetermined. An essential element defined by these institutions is property rights, for these establish who owns various commodities and place limits on what the owners can and cannot do with them. The U.S. and Canadian cases reveal that property rights to the income from natural resources and their control are subject to controversy and competition and are not clearly defined by institutions at one moment in time. The institutions themselves are an integral part of the competitors' strategies. Ambiguity and constant change prevail concerning the power and policies of political, legal, and economic institutions. Consequently a comprehensive economic model of natural resources should address the question of what role changing property rights and institutions play and what determines those changes. Models of property rights and institutions are inadequate, incomplete, and crude. The relevant economics literature is surveyed and the basic model of people voluntarily combining together to take collection action is formulated and analyzed in an environment of no institutional constraints. Next, the effect of preexisting institutions, which include a legal constitution and fixed geographic and legal jurisdictions, is imposed in order to examine how these affect collective decisions.

The overrriding consideration that makes a meaningful analysis of functional and regional competition over natural-resource income and control difficult to model and, indeed, is itself a cause of this competition is that ownership and property rights to the resource are defined ambiguously. Although private property rights are somewhat ill defined, the public and government rights are most unclear and most subject to change. When property rights are ambiguous, they are competed for, and the more ambiguous they are, the greater the likelihood that they can be altered. Furthermore, changes in economic conditions and markets and changes in technology render previous institutions less stable and property rights less certain. The case-study descriptions of U.S. and Canadian energy policies indicate that unstable conditions have prevailed since 1973.

The ambiguity of the public portion of property rights cannot be dispensed with by appealing to the founding institution: the explicit constitution and the implicit social contract. First of all, these institutions primarily establish a framework for limiting government authority and specifying how collective decisions are to be arrived at and enforced. Second, where natural-resouce ownership is specified, the institutions are open to interpretation. The U.S. Constitution has been interpreted in several ways with respect to state taxation of natural resources. It is particularly vague about horizontal relationships among similar political jurisdictions where much of the resource competition takes place. Although vertical interjurisdictional relationships are more clearly specified in the Constitution, these have changed dramatically over time, all within the confines of these documents. Although the Canadian Constitution (the BNA) appears to be specific in defining resource ownership, its interpretation became so ambiguous as to foster not only regional competition but talk of provincial secession and the necessity to reformulate that document.

The case studies in chapter 2 make obvious that actual ownership is but one of the components of property rights in natural resources. The public sector exercises its property rights by means of ownership and by taxation and various other methods of regulation. Ownership, taxation, and regulation affect the use of the resource and its income flows among factions in the economy and among generations. Because nonrenewable resources are irreplaceable and renewable resources may be damaged or extinguished entirely by human use, intergenerational economic efficiency and distribution of income and wealth must be considered as implications of natural-resource policy made in any single time period.

Although public-sector property rights to natural resources are ambiguous and changing because of economic and technological conditions and political realities, two property-right philosophies can be identified in the theoretical literature and from actual public-sector policies. One philosophy is to make certain that the explorers for and developers of natural resources pay the private and social costs arising from their activities. The second is that natural resources represent an endowment to all persons and, therefore, government is responsible for ensuring that the natural capital stock is maintained or, if exhausted, is replaced by man-made capital that benefits future generations. A number of instances have been identified in which property rights granted exclusively to private resource owners fail to make the private owners bear the full social consequences of resource extraction and use. If the public sector establishes appropriate ownership and tax and regulatory policies, full social costs can be placed on private owners, developers, and users of resources. These policies usurp a portion of the private owners' bundle of property rights.

The social cost that has received widespread attention since the late 1960s is environmental damage. Economists have devised ingenious methods of regulation and taxation that shift these costs to the polluter or in other ways internalize the costs, which ensure that all resources are used efficiently (Kneese and Herfindahl 1974; Kneese and Schultze 1975 p. 197).

Some have argued that the direct and indirect benefits to local communities and states in which natural-resource developments occur may be less than the costs of providing the necessary public services, such as police protection, education, and streets. The special concern is for boom towns, which grow and prosper as the resource is developed and extracted but collapse when the nonrenewable resource is exhausted or the renewable resource is no longer economically attractive. For the unlucky taxpayers who chose to remain, the extra costs of maintaining an underpopulated town may be substantial; for example, municipal bonded indebtedness may remain. A related social cost is that boom-town location is dictated by the location of the resource, which often is in otherwise isolated and undeveloped sites. Furthermore, in some states and provinces, natural-resource extraction is a primary employer and a critical export industry. Thus, jurisdictions depend on one or a few resource-based industries, and this makes them susceptible to the economic conditions facing those industries. Consequently public-sector revenues, expenditures, and the private economy may display greater fluctuations and exaggerate the world or national business cycle. Resource-induced variation in employment, income, and tax revenues creates economic instability or risk. Some observers argue that resource-extractive activities should compensate residents for the higher risks that they impose on local economies (Leistritz and Murdock 1981; Schulze, Brookshire, d'Arge, and Cummings 1981).

Finally, the sacrcity of natural and man-made capital and localized labor markets constrain total economic activity. If natural-resource development occurs, other projects must be deferred or abandoned. Moreover, natural-resource extraction may displace essential commodities and thereby induce the decline or death of preexisting industries. One example is competition over water use for energy development and residential, commercial, and agricultural uses. In the arid West, property rights to water belong to the first beneficial user and can subsequently be sold and transferred. Large amounts of water are required for secondary oil and gas recovery, oil-sand and oil-shale processing, coal-slurry pipelines, and mine dewatering, which affects local hydrology, to say nothing of energy-induced residential and commercial development. Agricultural use is likely to suffer because these activities reduce the incomes of farmers, and agriculturally based communities will suffer. Some observers advocate that these indirect costs—a diminished value of agricultural land and increased business risk—should be borne by resource development. The tax, regulatory, and public-ownership policies implied would all serve to alter property rights in natural resources.

A second philosophy holds that natural resources are an endowment and belong to past, present, and future generations. Although the legal title to the resource may be transferred to private hands, public-ownership rights to the value of the resource in situ remain. Furthermore, the government should act as steward for the property rights of future generations by ensuring that when the resource is extracted, the value of the natural capital is preserved as financial capital. If private markets operate efficiently, private owners will extract and use natural resources when they are more valuable in use than leaving them undisturbed. Should markets fail to achieve efficiency, government should intervene to ensure that extraction takes place at the socially optimal rate (Page 1977).

Government should also tax extraction and invest the proceeds so as to preserve the public-ownership component. When the resource is unextracted, private owners will make investment and extraction decisions so that the market value of property rights to the resource increases at the real (inflation adjusted) rate of interest. This means that the public's share is increasing at this same rate. When extraction takes place and taxes are collected, then government's stewardship role implies that financial investment should earn an equal rate of return, and this should be reinvested so that the real value of the capital stock is preserved. As long as private markets are efficient, the resource is extracted at the time its highest and best use is realized. However, private owners might not reinvest and might consume a portion of the proceeds. One line of argument holds that public policy should ensure that the value of the resource (excluding the cost of extracting it) is reinvested and preserved. However, nowhere in the theoretical or applied literature is the socially correct public-ownership interest in natural resources defined. There is also little reason to expect public bodies to define and exercise property rights to ensure that natural-resource wealth is used correctly or optimally. Rather, one would expect public policy to reflect the collective preferences of the political constituency. The core hypothesis of this book is that competitive behavior for the income from natural resources most accurately describes how public policy is determined and administered. Special-interest groups and subnational jurisdictions compete for resource ownership and control. Income redistribution is a powerful motivation. This process is analyzed after the reasons are discussed that make natural resources attractive and susceptible to ownership, taxation, and regulation by subnational levels of government.

## Special Characteristics of Natural Resources

Every natural material has specific physical and chemical properties, such as strength, hardness, and potential energy. However, it is not the special

properties of each separate resource that engender interest in their ownership and control; it is their economics. There are general factors that are the
foundation of conflicts over natural-resource ownership among private
individuals and public institutions.

The first is that the natural-resource capital is controlled by the laws of
nature and past human behavior. Our natural endowment and past extraction determine the stock of nonrenewable resources; growth rates and
human investment and harvest decisions determine the stock and total yield
of renewable natural resources. Natural stocks have fixed locations or are
relatively immobile. Nonrenewable natural resources are found in the
earth's crust heterogeneously. Surface water and groundwater are defined
by location. Generally water is most often found in quantities that are too
great or too small for human needs; moreover, the quantity fluctuates from
floods to droughts over cycles, which seemingly are impossible to predict.
Renewable natural resources depend critically on the climate, and animal
and plant species are usually adapted to and thrive in specialized environments, although migratory movements of almost inconceivable distances
occur in some species. Consequently most natural resources are concentrated by location (even air is localized to a degree by land masses and
weather systems) and in their natural state are for the most part useless to
humans unless they are extracted and, in most instances, processed. Thus,
nearly all natural resources are classified as being immobile.

Since natural resources are defined by location, they are nonuniformly
distributed. In most instances the richest and economically exploitable
resources are found in few and relatively restricted locations, although
resources of poorer quality are found in a wider and more-uniform distribution. A graphic example of the nonuniform distribution may be found in
the production and consumption of energy. As is true for most other
resources, energy use and consumption are primarily a function of the size
of the population and their income (assuming energy prices among regions
are differentiated only by transportation costs). Production of energy is
determined by the location of fuel resources and the technology to
transform and transport it to consumers. In our petroleum age, oil, natural
gas, and to a lesser extent coal are the primary energy sources, but energy
also is derived from renewable sources, which today are almost exclusively
hydropower, dependent on a consistent water flow with sufficient head,
and, to a far lesser extent, geothermal sources. Solar, wind, and other
renewable-energy sources that are less clearly defined by region, are becoming more economically attractive and by the turn of the century may supply
significant amounts of power.

The nonuniform distribution is apparent by a comparison of energy
production and consumption. Although in its computations, the DOE
neglects to include the location of the uranium fuel as energy production

and classifies production by the location of the nuclear power plant itself, and this factor muddies their tabulations a bit—U.S. uranium production is concentrated in New Mexico and Wyoming—it is worthwhile to look at the ratio of total energy production to total energy consumption computed from their data by state and for the United States as a whole. This ratio ranged from 0.0 to 5.1 in 1977–1978 and is shown in table 3–1. Although the United States as a whole produces about 80 percent of its energy domestically (it should be remembered that significant quantities of oil and natural gas are used as feedstocks for the chemical, plastic, and fertilizer industries), the location of energy production and consumption is not uniform. Thus massive net exporting and importing occurs among the states. Because most natural resources are locationally dependent and consumption is in large measure determined by population, income, and prices of intermediate and final (consumed) commodities, similar trade patterns can be shown to exist for other natural resources in their unprocessed state.

Because natural resources are either immobile or are expensive to relocate in their natural state, resource-rich locations possess potential monopoly or market power defined as existing when an individual or organization of individuals is aware they are able to affect market prices. The combined effect of the supply disruptions caused by the 1973 Middle East war and the OPEC embargo revealed the extent of market power possessed by the oil-exporting cartel. This power arises because of the world's energy demand and the concentration of known low-recovery-cost oil reserves located in OPEC countries. If other equally low-cost resources were located, competition among producing countries would reduce this market power, but no such bonanza has been found to date, nor is another of this magnitude likely to be found. By means of controlling production, the OPEC cartel is able to increase both the world price of oil and its share of oil revenues. Locations in which other reserves of scarce natural resources exist are able to exercise market power either by acting individually or in concert with others. Furthermore, the exercise of monopoly power not only transfers income and wealth, it causes resources to be used inefficiently and creates a loss for society.

Because natural resources possess physical and ownership characteristics that set them apart from man-made commodities, the public at large, special-interest groups concerned with the environment, and public policymakers have questioned the efficacy of the private marketplace's pricing and use of natural resources. A recurring theme heard from many sources and at many different times is that natural resources are unpriced or underpriced in private markets, and this leads to overuse and inadequate conservation. Public policy enacted to preserve public ownership of mineral rights and unique natural wonders, the conservation movement of the late nineteenth and early twentieth centuries, and the environmental movement

**Table 3-1**
**Ratio of Total Energy Production (1978) to Total Energy Consumption (1977)**

| State | Production-Consumption[a] | State | Production-Consumption |
|---|---|---|---|
| United States | 0.80 | | |
| Alabama | 0.57 | Montana | 2.45 |
| Alaska | 9.50 | Nebraska | 0.39 |
| Arizona | 0.35 | Nevada | 0.07 |
| Arkansas | 0.42 | New Hampshire | 0.06 |
| California | 0.85 | New Jersey | 0.10 |
| Colorado | 0.85 | New Mexico | 3.38 |
| Connecticut | 0.20 | New York | 0.12 |
| Delaware | 0.00 | North Carolina | 0.11 |
| Dist. of Columbia | 0.00 | North Dakota | 1.80 |
| Florida | 0.24 | Ohio | 0.28 |
| Georgia | 0.06 | Oklahoma | 2.27 |
| Hawaii | 0.00 | Oregon | 0.97 |
| Idaho | 0.39 | Pennsylvania | 0.59 |
| Illinois | 0.39 | Rhode Island | 0.00 |
| Indiana | 0.23 | South Carolina | 0.25 |
| Iowa | 0.03 | South Dakota | 0.32 |
| Kansas | 1.29 | Tennessee | 0.22 |
| Kentucky | 2.28 | Texas | 1.66 |
| Louisiana | 2.85 | Utah | 0.99 |
| Maine | 0.25 | Vermont | 0.39 |
| Maryland | 0.17 | Virginia | 0.67 |
| Massachusetts | 0.01 | Washington | 0.69 |
| Michigan | 0.19 | West Virginia | 1.69 |
| Minnesota | 0.11 | Wisconsin | 0.11 |
| Mississippi | 0.47 | Wyoming | 5.12 |
| Missouri | 0.09 | | |

Source: Computed from U.S. Department of Energy, Energy Information Administration, Energy Data Reports and Office of Energy Data, *Federal Energy Data System* (1977).

[a]*Production (1978)* in Btu's includes coal, natural gas, petroleum, hydropower, nuclear, goethermal, and other.

*Consumption (1978)* in Btu's includes gasoline, residual fuel oil, distillate fuel oil, diesel, jet fuel, liquified petroleum gases, kerosene, coal, natural gas, nuclear, hydro, and other.

of the 1970s have made these arguments. Widespread failure of private markets to perform properly would single out natural resources for special consideration by the public sector.

Man-made commodities are reproducible and depend primarily on human ingenuity, energy, and creativity. Because long-term economic growth, both in aggregate and on a per-capita basis, caused by technological innovation and specialization of labor has characterized the progress of civilization, markets for these goods and services are well developed and well understood. With billions of exchanges and production and consumption decisions taking place daily, market prices and the intrinsic value of man-made goods are well known and at least roughly balanced.

Natual resources, however, were endowed to humanity. Because they are determined by nature's laws, the extent and quality of most of them are either unknown or crudely understood compared to our own creations. Furthermore, the degree of uniqueness in each location, their scarcity, and their variation in quality creates uncertainty and ambiguity as to who owns the resource and, from an economist's viewpoint, their true value to society versus prices determined by exchanges of privately owned rights to them. Further, these factors mean that relatively few exchanges of these rights occur, and this leads to further uncertainty about the efficacy of market forces because relatively few people determine prices.

The case studies of the U.S. and Canadian regulation of energy and resource ownership reveal the reluctance of both the public and policymakers to allow the free reign to private markets that is willingly granted to markets for man-made commodities. An underlying theme is that private markets either underprice or overprice these resources relative to their true social value.

This concern has been the subject of much investigation by academic and government-based economists in the twentieth century, triggered by public-policy questions and the availability of research funds. On one hand these economists have concluded from theoretical models that markets coupled with clearly defined private ownership rights allocate natural resources efficiently among alternative uses and over time (Hotelling 1931; Page 1977). Empirical studies reveal that prices are valid indicators of resource scarcity (Barnett and Morse 1963; Smith 1968, 1979, 1980a, 1980b) and that their extraction, harvest, and use is unlikely to threaten human existence or produce a premature doomsday. Nevertheless, economists have identified a number of situations in which market fail to price or allocate natural resources appropriately. The unifying thread that runs through market-failure situations and the historical precedent for public-sector involvement in resource policy is that natural resources possess common property characteristics.

Different disciplines and interest groups define *common property* somewhat differently. An acceptable definition for our purposes is a situation where, in legal fact or in practice, the property rights to a scarce resource are shared among persons or institutions and the objectives and goals of these individuals are not identical. Thus the use of a common property is granted to many and in the limiting case is unrestricted. Because all natural resources were at one time owned by humanity at large as the natural endowment and public authorities have maintained an ownership interest in them by direct ownership, taxation, and regulation, all or part of the legal ownership lies with the body politic. Common property characteristics occur when use and access to a resource are very inexpensive or impossible to limit. There are institutional and technical causes. Whenever common-property aspects prevail, there is an incentive for the nonowner or partial (but undivided) owner to use up as much of the resource as quickly as possible before other owners exercise their claims. This leads to overuse and waste, which economists would attribute to the unpriced or underpriced aspect of the resource.

Common property is created by institutional imperfections in how property rights are defined and by the characteristics of certain commodities that make it difficult to exclude other users so that property rights are shared in practice even though they may be private under the law. For many natural resources, property rights are not clearly defined and are subject to frequent adjustments caused by changes in technology, law, and other institutions. Water is a prime example. Where water is plentiful, the law usually takes the position that anyone with access to it may use it, a common property definition. This is the fundamental assumption in the riparian definition of water rights. However, large-scale modern industry is capable of rendering water unfit for other uses, and certain consumptive uses may become so large as to threaten other downstream users. While institutions imply that water rights possess a zero price, the quality and sometimes quantity constraints mean that the true value of water to existing and potential future users is positive.

In the arid West, water rights are granted to the first beneficial user. This legal system is called *appropriative water rights,* and the owner can subsequently sell the rights to other users. Surface water and groundwater in these states were spoken for by agricultural and mining interests as economic development took place; thus water resources were fully appropriated early on. Over time water rights acquired market prices that have risen to thousands of dollars per acre-foot in New Mexico, Colorado, and other states governed by the appropriate system. However, uncertainties prevail as to the long-run amounts of surface waters where streamflows vary significantly and the extent of groundwater and the effects of hydrological interdependencies of groundwater and surface water and legal boundaries defined by law. Thus water rights are ambiguous and subject to continual contention in the courts. This interconnectedness and difficulty in enforcing private right gives a common-property aspect to appropriative water-right states.

When rights are owned outright by public authorities or partial rights are granted in the form of tax powers and regulatory authority, resource use and management acquires common-property attributes. One reason is that public ownership grants all citizens an ambiguously defined right to direct the use and income from the resource and, in certain cases, a right to use it themselves. Another reason is that the objectives of government officials are mixed and are not expected to be the same as those of private owners who seek to maximize the income and value of an undivided and clearly defined interest in their property. The goals of elected government officials are diverse and often vague; however, it is obvious that elected officials must first gain office and then stay in. Therefore, they will seek to enact legislation governing disposal, acquisition, and management of public property and regulatory property rights affecting privately owned resources so as to maximize votes and their tenure in office.

Appointed officials inform elected officials and administer the public sector often with wide discretion under broadly defined legislation. They become key components in the network of information flows between those in the private sector, other government agencies, and elected officials. Their personal objectives, while less distinct than for elected officials, frequently allude to the rubric of power. More-specific objectives include job security and the size of the agency's budget, which determines both their salary and their power. This requires serving the agency's constituencies—the elected officials who grant legal powers and vote on budgets and the particular groups that the agency most directly affects.

The groups in the private sector that have similar interests and whose well-being and economic success are affected by property rights controlled in the public sector have an incentive to organize and to lobby both elected officials and agencies. Industry trade organizations and consumer and public-interest groups represent these common interests and carry out information exchanges with legislators, agencies, and the public media. The constituencies that are highly diffused and whose income and wealth are only slightly affected by public-sector activity, however, have little incentive to organize, and the potential membership would not find it advantageous to contribute time or funds when the expected return is small.

The objectives of elected and appointed government officials and lobbying organizations imply various characteristics in the creation and administration of public policy. When public bodies own natural resources and the services that they produce outright or are granted partial property rights to regulate private action, certain behavior is predictable. Individuals who work for profit and nonprofit organizations in the private sector that benefit from or are damaged significantly by public policy seek to influence the public sector. Although those who are only slightly affected will be ineffectual, this wider public serves as an important constraint. Should the general voter became aware of the effects that individually are small but are large in aggregate, they may be aroused to action. Therefore it is expected that the stated purposes and effects of public policy prepared for consumption by the wider public address the broadly defined public interest. However, no organization or single objective represents the public interest because public policy affects private interests both positively and negatively and in differing degrees. The closest one could come to defining the public interest wherein everyone is made better off by public policy is the objective of economic efficiency. The more diffused and the lower the cost or benefit per capita, the less likely that the goal of efficiency or that of a private interest will be effectively represented. While rhetoric about the public interest may be used for propaganda purposes, it is unlikely to have a significant impact on public policy.

When specialized and well-organized special interests benefit from public policy, somebody must end up paying. The most likely candidates are the unrepresented and diffused interests—generally the taxpayers at large. It follows that one would predict that the true special-interest effects of public policy will be observed behind a smokescreen of the public interest. An implication is that the legislation enacting public policy and the agency decisions and regulations administering it will be deliberately complex so as to obfuscate their true effects. Once the veil is lifted, there are a number of expected characteristics of public policy pertaining to natural-resource ownership and control.

When units of government own some or all of the rights to a natural resource, one would expect that the rights or the services provided by the natural resource would be unpriced or underpriced to the special-interest beneficiaries in the private sector. Examples are readily apparent. The General Mining Law of 1872 grants the prospector-developer complete ownership rights to the land surface and to the resource in exchange for discovery and a modest investment. The Mineral Leasing Act of 1920 provides preferential bidding, which leads to below-market prices on certain tracts, although competitive bidding is the conventional means of disposal.

Studies made of government-owned utilities that sell water and electricity and other services dependent on natural resources show consistent underpricing to certain groups (Russell and Shelton 1974). One indication of this is that the rate of return on invested capital in publicly owned enterprises consistently falls below that achieved in privately owned utilities and for industry in general, and this discrepancy is magnified when one realizes that public enterprises need not pay corporate income taxes. This implies that some or all classes of utility consumers are being subsidized by means of underpricing, and the full social costs of resources being used are not being recovered. A corollary is that new capacity is constructed prematurely and the chosen technology is overly capital intensive. Studies of public-water-project investment and pricing decisions indicate that certain classes of customers are treated differentially and subsidized more heavily. For example, prices that decline as the amount of the service consumed increases are inappropriate because it is the large users who demand increased capacity and require greater peak-load capacity and thus additional investment. Postconstruction audits of water projects reveal that actual direct and indirect benefits and dollar revenues are less than costs. Public enterprises are supported by revenues from users and by tax prices charged for locating in the supplying jurisdiction. For example, the Metropolitan Water District in southern California, the Central Arizona Conservancy District, and numerous other water-supply and flood-control districts levy property taxes on all residents in their jurisdictions. User fees provide the remaining revenues. The benefits, however, are concentrated among agricultural interests and certain other specialized classes of users, and so the general residential and commercial users subsidize agricultural water users and others who receive above-average benefits.

Underpricing leads to overconsumption and a subsidy reflected in higher private rates of return for these uses and increased land prices. The subsidy gives an incentive for special-interest groups to lobby, which provides political support for the government agency and the sponsoring elected officials. Because the amount demanded of a product becomes greater at lower prices, underpricing also increases the required scale of the project and thus the power of the administering agency. Both are reasons for the agency to underprice to the best-organized and most politically effective interest groups. Including nonmeasurable and specific criteria in public projects, such as safety or fixed environmental standards in enabling legislation and regulation, is yet another means of subsidizing particular interest groups and at the same time serving the (mandated) public interest.

A similar situation occurs when public property rights are held as regulatory authority rather than in ownership. Privately owned telephone, water, sewer, electric, transportation, and natural-gas companies are regulated at the state and federal level and thus invariably afford protection from entry by potential competitors. This protection allows such firms to exercise monopoly power and to earn a higher rate of return on invested capital than if competition prevailed, although the true extent of this excess profit is generally concealed in arcane accounting practices so that the rate-making body appears to be controlling its charges. Furthermore, mandated levels and quality of service and regulated prices provide the public regulatory authority the ability to subsidize effective special interests that are customers of the regulated company or suppliers to it, to the detriment of the larger and poorly organized classes of customers or third parties, who in effect pay the bill. The use of environmental regulations on electric power plants both publicly and privately owned to benefit midwestern and eastern coal producers was discussed in chapter 2 (Ackerman and Hassler 1981). One could make the case that underpricing of oil and natural gas originally occurred because tax concessions made energy investment lucrative, and this increased output and brought about lower prices. The powerful oil lobby, not diffused consumer groups, brought this about. It was, then, the events of 1973 and 1979 that sent this system into disarray. However, despite regulation, consumers have been hurt in the long run while producers have benefited. The effects of government ownership and regulatory authority on private-interest groups, public agencies, and elected officials have received extensive attention in the literature (Posner 1975; Stigler 1971; Shapiro 1977; Russell and Shelton 1974).

The common-property effects are caused by the failure of institutions to define property rights unambiguously or by rewarding managers of publicly owned or regulated enterprise on a basis other than maximizing the value of the resource. When markets are competitive and property rights are assigned clearly, individual action in their own self-interest produces an efficient allocation of resources that maximizes both private and social welfare. Adam Smith sought to verify this correspondence and labeled it "the invisible hand." The common-property phenomenon may occur, however, because of institutional failures or because appropriate property rights cannot be assigned for technical reasons. This leads unconstrained markets to establish prices that fail to reflect the social benefits and costs of various activities, and therefore individuals seeking to maximize the following marketprice signals allocate resources inefficiently.

The technical causes for common-property difficulties arise because some resources, particularly natural resources, cannot be rationed by price; certain market exchanges result in direct effects on third parties that are unnegotiated and are involuntary exchanges; and the property rights of future generations cannot be validly represented by the living generation. In order for the market mechanism to act as an efficient means of allocating resources, prices need to reflect the true social costs and benefits of alternative uses of scarce natural and man-made resources. Institutional or technical causes for common property generally cause markets to fail in achieving this end. While institutional failures can be eliminated by means of appropriately specified and enforced property rights, technical causes may require government intervention, and in the process various parties are expected to benefit while others may be made worse off.

Perhaps the most widely recognized cause of common property is the technical impossibility or high cost of ascertaining what the scarce resource is and preventing others from using it. The notable examples of this situation are the air, water, and, sometimes, land. A widely acknowledged common-resource problem is fishing rights. Except for some inland lakes and streams, fishing rights are not treated as private property rights, and the fish themselves are unpriced because controlling entry to fishing grounds is difficult and expensive. This leads to excess fishing effort and increases the number of fishing vessels beyond the socially efficient level. The near-extinction of certain fish and whale species and decimation of large lobsters and valuable shellfish are well-known examples of overuse. Overgrazing in the vast plains and valleys of the western United States and Canada was a common property for these technical reasons when the cost of fencing and controlling access was prohibitive. Free dumping of harmful by-products from production and consumption activities into waterways and oceans and into the air produce pollution, which damages others and is technically difficult to discover, regulate, and control.

The ultimate of common property is called a public good by economists. When excluding others from using a resource is impossible and when the external cost or benefit is so widespread that everyone consumes the same amount of a commodity (for example, residents in a polluted airshed), and it is technically impossible or difficult to exclude people from consuming the bad (pollution) or the good (such as national defense), a public good is said to occur. The more-restrictive case occurs when only certain parties are affected by a production or consumption activity produced by a voluntary market exchange.

When a third party does not engage in the market exchange but is harmed or benefited, an externality is said to take place. The classic examples of externalities are sparks from a steam locomotive igniting farmers' fields and the nectar taken by bees from an apple orchard that produces honey for the beekeeper. In the case of externalities, third-party benefits or damages mean that it is theoretically possible for the various participants to negotiate a solution. This necessarily involves bribes and subsidies to induce behavioral changes, so that everyone is made better off, and this means that there are incentives for creating externalities and upon negotiation the externality is converted to a benefit for the perpetrator.

Externalities that affect more than a few people and public goods that affect everyone are unlikely to be negotiated. The reason is that some persons will benefit fromt he negotiations even if they fail to participate and fail to contribute to the required bribes and subsidies. Such individuals are called *free riders,* and their strategic behavior means that negotiations will tend to be unsuccessful. Thus a common-property problem will remain.

Because natural resources are either irreplaceable after extraction and use (nonrenewable) or their growth rate and stock is affected by extraction and use (renewable), current extraction alters the future stock and the availability to future generations. Since these generations are not around to make their preferences known and to negotiate over how the natural-resource stock is allocated over time, their property rights may not be adequately represented in private markets or in public policy. The effect on natural resources is critical, whereas it is less significant for reproducible, man-made commodities. It can be argued that the present generation does take the future into account because of the inheritance motive, and this argument may be valid for those resources in which property rights are clearly defined and which are privately owned. Public property rights to natural resources, however, may be allocated myopically, and some argue the same may be true for private ones (Page 1977). If the natural-resource stock is consumed today and is not replaced with equally productive man-made capital that does pass to future generations, then the future is made worse off. Uncertainty about what the future holds and what the ultimate economically exploitable reserves of natural resources are leads to difficulties in specifying how much capital stock should be endowed to future generations and what form it should take—in its natural state, as man-made physical capital, as knowledge, and as educational investment in the young. These intergenerational efficiency and equity issues are troublesome and intrinsically part of the natural-resource policy concerns.

It is clear that natural resources possess special characteristics of fixed location, heterogeneous and uncertain quality and quantity, nonuniform and ambiguous property rights vested in both the public and private sectors, nonstandard and relatively inactive markets for these property rights, and common-property characteristics caused by institutional factors and by the technical characteristics of these commodities. One effect of these characteristics is uncertainty as to whether prices and use rates determined in the marketplace represent the true social opportunity costs and whether market-induced distortions occur. There is also reason to suspect the appropriateness of public policy. For this reason and because common-property factors lead to underpricing, markets may fail to allocate the resource efficiently, and property rights to the resource may yield a higher rate of return than those in alternative investments and possess a higher instrinsic value than indicated by the market price. Not only may inefficiencies result, but all of the characteristics just described give rise to what economists call *economic rent*.

## Economic Rent

The concept of economic rent has been written about by economists since the eighteenth century, and as a result there are many definitions and applications, some of them conflicting and many obscure. The broadest definition is used here: economic rent is the difference between what people are willing to pay for a resource, or any other good or service (the market price), and the minimum amount owners would be willing to sell it for. This latter price, sometimes called the *reservation price,* is the minimum that someone will accept and still be willing to part with the commodity. The concept of economic rent is useful although somewhat maligned in economics. The criticism stems from the fact that what we observe are market prices or what people are currently paying. Reservation prices, however, are not directly observable, which means that economic rent can never can be known with certainty.

Economic rent has remained in the economic literature because in a theoretical model it can be assumed to be precisely measurable, and the concept is extremely useful. One of its more-important implications is that economic rents can be extracted and transferred without affecting how much of the commodity is produced. This is important because of the deep faith economists have in the role of markets and prices. When competition in markets and certain other conditions prevail, economists have rigorously demonstrated that market-determined resource allocation corresponds to efficient use of scarce resources. When true, any interference in the marketplace that affects prices, such as taxes and government regulations, distorts the production and allocation of resources into inefficient uses. However, if economic rents exist and if taxes or regulation only affect or extract part or all of those economic rents, no inefficiencies result. Clearly economic rents are an attractive target for those in both the public and private sectors of the economy because production is unaffected, and this implies that the burden of reallocating economic rents falls on their former owners and not on other individual sectors of the economy. However, when economic rents are reallocated by changes made in property rights to them, the distribution of income and wealth is altered. When the recipients have different tastes and preferences than the former owners, consumption patterns change, and this leads to resource reallocations that do not necessarily imply inefficiency or market failure.

There are multiple sources of economic rent associated with natural resources. The fundamental reason is the fact that natural resources are immobile. This usually implies that few alternative uses exist because the land, air, or water where the resources are found is frequently remote and often inhospitable and is worth far less in its next-best alternative. That is to say, opportunity costs are often small. Mining and oil-drilling sites in deserts, offshore in dangerous waters, and in extremely cold and hot climes are well known. Commercial fishing entails long journeys and the associated trials of the sea.

Value comes from the difference between what people are willing to pay for the resource as it is contained in finished products and the cost of finding, extracting, and processing it. This determines the value of the resource in situ. The opportunity cost for the earth or water containing the resource depends on its alternative uses, and for most resources this cost is small. In certain cases, this has allowed researchers to make the simplifying assumption that no alternative uses exist, and consequently the entire market price for property rights to a resource in situ, net of extraction, processing, and transportation costs, comprises economic rent because the opportunity cost is zero. Of course, this is never the case once the resource has been located, evaluated in detail, and extracted or harvested because other resources are used up in these processes. Because alternative uses exist for these natural and man-made resources, opportunity cost becomes positive, and when extraction and beneficiation take place, the natural resource becomes imbued with a positive opportunity cost. The discovery and extraction processes take place only because entrepreneurs believe that their investments will yield higher rates of return than in other alternatives, and thus natural resources compete with other uses of scarce economic resources.

Reservation price, if rational, is related to opportunity cost. It is sometimes measured as the price necessary to produce an income stream, which ensures that such investments yield a normal and reasonable rate of return on invested capital. Another way of estimating it is by computing the replacement cost for the commodity should it suddenly become unavailable. Although such means of estimating reservation price are helpful, they are not precise and may be misleading. This problem leads some experts to conclude that the inability to measure economic rents accurately makes it nonoperational and thus less meaningful in theoretical discussion (Gillis and McLure 1975). Many other economists hold a different opinion.

One of the sources of economic rent to natural resources is the immobility factor of the resource in situ, which implies that its opportunity cost is low unless, of course, the potential mine site is located in a place with a high opportunity cost, such as midtown Manhattan.

The second and somewhat related source of economic rent is that the resource is scarce. This means that relative to the potential demand, the amount that is easily and cheaply found, extracted, and harvested is insufficient. When the resource is a private good, people competing for it bid the price upward. Since the market price indicates what people are willing to pay for a commodity, it measures relative scarcity (for private-good aspects). Scarcity and the price determined in a market system have some specific definitions with respect to natural resources. All goods and services that possess nonzero prices are scarce in the sense that people are willing to pay for them (those things that engender positive benefits) or willing to pay to get rid of them (those things that engender negative benefits, such as polluted water and air or garbage).

Natural resources are special because they cannot be reproduced solely at the behest of people. A man-made item such as a movie film can be rescreened virtually without limit. This, in turn, means that time is of no special significance since reproduction is technically without limit. However, a nonrenewable natural resource can be found only in finite quantities, and the more that is used up today, the less will be available in the future. Renewable natural-resource growth is regulated by the laws of nature, and the time element can be varied only within rather narrow confines. Thus natural-resource scarcity inexorably involves time.

This special scarcity creates economic rents, at least potentially. However, it turns out that the concept of resource scarcity and economic rent corresponds only in part. The economic value engendered by scarcity is required in order to ensure that the resource is used efficiently over time. Markets ensure that the natural resource is allocated efficiently over time as long as scarcity value increases at a rate approximately equal to the rate of interest, and this growth, which is anticipated by resource owners, compensates them for retaining the resource stock and extracting it gradually over time. If this scarcity value were taken away, the incentive by private owners to allocate the resources efficiently would be removed, and current and intergenerational resource allocation would be distorted. In such cases, scarcity value falls outside the operational definition of economic rent used in this book. It turns out that only the constant and nongrowing portion of scarcity can be called economic rent.

A third source of economic rents evolves from the differential quality of natural resources. The cost and complexity of search, development, and extraction of ores and fuels from the earth's crust and renewable-resource harvests varies according to the ore grade (the ore grade is the percentage of the resource per unit of mined material), shape, depth, geology, and geochemistry for exhaustible resources and the distance to market, resource quality, climate, and the large number of factors that affect growth rates and quality for renewable resources. For example, the species and lumber quality of forests (fertility and productivity) varies, as does the quality of fisheries, agricultural lands, and water resources. These quality differentials cause the costs of discovery, harvesting, and processing, as well as the marketable product's price (for nonhomogeneous commodities), to be heterogeneous.

The poorest-quality resource being used is the highest-cost resource. Reserves of superior quality are less costly to extract, and reproducible natural resources grown on higher-quality environments produce greater yields and consequently lower costs per unit. In a competitive market economy, a single price prevails for every commodity at each particular location and point in time. Consequently producers with higher-quality natural resources and lower costs than from the most-costly resource being utilized (equal to market price when competition prevails) realize a higher net return. These differences are economic rents because if the spread between cost and price were taken away, the producer would continue in operation as long as the net proceeds were sufficient to cover costs and to provide sufficient incentive to keep operating.

Economic rents created by differential quality are called *Ricardian rents,* after the English economist David Ricardo who looked at the case of the differential quality of agricultural lands. Others have discussed and attempted to measure rents, which are created by other differential quality measures, and this has led many to believe that rents associated with natural resources are substantial. Take, for example, Saudi Arabian oil. It is widely reported that the total cost of production approximates $0.50 to less than $1 per barrel. If these estimates are true, the total economic rents to them are enormous.

The most spectacular sources of economic rents are called windfalls or bonanzas because of their unexpected quality and size. The OPEC case illustrates market windfall. When an unanticipated price increase or decrease takes place, whatever the cause, resource owners become wealthier or poorer, and economic rent increases or decreases. The 1973 war in the Middle East and the 1979 disruption of oil supplies from that region produced a windfall of unprecedented proportions for all oil-exporting countries. The panicked response in international oil markets and among oil-importing nations indicates that the price increases were not expected (for an excellent summary of the history of OPEC and the Middle Eastern oil situation, see Stoubaugh and Yergin 1979). Oil-price regulations in the United States and Canada invoked in response to these changes illustrate that these economic rents could be captured and redirected by the use of government power. Price regulation meant that the market windfalls to existing reserves in the United States and Canada were allocated to consumers.

A discovery of a new reserve of unforeseen size or quality is a second cause of a windfall. Resource owners find the value of their land increases enormously because of this knowledge. For example, when the first major find was made in Alaska's North Slope, the discovery confirmed and exceeded most expectations, and the market value of nearby leases skyrocketed. A final source of windfall rents is a purely artificial one. Changes in public policies, such as in regulation, spending, or taxes, which are impossible to predict accurately, create and destroy wealth. These gains and losses are windfall economic rents when they occur costlessly; however, the complexity of existing institutions precludes changes that affect private and public wealth from happening easily or without resistance. The potential losers are willing to fight the potential gainers for political control.

Another source of economic rents occurs when competitive markets fail and one person or group of persons has sufficient power to affect prices. This is called *market* or *monopoly power,* and its exercise creates returns above those necessary to attract investment capital. The excess return on investment is economic rent, and this source of economic rent persists only as long as the market power is retained.

It may also be argued that common-property and public-good characteristics, including externalities, create economic rents. These are not reflected in market prices but in the difference between the true social-opportunity cost of an activity that is greater than its market price and thus subsidizes the purchaser. Positive and negative externalities among private parties wherein the beneficiary or victim does not have to pay are also unpriced benefits. These are an implicit income or economic rent.

It is apparent that economic rents are created by the uniqueness, fixed location, and scarcity of natural resources; their differential quality and consequently differential cost of extraction and processing; windfalls created by discovery, the market, or government interference; monopoly or market power; and externalities and common-property characteristics that may be associated with their extraction, processing, and consumption. No matter what the source, these economic rents can be thought of as producing an explicit or implicit flow of income. If economic rent can be transferred without affecting the allocation of natural and man-made resources, then it is not only a seductive target for taxation but a target for any people who are able to utilize their power or skills in securing it. This provides incentives for people to act.

Economic rents flow to two groups: owners of productive services and consumers. The conventional classifications of productive services are labor, land, and capital. However, the traditional definition of land does not correspond to the lay notion, nor does it include all the attributes normally associated with natural resources. The land definition was formulated in the eighteenth century by David Ricardo as the irreducible powers of the soil. The source of economic rent he analyzed was caused by the differential quality of agricultural land. His notion was applied to all uses of land and was expanded by Von Thunen to include the advantages of location. However, natural-resource uniqueness and productitivy is clearly depletable. This includes the agricultural productivity of soils, the life-supporting properties of the environment, as well as those resources regarded as being nonrenewable. A natural resource assumes measurable value to society only after a purpose or use is found for it and the resource is located and its quality and extent become known, so little is known about the future value of natural resources. Future value stems from new knowledge and new uses; thus it becomes virtually impossible to place a current value on underpriced and unused resources.

The term *value* rather than *price* was chosen purposely because when market failures caused by externalities and public-good characteristics occur, a resource's social value and market price differ. There are virtually no natural resources that possess a zero current social value because future and, as yet, unknown uses exist. Also some people care about the mere existence of some resources and are theoretically willing to pay to preserve these; these range from scenic views to the most-obscure plant and animal species and genetic code of the most harmful or seemingly useless living things. In fact, every living thing making up the earth's gene pool has assumed greater value because of the recent discoveries of genetic manipulation and expectations about genetic engineering. It follows that the value of natural resources depends upon our present and future needs, technology, and knowledge. Thus any quantitative estimate of economic value and economic rents is uncertain and speculative. These uncertainties are in large part public goods, for private ownership cannot be assigned until discoveries are made.

The natural endowment and man-made capital begin as distinct concepts. However, as more is known about the specific characteristics of the stock of natural capital and the uses for its components, the distinction diminishes. The polar extreme occurs when comparing a natural resource that has potential but unspecified uses and unknown reserves of uncertain value. Compare this natural capital to a purely man-made investment, such as the knowledge and techniques to construct, program, and use computers. The natural resource is in its virgin state, and little or no human effort has been applied to discovering its extent, potential value, or use. In the latter case, society has diverted human resources away from immediate consumption activities to invest (defer consumption to the future), to develop, and to transfer knowledge to build computers and the technology to program and use them. This human investment or capital is measured both by the opportunity cost of past alternatives given up to develop these machines and knowledge and by the present value or worth of future benefits that this knowledge is expected to produce for humanity. The former measure of capital is favored by accountants and statisticians because it can be measured relatively easily, whereas the latter dominates business person's and investor's decisions and determines market values. As human investment is applied to natural resources, uncertainty as to its market worth is reduced, and the natural capital is integrated with man-made capital and comes to resemble it more. Nevertheless, the special properties that distinguish natural resources and give rise to economic rent remain.

Ownership of the bundle of private property rights is clearly defined for many commodities. There are two reasons for unambiguity of these bundles of rights. The first is that the rights are valuable to those who own them and to others who may be able to secure them; the second is that these rights can be defined, and control can be exercised over them. In order for these conditions to hold, there must be markets for these rights or their value must be ascertained by some other mechanism, and the technology and institutions must exist so that these rights can be enforced and regulated. Ownership of property rights is held by individuals and institutions in the private sector and by the institutions of the public sector, for property rights imply use and control, and these rights supersede the more limited concept of legal ownership. Furthermore, privately owned property rights include purely private goods, as well as the control of external and public-good effects. The same can be said of the public sector: it controls rights that are private, as well as public goods. Nothing inherent in public and private goods automatically places them in individual or government hands. Because technology and other factors affect markets and all these affect the utility and exercisability of property rights, the definition of property rights is in constant flux regardless of the state of legal ownership and institutional responsibilities and mandates. It is often said that one of the primary causes of conflict over property rights is that technological and market changes occur rapidly, whereas institutional structure and legal definitions of ownership change slowly. For this reason, institutions are inevitably years or decades behind economic and social reality.

Because the true present and future value of natural resources is uncertain and because common-property characteristics pervade, property rights to virgin and unused natural resources are ambiguous. As discovery of the resource and uses for it occur and development of it and markets for it develop, property rights to the resource in situ become more clearly and unambiguously defined because of its market value and integration with man-made capital. Nonetheless, obviously defined property rights to natural resources are valuable and competed for because of actual and perceived economic rent.

An attribute of economic rent is that it can be transferred and shifted, and those who are affected, no matter what the outcome, will not alter their decisions about supplying or using the resource that produced rents. This does not imply, however, that there is no resistance to the transfer, for ownership of an economic rent and its explicit or implicit flow of income means that owners possess an incentive and capability to compete for control, and those who wish to obtain the rent are willing to expend capital in the attempt. The ownership rights to explicit and implicit income streams associated with economic rent are established by tradition, public and private institutions, and the legal structure. Economists call the assignment of these rights at a particular point in time the *initial endowment.* Evidence that economic rents exist or, just as important, are thought to exist is readily apparent. This belief is enough to induce nonrecipients to attempt to secure the economic rents accruing to others and for the present owners to retain their endowments for themselves. The search for and attempts to transfer and secure economic rents have given rise to models of individual and collective behavior and the designation of a rent-seeking society. To a large extent, the ownership and transfer of property rights occur voluntarily in the private sector, and many of these transfers involve economic rent. These sales, leases, options, and other contractual arrangements are well known and will not be discussed further. Individuals who are rent seekers also have incentives to employ involuntary transfers to achieve their ends. Coerced transfers are linked most closely with externalities, public goods, and the power of the public sector. One attribute of externalities and public goods is the associated involuntary transfer.

A most important fact is that property rights are defined and changed within legal, legislative, and social systems. As a result individuals and organized groups of individuals can carry out activities through the court system, lobbying in legislatures, and influencing government bureaucrats and elected officials in various ways in order to change those bundles of rights (for a survey of the property-rights literature in economics, see Furubota and Pejovich 1972). Government activities change property rights in a number of ways. A useful classification is direct and indirect methods. Direct methods result from redefining property rights by court decisions, legislation, and regulation. These changes are reflected in the market price of ownership rights. The indirect methods occur through the fiscal mechanism of government taxation and expenditures that reduce or enhance the income stream coming from ownership rights. These changes are capitalized into the market prices of these ownership rights. Because the economy is interdependent and complex, it sometimes happens that when price changes are induced, the distribution of economic rents may change in ways unforeseen by those who were originally seeking to alter property rights. Although these effects have not been studied closely for natural resources, there have been some classic studies of the property-rights effects of zoning and controlled growth of real-estate development.

The use of courts and legislation to affect the bundle of property rights directly is relatively straightforward. Assessment of damages and awards in court cases and the rights to do and prohibitions from doing certain things under statute law and court opinions is clear. The effects of taxes and government expenditures on the flow of income (economic rents), its impact on market prices, and how these affect property rights are analyzable, if indirect. It is perhaps the interrelationships of regulation and the interest groups that establish and administer government intervention where the effects on economic rents and property rights are more subtle.

A number of economists have sought to explain government regulation as the result of interest groups' efforts to secure economic rents. George Stigler's (1971) publication in which he analyzes economic regulation in the economic tradition of supply and demand is becoming known as one of the seminal works. Those who seek to use public resources and the coercive power of government to improve their economic status (securing economic rents) are the demanders for regulation. The character of the political process shows how these ends can be met, and the political system and its actors determine the supply of regulation. Stigler's premise is that regulation is not thrust upon those who are affected but is sought and that economic regulation is not implemented to serve some amorphous public good or public interest but rather to serve economic interests.

As one example, he cites the oil-import quotas that were in effect in the United States from 1959 until 1974. The stated purpose of quotas was protection of the public by means of developing a domestic industry that would ensure a supply of oil in times of war or emergency. Stigler indicates that the moving power behind this legislation and resulting regulation was the oil industry itself. Of course, the result was the more-rapid exhaustion of domestic reserves and a higher price to consumers, estimated to be about $5 billion annually in 1970. Stigler points out that a tariff on imported oil would have restricted imports more efficiently than the regulation, and he estimates it would have cost approximately $2.5 billion annually to pay direct subsidies to domestic producers to achieve the same economic rent as produced by the quotas. He asks, "Why then the quota system?" The answer is that economic rents—in this case, higher profits to domestic oil producers—attract rent seekers, and a direct-subsidy system would have attracted the entry of new firms into domestic oil production, thus dissipating rents to established producers. He points out that direct subsidies are preferred to regulation, whose ultimate benefits are more obscure, only when it is difficult for new entrants to respond to cash payments. Examples are industries where entry is difficult, such as airmail carriers, the domestic merchant marine, and education. Some industries seek regulation to prevent new entrants and retard the growth of new firms: the Civil Aeronautics Board, which previous to deregulation awarded airline routes; the Federal Deposit Insurance Corporation and other agencies that regulate banks and laws that restrict branch banking both within states and interstate banking; and all industries that seek tariff or quota protection, such as the domestic automobile, shoe, textile, and steel industries.

Another effect of regulation on property rights and the creation and retention of economic rents is through regulating substitute and complementary commodities. For example, air carriers receive indirect complementary commodities. For example, air carriers receive indirect financial aid by airmail and airport-construction subsidies. The dairy industry historically has sought regulation to restrict or reduce margarine consumption (substitutes). Stigler cites yet another means for regulation to affect rents as price fixing. Examples include the Interstate Commerce Commission, which regulates both prices and entry into interstate common-carrier motor transport and railroads. The former prohibition on banks' paying interest on checking accounts and the regulated rates on savings accounts and occupational licensing are yet other examples. Regulatory controls, which affect the distribution of economic rents, include not only direct regulation of prices, production, consumption, and control of new entrants but also controls over new construction, land use and land abandonment, and availability of utility services.

Stigler concludes that regulation is insidious and costly. It affects the number of producing firms and their technology, as well as consumers. The procedural safeguards that regulation is thought to possess are costly and ineffective. The political process gives access to powerful special-interest groups who use regulation for their own benefit.

In an equally well-known article Posner (1971) is more specific about how regulation is employed by groups beyond those who are being regulated, to redirect income streams from economic rents. He calls this the prevalence of regulators to require internal subsidies, more frequently called *cross-subsidization,* to remunerative services out of the profits or rents from other services. The effect is to use regulatory power to redirect economic rents. Posner calls this *taxation by regulation,* for he notes that this redistributive function of government is traditionally carried out by means of the governmental budgets—taxation and expenditures. Some interesting examples are the requirement that American Telephone and Telegraph Company allows free access to the National Education Network for communications and that long-distance telephone charges exceed their costs in order to subsidize local service. Other examples include state regulatory authorities' requiring automobile insurance companies to accept high-risk drivers at subsidized rates and the Federal Power Commission (FPC) and its successor, the Federal Energy Regulator Commission (FERC), setting natural-gas prices at less than its scarcity rent, which has induced past and present overconsumption at the expense of future consumers.

Posner and other economists indicate that cross-subsidization occurs, and consequently rents are redirected any time that price deviates from the incremental cost of producing one more unit (marginal cost). Since competitive markets ensure that equilibrium prices equal marginal cost, subsidization occurs only when some participants have market power or use the coercive powers of government (taxation, expenditures, and regulation).

A large number of economists have analyzed how changes in property rights carried out through the public sector redistribute economic rents and how the methods used to transfer rents reallocate society's scarce resources. The motivation is to secure economic rents, and they have labeled this behavior the *rent-seeking society.* Among the contributors to this movement are Tullock (1967), Stigler (1971), Posner (1971, 1975), Barzel (1974), Cheung (1974), Buchanan (1968), Libecap and Johnson (1979), and Foster (1981). These researchers have developed theoretical models, conducted case studies, and tested theories empirically in describing rent-seeking behavior. The literature indicates that the rent-seeking hypothesis is valid and provides insights into individual and group behavior. However, the theory has been applied to collective behavior infrequently (Stigler 1974) and has yet to be applied to the distribution of rents accruing from natural resources. In the next section, this concept is applied both to resources and, more particularly, to how collective action may be used to shift economic rents. Before we examine the behavioral models, we need to understand some of the implications of the rent-seeking behavior identified and hypothesized by the researchers cited above.

The first implication follows from the basic premise of economic theory that people act in their own self-interest and do so by maximizing profits (rent) and satisfaction. What this implies is that whenever individuals identify economic rents, they seek to secure and capture them for themselves. In so doing, they will use resources up to the probable amount of the rents they hope to capture. If information concerning sources of rents and the private and public means to secure them were certain in this effectiveness, resources on such activities as competition in markets, court cases, lobbying, campaign contributions, bribery, and many other activities would equal the total amounts of rent in a society (Foster 1981; Harberger 1974b chap. 7; Krueger 1974; Posner 1975). Researchers have called this result the tendency for rent-seeking behavior to dissipate economic rents. The outcome is undesirable because had those resources been applied to activities that were productive from society's as opposed to the individual's viewpoint, greater net production and consumption would have occurred. Thus rent-seeking behavior may result in dissipation and cause an inefficient allocation of resources.

This result also implies that individuals will use all means possible—both legal and illegal (extortion is one of the more-effective means employed by some rent seekers)—to secure rents. Furthermore, because of the coercive power that government possesses, individuals and collective groups of individuals will seek to use that coercive power for their own ends in retaining, securing, and creating economic rents. Some researchers (Kreuger 1974; Foster 1981) believe attempts to manipulate government regulatory powers absorb significant resources.

Although using collective action in seeking rents in being developed in the professional economics literature, it is a clear implication of rent-seeking behavior. Furthermore, natural-resource rents appear to be particularly lucrative targets. The first reason is that the location of the resource is fixed or controllable in virtually all cases (migrant herds, navigable waters, and schools of fish are exceptions). This characteristic is critical because the potential mobility of people and man-made capital makes capturing rents from these productive factors more difficult. When resources are mobile, geographic areas and government jurisdictions seek to attract activities that produce net economic benefits to existing residents. The resulting competition makes it difficult, and some would say impossible, for governments or other collective groups to capture rents. This is not the case, however, for immobile natural resources.

The implication corresponds to the conclusions of the seminal work by Tiebout (1956). He assumed that many political jurisdictions exist and that all resources are perfectly mobile. This implies that the movement is costless and instantaneous. Tiebout makes the analogy of the attractiveness of the tax and expenditure fiscal package of local government acting like prices in competitive markets. Competition for residents and the resources that accompany them force subnational governments to utilize their budget and regulatory powers efficiently. His theory also implies, although he did not discuss this implication, that no individual receiving economic rent would move to a jurisdiction (or would leave the one they reside in) if the possibility of involuntary rent transfers might arise. Thus jurisdictions would not take actions to transfer economic rents.

This conclusion is related to the often-cited conclusion of Musgrave (1959) that subnational governments are illadvised to attempt to carry out income redistributive programs, and such attempts will be counterproductive. The reason, of course, is that those coerced to relinquish income, which includes economic rent, will migrate. However, the immobile nature of natural resources and its associated rent prevents migration and removes the inhibition. Natural resources, which are fixed in location and which enjoy cost advantages over resources found in other locations, earn economic rents. Among the ways these rents may be captured is by taxes and regulation. Effectiveness in exporting the burdens of taxes and regulations invoked by state and local governments onto those in other regions creates interregional income transfers, and this net benefit is particularly attractive to resource-rich jurisdictions.

In order for individuals and special interests to direct the police and fiscal powers of government to their benefit, they need to affect the legislative, administrative, or judicial processes. One decisive and effective way of accomplishing this is by means of collective action. Under a constitution, this means garnering sufficient support to form a majority, a voluntary coalition of individuals who use their collective strength to achieve common objectives by means of controlling the state. Under a constitution, the size and powers of the majority and the acceptable ways to achieve a majority are specified in rules of order and conduct.

## Two Models of Collective Behavior

Two models of collective behavior are examined in this section. A number of simplifying assumptions are made in the first model in order to relate it to the economic theory just surveyed. The most important of these is that no constraints exist on how government jurisdictions are formed or on their powers. In other words, the situation is one of a preconstitutional state, although the assignment of property rights to the initial endowment is assumed to have taken place and the size of the majority necessary to constitute collective action has been established. In order to introduce realism into the models, the assumption of no national government and federal system is relaxed in the second model of collective behavior. A federal structure of government entailing fixed jurisdictions and constitutional constraints specifying limits on collective powers is introduced. The implications of the two models are examined in two ways: to show how collective activity and local government might be expected to arise and how the implementation of a federal system of a constitution and various constraints or institutions affect the manner in which government authority is used to transfer economic rents.

Social scientists construct models and perform simulations of public policy and other conditions on their models in order to predict, analyze, and understand how the economic and social mechanism operates. The economist, however, is at an advantage over the other social scientists because the variables of primary interest, such as prices, quantities of goods and services, incomes, and so forth, are quantified and an enormous amount of this information has already been collected by private and government entities. Economic models are invariably quantitative and thus can be expressed mathematically.

Property rights and the institutions that determine these rights are more difficult to classify and often are impossible to describe objectively and quantitatively. These are the concern of sociologists, political scientists, social psychologists, and, to a lesser extent, economists. Although economists have attempted to incorporate institutional aspects into their modeling efforts, in most exercises institutions are assumed to be given and property rights assigned. Thus the first model concentrates on how individuals have an incentive to combine collectively in order to capture and distribute economic rents associated with natural resources by means of a mandated redefinition of property rights. The effects of a constitution, a federal system of government, and prevailing government ownership, taxation, and regulation are taken up in the second model.

The previous discussions make it clear that the rent-seeking objective is plausible. Collective decisions are assumed in the first model to enable a jurisdiction to capture and redistribute economic rents costlessly. Thus one institution is allowed—that of the coercive state.

The assumptions made in the first model are that individuals own all man-made and natural resources (called the *initial endowment*), that natural resources are immobile, and that transaction costs in reaching agreement to take collective action are zero. These imply that no constraints inhibit the formation or power of collective activity and government jurisdictions. Furthermore, it is assumed that the purpose of collective decision making that results in the founding and operation of governments is to transfer and secure economic rents (a rent-seeking society both in private agreements and in the public sector).

Before the structural details of this first model of behavior are examined, some speculative conclusions surface immediately. If consensus can be achieved without cost, then it appears that government's coercive behavior, whether by ownership, regulation, or fiscal powers, can be used to capture economic rents and transfer them to whomever controls the jurisdiction. Furthermore, if the coercive acts are carried out swiftly and with certainty and if those affected can be made to believe these actions are conclusive, it may be possible to secure and transfer rents while expending few resources. If this takes place, then rent dissipation is curtailed because of the unique coercive and decisive power of the state. Being immobile, there is no escape from these transfer measures by owners' moving to another location or by other means of avoidance other than seeking to alter collective decisions.

There is an additional consideration. The formation of government jurisdictions that contain large reserves of relatively low-cost natural resources may attain market power over consumers residing outside those jurisdictions. Market power can be exploited to create rents by means of curtailing output, increasing price, and in the process increasing the total wealth of the resource-rich jurisdiction. The limits on collective action to exploit market power are determined by the characteristics of the supply funcions of other resource-producing areas and the demand for the resource, the most important being the cost of substituting other resources for the one whose supply is being artificially manipulated (Gillis and McLure 1975).

The motivation for individuals to combine voluntarily for collective decision making is that they are made better off by such action. Those whose welfare would not improve by combining do not join the coalition. As long as each coalition creates no external effects on others, the process of collective decision making serves to internalize externalities. This type of collective decision making implies a democratic rule of unanimity within the coalition because all agreements are voluntary. Under these conditions, collective decisions improve the efficiency of the allocation of resources within the coalition by correcting for external effects that are not taken into account by individual agreements in the marketplace. Economists starting in the nineteenth century have agreed that the rule of unanimity ensures that coercion is prevented and that economic efficiency is enhanced. They have also identified the reasons why this type of collective decision making does not solve the difficulties introduced by externalities and public goods.

The first difficulty is that the public goods or bads constitute involuntary consumption, and those who are affected cannot be excluded from the benefits or costs. When benefits are involved, the beneficiary need not join in the collective action and the costs it may incur in order to consume the public good. This is the free-rider problem. Furthermore, externalities and public goods may fail to be internalized by collective decisions because of information, administration, enforcement, and other negotiation costs. Finally, it is unlikely that all residents in the vicinity of an immobile natural resource possess similar interests and that those owning resource rents would gain by joining a collective formed for this purpose of redistributing economic rents.

Extensive evidence shows that jurisdiction-wide unanimity is unlikely to be achieved in practice. For example, the Polish Diet operated under a unanimity rule from the mid-seventeenth century to the end of the eighteenth century. Any member could shout out "I disapprove," and this killed the possibility that the item under consideration would be accepted. Needless to say, nothing positive was accomplished, and the status quo remained intact. The reason unanimity is nonoperational is that even policies that enhance the net productivity of an economy and are hence efficient and superior to the status quo are unlikely to be approved unanimously. Even though the coalition can arrange decisions and compensation so that no individual is made worse off and some are made better off, defeat is likely because of strategic behavior. Someone will oppose a decision that meets the criteria of hurting none and improving the welfare of some people because his or her vote is required. Knowing this, strategists will hold out in order to increase their own or their constituents' net benefits. This is why collective decision making and pragmatic politics requires majorities and, by implication, coercion of minority interests. Even in the smallest and most-homogeneous organization, unanimity is rarely required (some religious orders and juries are exceptions).

Interestingly enough, under certain conditions the simple majority rule achieves efficiency, and thus the same resource allocation is achieved as under unanimity rules. This becomes possible when multiple issues are involved, voters possess heterogeneous preferences, and vote trading and negotiations among the voters are permitted. For example, Haefele (1971) has shown that under a representative form of government when alternatives to be voted on are mutually exclusive, issues are independent, and vote trading (negotiations and compromise) is possible (zero negotiations costs are assumed), collective choice allocates resources efficiently. This occurs because voters make trade-offs or exchanges among each other based on these different preferences, and vote-trading arrangements are made voluntarily, this pseudo-market results in an efficient resource allocation approximating one derived from a unanimity voting rule. Furthermore, Haefle shows that for a given set of issues and under rules that approximate a two-party system, the collective outcomes correspond to those found under the more-restrictive assumptions. Thus, representative legislatures with vote trading arrive at the same conclusions as constituents bargaining directly with each other, and so a referendum-type of voting may be unnecessary and undesirable.

The free-rider problem, however, is not solved by vote trading. The economists Lindahl, Bowen, and Samuelson first defined an externality that affects everyone equally (obviously a limiting case) as a public good (or a public bad if the effects are negative) (Musgrave 1959). They show that only through collective action can the correct or efficient level of the public good be provided. However, strategic behavior induces people not to reveal their true preferences because persons cannot be excluded from enjoying the benefits of the good. The strategic behavior is to enjoy the benefits but not reveal one's preferences and willingness to pay for them. Voting schemes have been developed that circumvent the free-rider problem. One, proposed by Clarke and updated by Tullock and Tideman (1976), requires that individuals pay for their votes. The charge, or Clarke Tax, equals the net costs to others (externalities) that result from including that individual's vote in the decision process. Although the tax resolves the strategic behavior problem, its computation and implementation are clearly impractical.

Economists have investigated another approach, which is most appropriate when externalities are not pure public goods. Impure public goods are ordinary externalities for they affect only certain people, and a degree of exclusion is possible. This implies jurisdiction size is variable because nonresidents can be excluded. Although the theories and literature associated with the possibility are diverse, its implications are readily understandable. Recall the previous reference to Tiebout (1956) and his theory of how local units of government competing for residents results in efficient government policies. His model avoids the free-rider and unanimity problems of collective choice by observing that people "vote with their feet." The implication is that each community will contain like-minded people. In effect, flexible jurisdiction size encourages the formation of coalitions whose collective actions satisfy all of its members, or else they would move to a more-amenable jurisdiction. This theory is one of many that utilize the concept of coalitions (some of these are reviewed next in order to determine their implications about the formation of jurisdictions that seek economic rent).

The Tiebout solution is obviously inapplicable for natural resources because of their immobility. In fact, people and economic goods and services are costly to move as well, thus limiting the applicability of his theory. Furthermore, the existence of externalities and public goods causes Tiebout's result to fail theoretically. It can be shown that with externalities and public goods, people may be better off to combine into larger, heterogeneous communities; however, it may be impossible for them to reach a collective decision to do so—a failure of the Tiebout hypothesis (Atkinson and Stiglitz 1979). Furthermore, interdependence among communities may imply that income transfers may be necessary to achieve economic efficiency.

Oates (1972) utilizes the concept of public goods whose boundaries vary to derive a theory of fiscal federalism. He concludes that the unit of government should be large enough to internalize external effects but kept as small as possible to minimize negotiation costs and the free-rider problem. Gokturk (1980) models the cost of producing the commodities displaying externalities allows for location to be variable and, most important, considers externalities that may affect those outside the coalition. His model resembles one in which the coalitions formed are political jurisdictions. He proves that coalitions will be formed, will be stable, and will result in an efficient allocation of resources.

Davis (1970) shows that coalitions will form to concentrate benefits of collective action and to disperse (externalities) the costs of their actions among the larger population. He assumes that one jurisdiction exists and is fixed and that majority rule prevails. A coalition that controls 50 percent plus one vote can dominate collective action. He demonstrates that collective actions will be taken that result in the redistribution of income in favor of the ruling coalition, and the new distribution will be downward. However, he also finds it is impossible to predict the extent to which redistribution will occur and its final incidence. While insightful, his model fails to consider multiple competing jurisdictions and the immobility of natural resources.

The reason for reviewing those concepts is to provide a basis for the first model. Coalition theory is helpful for it shows that no individual joins unless he or she is better off for doing so. Given that jurisdictions are not fixed, we assume that stable coalitions and jurisdictions of subnational governments can be created and are synonymous. Whenever a coalition forms where natural resources are located, it will seek to maximize benefits and exploit the immobile characteristic. The literature is suggestive that separate coalitions will form in distinct producing and consuming areas. If a majority rule prevails, it can impose its power on nonruling minorities. In this case collective decisions will occur more readily, and income redistribution from resource owners and nonresident consumers to jurisdiction residents will occur. If unanimity prevails, jurisdictions containing natural-resource owners and nonowning residents will fail to form unless the bundle of property rights assigned to resource owners are weak, externalities from resource extraction and processing exist, and redistribution of rents from those outside to those inside the coalition is possible.

The first model represents the intriguing possibility that if transactions costs for the formation of the coalitions are zero, either a majority rule or unanimity is specified and no constitutional constraints with regard to the coercive power of government exist, coalitions and jurisdictions may expropriate resource-related economic rents without dissipating them. In the majority-rule case, a coalition of nonresource owners will transfer resource rents to its members. In the unanimity case, a coalition will form and be successful only to the extent that it is able to create economic rent through exercising its market power over those residing outside the jurisdiction by exporting natural-resource products. Natural-resource owners will join only if they are made as well off under the coalition as without it. The transfers will occur because of the unique coercive power of collective action and the existence of market power. This assertion is speculative and must be modified when constitutional limitations are imposed at the national and subnational levels. Before this additional complication is introduced, this first model is refined to show coalition costs and benefits and what the size of jurisdictions may be.

*Collective Behavior Unconstrained by a*
*Federal Constitution*

The existence of economic rents and the incentive for people individually and collectively to compete for those rents introduces additional complexity into the model of collective behavior. If the private sector has identified, competed for, and captured economic rents (property rights to the initial endowment are assumed to have been established), this behavior may make it more difficult for collective action to capture those rents. Those competitors are unlikely to be totally effective, for collective action invokes the coercive power of government, and this is surely a more-effective tool than those available in the private sector. It could be further argued that governments are better equipped to identify where rents exist because of their powers of data collection and analysis not available to private organizations (see Krueger 1974 on rent identification and the distribution of rent).

The coercive power of the public sector also creates the incentive to utilize collective action to create economic rents by means of exercising market power. One example is when the burden of taxes can be passed forward to consumers in other jurisdictions (called *tax exporting*). When this occurs, the benefits to local jurisdictions will increase, and since these rents would not have been dissipated previously, they are thus more certain of being captured (see Foster 1981).

The model of collective rent seeking stresses the following factors:

1.  Economic rents are characteristic of certain geographical locations because of natural resources.

2. The coercive power of government directed by collective decisions and in the absence of federal constitutional constraints is likely to enable the local jurisdiction to capture and redistribute economic rent efficiently.
3. Although competitive rent seeking by individual members in the jurisdiction and those outside it undoubtedly will take place, public authority will be used to usurp those efforts and reduce the likelihood that rents will be dissipated.

The probability that a local jurisdiction will be formed under either majority or unanimity rule depends on the amount of rent that can be captured and subsequently distributed to its membership. One way to estimate the potential amount that might be captured and distributed is to evaluate the benefits of resource development and extraction to a community that has resource incomes paid to those in the jurisdictions which exceed alternative use of their time and resources plus economic rents captured and the accompanying public bad and externality costs that are borne directly or indirectly by the coalition members. The difference between aggregate benefits and costs reveals the potential gain or net benefits for collective action. The viability and stability of a coalition depend on what each individual perceives as her or his personal gains and losses. When average per-capita benefits exceed per-capita costs, the coalition is feasible. The greater the difference or net benefits per capita, the more likely the coalition will be formed. And since the benefits and costs depend on the size of the coalition and whether the majority or unanimity rule applies, the jurisdiction size that achieves the maximum net benefits per capita is the most likely to be formed because it can distribute more to its membership than can any alternative jurisdiction.

The benefits of natural-resource development are produced almost exclusively by the direct and indirect economic activity engendered by the discovery, extraction, and processing of the resource. Jobs and income come immediately to mind as benefits both for those directly employed and those affected by secondary and tertiary effects as this source of income works its way through the economy. Furthermore, land and capital owners who are jurisdiction residents will benefit directly if they are owners of resource industries being developed or if the associated increased economic activity indirectly shifts demand for other business enterprises. The difference between income and the reservation price of resources given up to produce this income represents economic rent. The portion of economic rent that accrues to jurisdiction residents cannot be transferred in the unanimity-rule case but is pertinent in the majority-rule case. The local government jurisdiction may capture some or all of the economic rents escaping the jurisdiction to nonresident resource and capital owners or to consumers by underpricing and unexercised market power either directly through ownership and confiscation or indirectly through taxation and regulation. These captured rents can be redistributed to coalition members in the jurisdiction in a manner that ensures that no one is made worse off and there is unanimous agreement with the government policies. If majority rule prevails, collective choice may also entail redistributing economic rents from resident owners or resources and other immobile capital to majority voters in the jurisdiction. Thereby residents can be induced to join the coalition.

Furthermore, the lack of constraints on jurisdiction size and government behavior means that public policy will include confiscation and cash grants in ways that enhance the formation and stability of the coalition (in either the majority rules or unanimity case). Since each individual performs his or her own calculus on whether to agree to the collective action, the concessions made to each individual may differ. Uniformity and equity in public policy would not be expected. The restricted case of majority rule instead of a unanimous coalition would ensure even more diversity in income redistribution because of the ability to take from the minority. For coalitions to form, the exploitation of the natural resource would be required to produce net benefits (economic rents) in order to have surplus income. This could be so distributed as to make those joining the coalition better off without diminishing the welfare of anyone in the coalition to the extent that they might leave it.

The costs of natural-resource exploitation are more difficult to pinpoint and measure than the benefits. The first are the forgone opportunities caused by its development and extraction. For nonrenewable resources, the scarcity and differential quality rent is used up as extraction place. Furthermore, the exploitation process may preclude alternative productive activities from taking place, such as tourism, agriculture, or development of other natural resources. The development may also alter the social fabric and cohesiveness of the local community. The destructive nature of resource-related boom towns is well documented in the literature (Denise and Ervin 1979; Leistritz and Murdock 1981). Exploitation of the resource may generate negative externalities for the community, such as air, water, or noise pollution. Also this development may require additional public expenditures for transportation, fire and police protection, schools, and other requirements whose cost falls on the local jurisdiction. Some resource development, particularly exhaustible resources, takes many years before production occurs and the tax reveneus based on extraction begin to flow, although the requirement for public services is immediate. The timing differentials between costs and benefits can be evaluated as a potential cost element. Finally, resource-related development will destabilize a local economy and may produce local inflation in excess of the national rate, along with traffic congestion and longer checkout lines to purchase local goods and services. Another cost factor is dependence on a single industry, which increases risk to a local economy. An economic recession, change in technology, or extinction or exhaustion of the resource can be devastating to a single-industry community. This is often labeled the boom-bust cycle and is characteristic of resource-based economies (see Kresge 1980 for the Alaska case).

Subtracting costs from benefits produces the net benefits from resource development for every potential jurisdiction that physically includes natural resources. The size of the jurisdiction or coalition that enjoys the greatest potential net benefits per capita is the one most likely to be formed for the purpose of capturing those net benefits and distributing them to its members. This calculus can be formalized and made explicit. Average per-capita benefits, $B$, are a function of: the quantity of the resource extracted, $Q$, in each time period, and this engenders economic activity by private markets; the public benefits of captured rents that are distributed to coalition members, and these are dependent on output, $T(Q)$; and the size of the jurisdiction, $S$, for the larger it is, the greater are the resources under control and in most cases the greater the economic leverage (market power) it has over markets outside the jurisdiction. Thus the benefit function is: $B = B[Q,T(Q),S]$. Average per-capita costs, $C$, are a function of: the amount of the resource extracted, $Q$, which summarizes direct, external, and public-good costs falling on the private sector; the necessary government expenditures, $E(Q)$, which indirectly depend on output, $Q$; and the size of the jurisdiction, $S$. Thus the cost function is $C = [Q,E(Q),S]$. Within each potential jurisdiction, $S$, a level of resource use and production, $Q$, can be found that maximizes the difference between benefits, $B$, and costs, $C$. The optimum size of the jurisdiction can then be derived as a second stage by evaluating each sized jurisdiction, $S$. The optimal output level $(Q^*)$ and the jurisdiction size $(S^*)$ occurs where per-capita marginal benefits engendered by output and jurisdiction size equals the comparable per-capita marginal costs or simultaneously: $MB_Q = MC_Q$ and $MB_S = MC_S$. When these marginal conditions hold, the optimum jurisdiction size and the corresponding level of output are revealed.

*Assume that the optimum level of output, Q, is known for each possible jurisdiction size, S,* in geographical terms. Start by assuming that no economic rents are captured and transferred by collective action so that rent transfers are removed from estimated benefits to members of the ruling coalition. The effect of jurisdiction size on net benefits per capita, although speculative, is depicted in figure 3-1. The vertical axis measures average net benefits per individual member of the ruling coalition, and the horizontal axis shows the jurisdiction size. The no-rent-capture situation is shown as a solid line. A viable resource-development project in the public or private sector must create positive net benefits, or it should not be undertaken, and so far large jurisdictions, net benefits per capita are positive. For jurisdictions near the resource project, individual net benefits are likely to be

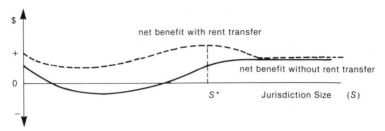

**Figure 3-1.** Net Benefits and Jurisdiction Size

positive because of direct and induced employment and economic activity. This may occur even if the majority of economic rents belong to consumers and owners of land and capital who do not live in the jurisdiction. It is also possible that within noise-, smoke-, and water-contamination range, the project's average per-capita net benefits may become negative for the majority of residents who would be induced to form a ruling coalition. This could be caused by pollution that more severely affects adjacent industries and consumers who are downstream or downwind of the extractive activity or because of burdensome taxes required for highway and school construction that benefit those nearby the project but whose cost is distributed over the large-sized jurisdiction. The effects of the jurisdiction size on benefits and costs in resource projects have been noted by a number of researchers (see, for example, Cummings and Schulze 1978; Krutill and Fisher 1978).

The solid per-capita net benefit curve in figure 3-1 reveals how the average citizen is affected by a resource development. The assumed example shows that when rent capture and transfer is ignored, the hypothetical project produces net benefits close to the location of the natural resource because of employment and induced economic growth. However, the public services supplied to these residents must be paid for, and it is assumed that air, water, and noise pollution is produced whose costs swamp the direct benefits of the project for those who live outside the employment commuting range. Within this range, per-capita costs exceed benefits, and the net benefits (solid line) are negative. Beyond a certain range, pollution is dissipated, and tax costs are widely distributed over many individuals. Therefore, net per-capita benefits again become positive. Of course, this function is hypothetical although it is possible.

Now consider that potential ruling coalitions in jurisdictions are unfettered and seek to maximize net benefits for their membership. A change will occur because of rent capture and transfer. Economic rents leaving the jurisdiction will be captured and transferred to residents, for resource immobility makes this possible. The majority-rule regime is more speculative than the unanimity case, for it would increase net benefits to its members at the expense of the capital and resource-owning minority as well as from nonmembers. The shape of the net-benefit function (shown in figure 3-1 as a dashed line) includes rent capture. Although its shape is conjectural, as long as some rent recipients, as resource owners or consumers, live outside the jurisdiction and their rent is socialized by coercive government acts and redistributed, the net-benefit function will shift upward by the amount of rent captured per capita. The dashed line depicting this implies that the optimal jurisdiction size (the peak at $S^*$), where per-capita net benefits are maximized, is larger than the local jurisdiction but smaller than the nation. As long as the subnational jurisdiction captures rents and does not dissipate them or create inefficiencies, the bigger jurisdictions will receive the same net benefit, for only the distribution of rents will be changed and the lines with and without rent transfer will correspond at large jurisdiction sizes. Note that the subnational jurisdiction has an incentive to create rents by restricting output ($Q$) and inducing higher prices if the jurisdiction has market power. This effect has been included implicitly in figure 3-1 since the level of output is assumed to be optimal for each jurisdiction size. The effect of monopolization on output by rent-maximizing jurisdictions is shown at the top of figure 3-1. A small jurisdiction has no monopoly power when alternative sources exist. However, as the jurisdiction size increases and includes greater amounts of the natural resource and production capacity, market power grows. This produces a dip in the level of output for jurisdictions that are large enough to exert market power but not so large as to preclude exporting the effects of higher prices onto consumers residing outside the jurisdiction.

Whenever economic rents are shifted into a jurisdiction from outside it, the transfer is called *exporting*. Because the loss occurs outside the jurisdiction, the burden is exported and the benefit is imported. There are several sources for exporting rents for a jurisdiction in which resources are located. The most obvious are from owners of resources in situ and from owners of capital (the means to locate, extract, and process the resource) who live outside the jurisdiction. The simplest way to transfer the rent is by expropriation. However, in this case management of operations is transferred as well. Forced profit or equity sharing, royalty and other leasing arrangements, taxation, and regulation can be used to expropriate all but the last incremental rent and still leave management and the remaining property rights with the owners, for it is still in their interest to retain ownership and operational control. They abandon developments only when their remaining property rights are entirely worthless.

The second source of rent is from consumers who reside outside the jurisdiction. A form of economic rents accrues to consumers who are willing to pay more for some of the resource than they are currently paying. This is called *consumer surplus;* it is the difference between the current amount spent on consumption and the amount spent under a hypothetical offer of all or nothing. However, this bargain to extract the surplus is not possible as long as alternative sources for the resource exist. The best that a jurisdiction can do is to restrict output ($Q$) and increase rents extracted from the consumer until the point that the maximum amount of rent and surplus is transferred. This may be possible only when the jurisdiction contains high-quality and low-cost reserves (for a more detailed explanation and examination of this rent transfer, see Shelton and Morgan 1977; Gillis 1979; Gillis and McLure 1975). Output restriction results in higher prices to consumers, a higher price for the resource, and lowered production, resulting in a net economic loss to society at large.

The most successful coalition-jurisdiction is the one that captures and transfers the greatest net benefits to its members; this is depicted in figure 3-1 as $S^*$. This gives the organization an incentive to not dissipate the rents but to preserve them and create them by exercising market power so that members are made better off. The coercive power or collective action implies that capture and transfer can be made with a minimum of dissipation. Potential jurisdictions compete for membership, which is necessary before collective decisions are made. The one that maximizes the benefits to its members is the one most probably formed. Assuming it is effective, it dominates all potentially smaller and larger jurisdictions and shelters its constituents from having their rents captured by others. It is conceivable that when collective choice effectively captures rents, it acts as a deterrent to other rent seekers and prevents dissipation.

*Second Model of Collective Action: Adding Institutions*

The world as depicted in the first model is highly unrealistic, for in actuality property rights are divided among many entitites and individuals, a constitution and complex federal structure of governments exists, and government authorities possess police powers to achieve safety, health, and general-welfare objectives. There is a large body of statutory and common law, and extensive government regulation of private activities at levels prevails. Furthermore, these institutions are undergoing revision and change. Thus a complete predictive model would include all economic and institutional factors as variables to be explained. The difficulties in a complete approach are immediately apparent, however. Economic variables are quantitative, and they change with relatively rapid frequency. Variables describing institutions are mostly qualitative, and the structure of institutions changes relatively slowly. The large differences in rates of change make it difficult to integrate an economic model, which works best over the time period when institutions are stable, with an institutional one in which the determinants of institutional change are vast and the accompanying changes in property rights are difficult to analyze after they have occurred, much less predict.

An institutional model must begin by establishing the initial conditions from which changes will be described. This is a difficult task in itself because of the large number of institutions and how they determine the prevailing property rights. In a complex society, legally defined and pragmatic politics and social relationships make it difficult to discern what property rights actually prevail. This complexity also means that many people and organizations are able to exercise property right so that a large number of special interest would also have to be described. Another result is that participants are also unsure about the structure of property rights, which makes the entire structure itself uncertain. The perceived and actual uncertainty enhances the incentives for various participants to seek to shift the structure of property rights to their benefit, and it is from this competition that changes ultimately occur. Thus the quest to identify and capture economic rents is ongoing, and the public sector becomes an important instrument in the process.

The past and present structure of property rights and institutions has been determined by the competition for economic rents and not as an idealized assignment based on welfare maximization and economic efficiency or other definable and measurable goals, so the outcome is difficult to predict. The case studies of the United States and Canada reveal how competition and exogenous and unpredictable events have affected resource prices and rents to various jurisdictions. As the number of causative factors becomes greater and the role of individual personalities becomes more important, and the effect of random events growth in importance predictability becomes more difficult. The competition, its many participants and their objectives, and the uncertainty cause the institutional framework to change gradually. A desirable effect of this slow change is that stability is produced, which allows the occurrence of the activities of production, investing, saving, and consuming, which would otherwise not take place if change was too rapid and uncertainty too great. It also makes modeling both the existing order of things and changes difficult. How, then, does one go about incorporating this institutional structure into a model that describes how the collective choice and the public sector affect natural-resource use and the regional distribution of resource rents?

*Model of Collective Action—Constrained*

The constitutional constraints involve fixing jurisdictional boundaries and imposing limits on government authority, and the formal structure of government is but one of many constraints. The broad concept of taking places a major limitation on collective behavior hypothesized in the first model. In Western political philosophy, the outright confiscation of property is prohibited except in restricted circumstances. Under the doctrine of the police powers, the state is responsible for an empowered to provide for the general safety, health, and welfare of society. These powers include those of regulation and taxation, but not of taking. Under eminent domain, private property can be taken, but just compensation must be paid. Thus, direct expropriation of resource ownership and economic rents is ruled out, although more-subtle forms of taking under the police powers are possible and are exercised in the guise of regulation. A constitution reserves certain powers for declared levels of government. These may include the ownership of land or mineral right if these have never been transferred to private ownership. In the United States, extensive land is held by the federal and state governments, and in commonwealth countries, the provinces or states retain ownership of all mineral rights until they are leased or sold. In many governments, fisheries are considered to be common resource properties, which are owned and administered by the state.

The U.S. Constitution and Canadian BNA state in broad terms that no jurisdiction may impose constraints on interstate commerce and that taxes shall be levied uniformly. The interstate commerce clause has been referred to as "the great silence" because of its generality. The U.S. courts have ruled numerous times on cases that have specified the content of the commerce clause. The requirement of federal and state constitutions that taxes be levied uniformly restricts efforts to capture differential economic rents among resources, sites, and firms. Furthermore, there are numerous safeguards in the U.S. Constitution to protect the rights of individuals and minorities through procedural safeguards and the structure of government. What are the effects of these constraints on the behavior of units of government, and, more specifically, how do they restrict the ability to capture and transfer economic rent?

Foremost is that rents cannot be confiscated, and fixed political jurisdictions are unlikely to correspond with those sizes that maximize net benefits derived in the first model. These constraints make it virtually impossible to negotiate over and carry out pure rent and income transfer directly by confiscation and ownership. Indirect transfers by taxes and regulation are an order of magnitude more complex to negotiate and carry out. We speculate that the effect of the constitutional constraints is to make it more difficult to transfer economic rents within and among jurisdictions, and the complexities of using indirect methods of taxation, expenditures, and regulation will result in a greater dissipation of rent. The constraints may also encourage interjurisdictional competition because no single existing jurisdiction will be the optimal size.

The complexities become even greater at the local level where price, siting, health, safety, building, zoning, and a myriad of other regulations affect plants and mines. These measures, along with taxation, can be used to transfer and create rents (see Posner 1971). Some observers have noted that the mere presence of natural resources and belief in their bonanza potential have created expectations of economic rents and incentives to capture them (for example, Wisconsin enacted new mining taxes in 1979 on a copper deposit before development had started). The presence of complexly interrelated institutions itself introduces uncertainty as to what property rights are and how they may be changed in the future. This uncertainty provides for added incentive to compete for rents.

The result is the use of indirect means for jurisdictions' capturing and transferring rents, interjurisdictional competition, and occasional formal or de facto cooperation among jurisdictions in order to maximize net benefits. Fixed and overlapping jurisdictions (the same area is affected by state, local, and county governments, school districts, and an array of special units of government that possess tax and regulatory authority such as special assessment districts for utilities and flood control) will undoubtedly foster jurisdictional competition. In a dynamic world, the competition will be ongoing until the natural resource is depleted or produces no rents. Exogenous economic shocks that affect actual and perceived rents will alter the nature of this competition; one result may be the inefficient use of resources and dissipation of rents. The only way in which these hypotheses can be tested is by looking at actual experiences.

The purpose of a model is to identify, disaggregate, and analyze the important determinants of the phenomenon of interest. The difficulty with applying this technique in analyzing the effect of institutions is that there are many interdependent institutions that determine property rights, and the structure of these rights changes at divergent rates, albeit gradually, over time. It is difficult to distinguish which institutions and determinants are the critical ones, and therefore abstracting and modeling is difficult. Furthermore, little in the professional literature addresses these problems, as it is uncharted territory. Given this situation, attempts at analytical modeling are premature; the only alternative is to apply the case-study approach.

The events described in chapter 2 can be interpreted as case studies. What can be learned from these descriptions? Most apparent is that special interests representing consumers, industries, and regions compete for the economic rent associated with natural-resource development and use. Because there is such extensive evidence of this competition and how the implied costs and benefits to various groups have changed over time, it is clear that in the process rents have been dissipated. Next, the structure of existing institutions and uncertainty over who controls what property right creates a continuous battle in which special interests make probes, defenses, rebuttals, and counterattacks and employ an expanse of strategies. In the case of energy, the major catalysts for change has been world events and actual or potential supply disruptions. This implies that the complexity of existing institutions and the surprises brought about by world events create uncertainty and therefore future unpredictability. And if changes are unpredictable, it is futile to attempt to model the phenomena. The circumstantial evidence garnered from these case studies also confirms that no government agency of entity necessarily pursues a goal designed to achieve economic efficiency. Using the public sector to redirect natural-resource income invariably redistributes economic rent, but it also produces inefficient use of natural and man-made resources and therefore waste.

These implications are reinforced by looking at the Lower Colorado River. The Colorado River Compact of 1922 divided the property rights to this oasis found in an arid Southwest. However, several important dimensions were overlooked, which led to competition among regions and separate interest groups. The 1922 compact and the 1944 Colorado River Treaty with Mexico divided surplus streamflow among states and users; however, the total amount allocated was greater than the average streamflow that could be expected. So as dam and irrigation projects exercised the options on water use, conflicts over quantity were inevitable (see *Natural Resources Journal,* special issue, 1975). Furthermore, water quality was not specified in any agreement. Irrigation in arid climates increases the salinity to downstream users. The headwaters of the Colorado contain approximately 50 parts per million (ppm) of inorganic salts, but by the time the water leaves the Imperial Valley, salt concentrations rise to 870 ppm, which reduces agricultural productivity and increases corrosion of equipment. The Wellton-Mohawk Project in Arizona in which saline water is pumped into the river and the Glen Canyon Dam, coming on line in 1961 and reducing the river's flow, increased the salinity from 800 ppm in 1960 to 1,500 ppm in 1962, a change that did not sit well with the agricultural interests in the Mexicali Valley or with the Mexican government. In 1972 President Nixon appointed a special representative to resolve the conflict.

The solution typifies how regional conflicts have been solved in practice. The situation is a classic one of an externality in which a third party, in this case Mexican agricultural producers in the Mexicali Valley, suffers damages because of the actions of upstream users. Economic theory indicates that the victims could negotiate a solution with the polluters by means of bribing them to reduce salinity, and all parties would come out ahead. However, this is not the solution that was forthcoming. The regional and international nature of the conflict was resolved by making all of the direct participants net beneficiaries and passing on the costs to the unknowing general body of taxpayers in the United States. This is known as distributive solution, and it typifies a situation in which the victim has other bargaining chips to use in negotiations. The agreement, Minute 242, committed the U.S. government to construct a desalting plant on the Colorado River by 1978 (later rescheduled for a 1986 completion date) and to divert saline water from the Wellton-Mohawk project in lined canals. In the negotiations, U.S. agricultural interests were guaranteed that they would lose no financial benefits or water rights in the process, a constraint necessary to achieve political support. A distributive solution is virtually ensured success because the first step is to form coalitions at the local level and to guarantee that no one at this level will lose. The United States was willing to supply higher-quality water to Mexico at no cost, a net benefit, because of other considerations, including trade concessions, transfrontier labor and immigration problems, and international goodwill.

Once local, state, and regional support for the project was achieved by means of these guarantees, a coalition of special interests was cemented and a program was passed at the national level. There an argument could be made among legislators that the nation as a whole benefits and that the public at large should pay for it by higher taxes. Legislators from other jurisdictions and constituencies were made supporters in political pork-barrel negotiations in which they were assured support on their own projects in exchange for their support on the desalinization project, a process of negotiation and coalition building known as *logrolling*. The result is large expenditures on water and other public-works projects paid for in small increments by millions of taxpayers who remain unaware of the costs. This is another attribute of negotiated political solutions: the costs are diffused and disguised. Not only is the final solution expensive, it is inefficient. Logrolling and actual social costs masquerading as net national benefits result in public investment that yields negative economic returns (costs exceed benefits), but regional interests and logrolling nevertheless get them through.

It can be shown that a directly negotiated solution among the agricultural interests could have achieved an efficient solution. A cheaper solution, for example, would be to change upstream irrigation methods and greater upstream water discharges would lower salt concentrations. However, the distributive solution, in which no one has to pay for relief of the damages and guaranteeing the status quo in terms of water quantity and quality, imposed constraints on the solution, which produced the inefficiency and made a directly negotiated solution infeasible. This example illustrates that real-world political constraints make the outcome of regional conflicts and competition for resource-related revenues and benefits unpredictable and result in the dissipation of rents. Any situation in which the active parties do not face both the true costs and the benefits of a decision is certain to result in an inefficient solution. This confirms the tentative implications of regional competition in the presence of real-world institutional constraints and explicit and implicit property rights as being unpredictable and dissipating economic rent by inefficient resource use and the willingness of affected parties to spend in order to capture rents.

Although purely economic models are unable to deal with realistic institutional considerations, such as in this example, they are nevertheless helpful. First, they are able to incorporate the technical aspects and market implications of externalities, public goods, and common-property characteristics associated with natural resources. Once such models are constructed, they indicate the source of economic rents, their magnitude, and, when property rights are specified, the likely recipient of those rents. The models, therefore, predict how natural resources and man-made resources are allocated and where market failures are likely to occur. They also support policy evaluation by means of predicting who shares the burdens and benefits of tax, regulatory, and other policies and how those policies affect economic efficiency.

# 4

# Modeling Natural Resources

We frequently hear and read of elected officials, special-interest groups, lobbyists, business persons, academics, and others referring to forecasts and analyses based on economic models. Policy decisions are often made based on results from models, sometimes with disastrous results when the model failed to predict accurately or users failed to understand its limitations. Properly used, models are employed for predicting, simulating various possible conditions to evaluate the effects of public policy, and explaining past events. Therefore, those concerned with natural-resource and materials policy need to be aware of the capabilities and limitations of economic models and modeling techniques.

The purpose of a model is to help explain the world around us. A model is a simplifying description of certain aspects of reality. In order to be worthwhile, a model must be sufficiently complex so that it describes the phenomenon of interest accurately yet simply enough so that it can be produced, comprehended, and used to answer the questions that underlies its construction.

In the physical sciences a distinction can generally be made between pure and applied models. A pure model is one that is highly abstract and simplified. It rarely helps us to understand how to manipulate and control the world, for its sole purpose is to discover basic knowledge. An applied model is one that helps solve practical problems—for example, making refined petroleum products from crude oil. Its specifications are dictated by the problem at hand, and it invariably rests on knowledge garnered from purely scientific models. Ecnomics and the social sciences are concerned with human behavior, and, therefore, the distinction between pure and applied models is not clear-cut. Although the separate motivations for understanding and for problem solving and application remain valid in social sciences, the distinction is less pronounced.

What social science models should accomplish is understanding past events, predicting future ones, and analyzing the effect of alternative policies. Not all models are effective in achieving these three ends simultaneously, and some are ineffective for any purpose. Those who decide to utilize information derived from a model must understand their inherent general limitations and techniques and those that pertain to the specific model used.

137

They must never forget the caveats that are both implicit and explicit when using results derived from a model.

Economics is most broadly described as the study of choice involving scarce resources. A model enables an understanding of what those choices are and the implications of each alternative. In order to analyze choice, users must specify the factors that restrict the number of alternatives. In economic models these can be described as constraints, which determine what is feasible. The primary constraint is the stock of natural and man-made resources that exist at any point in time. Both resources can be thought of as the stock of capital where capital is something that can be consumed today or consumption can be deferred to the future. Nonrenewable natural resources were created before human arrival and are irreversibly depleted with use, whereas reproducible natural resources grow over time as determined by their intrinsic properties and human intervention. Man-made capital produces services over time, such as a single-family residence or a machine, and is fully augmentable, but it requires resource inputs to maintain and to construct. The discovery, construction, and use of both kinds of capital is governed by the laws of nature. Our knowledge of those laws and the practical application of them defines our technology; this is the second primary constraint. Resource and technology constraints together circumscribe what is possible or feasible and thus the alternative choices. Individual and collective goals and objectives express what is preferred or desirable, and matching these with what is feasible reduces the number of choices.

In purely descriptive or positive economic models, this matching predicts which alternatives people will choose. With models in which alternatives are evaluated, choices are ranked according to what is better and what is worse. These later models involve judgments and are labeled *normative*. The most widely accepted normative goal is economic efficiency. This description makes it clear that any analysis of past or future decisions involving scarce resources is an economic model. Thus either describing past decision making or evaluating future options involving resources requires an economic model. The model itself may range from an intuitive or judgmental one in which the internal relationships are not spelled out to completely specified quantitative models that are so large and complex they must be run on computers. Consequently, the question of when to model is a moot one because it will inevitably be a requirement.

The more-critical question is who should become involved in developing and supervising model construction. Those who are experienced with model building, particularly models used for policy evaluation, agree that model development and use of model output cannot take place immediately. Policymakers and their close advisers must be exposed to both the explanations and predictions that are produced by a model (output), and they must understand and agree with the model's basic precepts and internal structure.

The underlying structure of all models is made up of three processes, which are developed sequentially by the modeler and which the user must be aware of. The first process the modelers who have been trained in both economic theory and statistical methods acquaint themselves with is the nature of the problem to be analyzed and the historical and institutional context in which decisions involving scarce resources are made. This leads to formulating a set of simplifying assumptions. Although there is a long-standing dispute among intellectuals over how realistic these assumptions must be, the consensus holds that the assumptions, while abstractions, must correspond with the model users' perceptions of the real world. The second step is to trace through the possible implications of the chosen set of assumptions. These consist of general statements concerning how decisions are arrived at or what the decisions would be under various sets of circumstances. Those hypotheses that are developed from this process should be testable either by means of formal statistical tests or, at a minimum, by means of heuristic methods and observation of past events. The objective for a completed model is to validate it by means of empirical tests and to ensure that the structure of the model itself is internally consistent and complete or comprehensive enough to address the original questions or problems. At any stage in this third process, weakness or shortcomings may be rectified by returning to the starting point and reinitiating the entire procedure.

The model user who unquestioningly takes the results, analysis, predictions, or outcomes simulated by assuming future circumstances is making a serious mistake. Users must be aware of how the model builder proceeded through the steps, for the assumptions and internal operation of a model determine what questions the model validly answers and the particular conditions the model is suitable for. Furthermore, any model producing quantifiable outputs contains internal quantified relationships, which depend on data, scientific knowledge, or plausible assumptions. Users need to know the source of these data and the accuracy, timeliness, and the definitions and implicit assumptions underlying the data.

The thoroughness and professionalism of the model builder most prone to flaws and breakdowns are weaknesses with respect to the internal validity of the model and its documentation. Validity shortcomings occur because the model builder seeks to achieve two goals, which occasionally are conflicting. One goals is to construct a model that fits or explains data accurately. The second is to construct the model so that it corresponds to the accepted orthodoxy and theory of economics and other disciplines. A well-conceived model will achieve the goal of empirical accuracy and logical consistency simultaneously. However, inadequate data or poorly conceived theory mean that one or both goals may fail to be achieved, and the modeler who is less than professional or lack adequate statistical or economic training will be unable to satisfy both goals. At one extreme is the pure empiricist who gathers large amounts of data and manipulates them until relationships are constructed that "explain" past events accurately. At its nadir, this becomes an exercise in statistical correlation, and the product fails to be an economic model. Astute users should be able to detect such exercises and will be advised to place no faith in their ability to predict accurately in the future because there is no logic or system underlying the model. At the other extreme lies the theoretically elegant but nonfunctional model. The implications of such a model may be so complex that existing statistical techniques and data are inadequate to allow for testing it and making it empirically operational. While the well-known proof by Goedel demonstrates that no system can simultaneously be both complete and consistent, the proficient model builder strives for plausibility and internal consistency within the model, as well as making it empirically verifiable. The theoretical structure of a model must be such that the implications or predictions that are tested are analytically derived and not rigidly determined tautologically from the model structure or data.

A major shortcoming, which exists at least to some degree in all models, is inadequate documentation. Complete documentation allows any user to replicate the formulation and empirical estimation of the model. Acceptable documentation requires that the model's assumptions, implications, and hypotheses to be tested are explained clearly and completely; that the computer structure of the model be detailed with a flowchart; and that the data source be specified. Resource and time constraints inevitably make the goal of transferability and replication unachievable and thus ensure that the internal structure and consistency of the model can never be independently verified. Unfortunately, this means that those who use the model or its results must perform an act of faith. Obviously if the modelers are competent and ideologically unbiased, this act is an acceptable risk. In other cases, this is asking too much of faith because even for the most competent, there is a natural predilection to ignore potential difficulties. Often a model and its output are produced under severe time and resource constraints. The result is poor documentation and a high likelihood for error. In a well-documented model, all explicit and implicit assumptions are laid out, and all nonobvious adjustments to the model structure or data are clearly explained. Furthermore, the honest model builder describes the limitations and caveats inherent in the model and the methods used. For the others, the user must ferret out the implicit assumptions and deduce what the unstated but potential caveats and limitations are.

Economic modeling is approached in one of two directions: from the bottom up (micromodels) and from the top down (macromodels). A macromodel encompasses a broad picture and describes how the entire economy or a large sector of it functions. Models that begin with individual behavior and describe how a single sector or component in the economy functions are called micromodels. These seek to explain the relationships among detailed and disaggregated data, whereas the variables in macromodels are highly aggregated, which obscures the detailed functioning of the economy. Techniques also distinguish models. At one extreme is the conceptual model builder who integrates forecasts made by others, nonquantifiable data, and intuition to form a conceptual model. At the other end of the spectrum lies the quantitative model builder. All information and relationships must be theoretically and empirically measurable as numbers and equations, and so their devotion to the computer is nearly religious.

One way to distinguish between micromodels and macromodels is by observing the role of prices. In microeconomic models, prices constitute the key role in determining how individuals behave, and prices result from individuals acting in the marketplace. In macroeconomic models, aggregated price (as measured by price indexes) frequently plays a passive rather than a determining role; these indexes have proved notoriously difficult to predict and explain. The persistent worldwide inflation that began in the early 1970s has shown the requirement for including more price-sensitive information in macromodels. Further, the advent of low-cost, large-scale computer power has permitted the integration of dissaggregated relationships and data into macromodels. In a general equilibrium model, individual prices are included and explained; however, the model may include many commodities and economic sectors and take place on a large scale. Both macromodels and general equilibrium models are discussed in this chapter. Microeconomic models of individual behavior with respect to natural-resource exploration, exploitation, consumption, taxation, and regulation are reviewed in chapter 5.

The classical economic view of the economy is one of a perceptual machine. Firms and individuals are producers (the basic factors of production are land, labor, and capital) and produced goods and services (commodities) are either inputs into other production processes or are consumed. The world is static because services of labor and capital are assumed to be continuously renewable, and land (defined by David Ricardo as the irreducible powers of the soil) does not deteriorate. Money allows transactions to take place more easily than would be the case of barter and in this role becomes a common unit, measuring the flows of different kinds of goods and services.

For all sectors of the economy except for government, money inflows (income) must balance money outflows (expenditures), plus changes in accumulated savings and capital. Government may operate at a deficit or a surplus. It is responsible for regulating the amount of money in the economy, and in carrying out these two roles, it determines inflation and affects economic growth and unemployment. Since it is the flow of real goods and services through the production processes and to ultimate consumption that benefits people, money is sometimes referred to as a veil. The classical view is that inflation occurs when the monetary authorities increase the money supply faster than real growth (increases in the production of commodities) in the economy. Thus the money veil means that prices and dollar incomes increase proportionally, but real (deflated) magnitudes remain unaltered by monetary policy.

The impetus to model the economy (macromodels) has come more from the requirement for public-policy analysis and forecasting than out of pure intellectual curiosity, activities that were given momentum by the Great Depression. Unemployment, economic growth, utilization of plant and equipment, income distribution, and economic and financial stability are among the major concerns of policymakers. The theories of John Maynard Keynes (1936) and his emphasis on the role of government's economic policies led to the formation of policy-oriented macromodels. Jan Tinberger, Lawrence Klein, Wassily Leontief, and the originator of national income accounts, Simon Kuznets, are among the most-famous originators of macromodels.

The advent of inexpensive large-scale computing power in the 1960s meant that empirical models of the economy could be constructed, analyzed, solved, and run with different policies and assumed levels of exogenous variables (scenarios) to see how the economy would probably behave. This progress allowed the confidence of macromodel builders and forecasters to reach its zenith in the late 1960s and early 1970s. However, the reputations of forecasters became tarnished as they failed to anticipate the seriousness and persistence of inflation, although it was initially correctly forecast and understood at its origination during the Vietnam war.

President Johnson was alerted that the enormous increases in spending on the Vietnam war and the social programs of the war on poverty would cause inflation unless taxes were increased. He ignored his economic advisers. President Nixon's price and wage controls in 1971 and the Middle East war, the resulting oil embargo, and the quadrupling of oil prices were all unanticipated events, which models based on past economic behavior were unable to explain and thus were unable to supply accurate policy analysis. There is no reason to expect economic models built on the past to have anticipated those events, for they had no previous precedent and the models assumed the structure of the economy would continue in the future as it had behaved in the past. These shocks not only jarred current events but affected how people behaved thereafter and so substantially changed the basic structure of the economy. Economic models rest on the premise that people will behave in the future as they have in the past. These behavioral changes sent the model builders back to their drawing boards (more data collection and computer analysis, and endless professional papers and conferences) in efforts to reformulate and improve their progeny. The inability of macromodels to predict accurately and the apparent changing structure of the economy reduced the confidence of public policymakers and the public in economic models and forecasts. It is interesting that President Reagan formulated his initial budget based on a model of the economy that was never revealed publicly. The Claremont Graduate School (California) researcher responsible refused to make the specific structure of his model available for scrutiny to the public and academicians.

National income accounts are used to measure the flows of goods and services, and they are measured in either nominal (current dollars) or real (constant purchasing power dollars) money units. These accounts are defined so that output of final goods and services (the gross national product) is used up in consumption, investment, government spending, and net importing activities. This identity ensures that gross national product (GNP) equals income. This, in turn, means that costs of production and prices are interrelated.

All macroeconomic models reflect these underlying accounting identities but differ significantly with regard to other roles that money, prices, people's expectations, and wealth may have on consumer and producer behavior. These differences are the foundations for disputes among theoreticians and macromodel builders and explain why reputable economists' forecasts and policy recommendations can be at such great odds.

Conventional economic models consider government policy as an exogenous factor determined outside of the model. However, the models of collective choice referred to in chapter 3 concentrate on how individuals and interest groups affect public policy, thus explaining how public policy is formed. These models are closely related in structure and operation to microeconomic models.

In macroeconomic models, investment is undertaken by government and by private individuals and firms. Private investment is made by individuals and firms in anticipation of future profits because investment is expected to increase production. In practice any good or service expected to provide service for more than one year is classified as an investment, and the sum of past investment minus depreciation equals total man-made capital. Since investments use produced goods and the services of land, labor, and capital, the conventional model does not account for the services of natural resources.

In the 1970s a group of model builders outside of the mainstream economics profession considered factors that had been neglected heretofore in macroeconomic models—natural resources. Meadows et al. (1972) started the movement with research and the publication of *Limits to Growth*. The Club of Rome group constructed world models that emphasized the role of renewable and nonrenewable resources and the feedback effects of pollution and population growth on the environment, which the conventional macromodel builders had neglected to account for. Jay Forrester of MIT made his contribution in *World Dynamics,* published in 1971. Their prognostications could be called pessimistic at best. The events of the mid-1970s—OPEC, the Soviet grain-purchase debacle, and the subsequent skyrocketing of virtually all natural-resource prices—lent credence to the dismal forecast of these natural-resource "doom" groups. The specter of resource exhaustion and extinction of many species, perhaps including humans, from overpopulation, a consumption-oriented society, and pollution jarred some economists and others into considering natural resources more explicitly in models. Although the mainstream economists criticized this group for failing to account for the technological change and important economic considerations (Cole et al. 1973), this movement had a significant impact.

Although the traditional economic problems of unemployment, stagnant growth, inflation, and variation in the business cycle are far from being solved, the limitations in conventional models brought out by these innovators indicated that the constraints of renewable and nonrenewable natural resources needed to be explicitly introduced into economic models. This required expanding the traditional model of infinitely renewable production and consumption growing without limit.

Some of the models that include natural resources are revamped models from the past, but many are original theoretical concepts and empirical applications that have occurred in both macromodels and micromodels (Solow 1974a). Another important source has come from advances made in engineering models of physical processes and integrated with economic models (for an example, see Vaughn and Russell 1975). Macroeconomic models of growth were modified to include natural-resource constraints and to consider the trade-offs between accumulation of man-made capital, knowledge, and natural resources. Their conclusions vary from confirming those of the pessimists to ones showing that natural-resource depletion can be compensated for by technological advances and accumulation of man-made capital (Smith 1979 and 1980) (Peterson and Fisher 1977).

These advances recognize two facts that previous models had neglected. The first is that failures of the market mechanism in achieving the efficient use of resources are not aberrations and isolated events but are significant and pervasive for nearly all production and consumption (see Ayers and Kneese 1969). The second is that changes in the international political and economic structure and failure to include natural-resource constraints and the physical laws of nature have reduced the capabilities that conventional economic models have to analyze and to predict.

**Economic Models and the Physical Laws**

All economic production and consumption activity ultimately rests on physical energy and materials, and the use and transformation of these are regulated by natural laws. Materials use involves successive stages of discovery, development, extraction, processing, manufacturing, transportation, distribution, and finally consumption and other means of disposal. The fundamental law of the preservation of energy and mass means that all these activities produce both products and services that are useful, along with waste. Harmful by-products and damaging emissions—for example, noise and long-lived toxic residuals—are returned to the environment, where they cause current and future problems. Economic models that explicitly recognize the exhaustibility of nonrenewable resources and the constraints imposed by the natural order of the ecosystem are required to account for these balances of energy and materials. The complex physical as well as economic interdependencies and the limited supplies of natural resources need to be integrated into models of economic and social behavior. An initial problem is that the services of the environment and certain natural resources are not owned or exchanged and therefore do not acquire market prices. The social value of natural resources that are unvalued or undervalued in the marketplace, such as air, water, and a variety of services from land (common property), need to be accounted for, particularly in models used for evaluation of public policy. Humanity as expressed in private conduct and public policy must be aware that despite the advances in knowledge and technology, it cannot replace natural resources or completely regulate natural phenomena with investments (man-made capital), and the very technological advances that have been so successful in driving economic and productivity growth may threaten the very natural system that supports humanity.

The critical services that the natural endowment provides deserve listing. The first is the sun, which provides the climate necessary for the development and sustenance of life. Photosynthesis is the process of utilizing solar energy, which provides all food and fuels (albeit with millions of years lag) and maintains the atmosphere. The other inputs are water and carbon dioxide, which produce oxygen, cellulose, and glucose and plants to synthesize these into the complex amino acids necessary for life. Water is a basic element of life. It is necessary for agriculture and maintaining the climate. These materials make up the oxygen and carbon dioxide cycle, which combustion of fossil fuels may ultimately disrupt by pollution and warming of the earth's surface. The nitrogen necessary for higher plants and animals is fixed to a degree by geophysical and industrial processes but primarily by bacteria in conjunction with legume plants. In decay, complex organic structures are decomposed, insuring that the structure of organic materials is kept in balance. The process also ensures that nearly all energy in organic materials is used up. These materials and processes are interrelated in a way that simultaneously ensures long-run stability within a context of change (evolution).

The value of diverse and complex genetic structures contained in all living things is only recently beginning to become known through selective cross-breeding and the evolving science of genetic engineering. People's stake in the ecosystem is enormous, yet it is in large part underappreciated and unpriced. Because of technological advances and the growth of world-wide population, it has become possible to so disturb natural balances that destabilization and catastrophe could occur. Although nonrenewable resources and land are owned by private individuals and government, externalities associated with their use create a related set of market failures. This specter should be a concern of all those who intend to construct economic models that include natural phenomena. For the most part, fundamental natural relationships are unrecognized in economic models, for they lie outside the conventional paradigms of consumption and production activities. The implications of these relationships, particularly those involving policy evaluation, should be included in economic models. The direct way to accomplish this is by explicitly including basic physical laws in the specifications of models.

This can be accomplished by expanding the conventional concept of scarcity as used by economists. A commodity is considered scarce when resources must be used up to produce it and people are willing to pay for it. The laws of nature are all-encompassing, for the preservation of energy and mass (materials balance) means that every process uses scarce resources, but externalities and public-goods characteristics cause markets to fail and prices not to reflect true social opportunity costs. Myopia and limited knowledge and social institutions fail to make people recognize the value of scarce natural resources, and thus they may command a zero price or a price less than their social value. Nevertheless, one should strive for ways to estimate and include the social value of natural resources (their *shadow prices*) in models. A shadow price is the true scarcity value of a commodity, and these may deviate from market prices. This notion corresponds to the concept of implicit economic and externalities mentioned in chapter 3.

Furthermore, economic and social behavior are determined both in the private sector, where markets and prices dominate, and in the public sector, where political decisions dominate. Collective choice and, by implication, the formation of public policy needs to be understood. In the last decade, more-sophisticated models have been developed to show how collective behavior is made and how it changes, how individuals respond to what they expect public policy will be, and how the assignment and transfer of property rights and the institutions that govern them have been developed. Models of collective choice were touched on in chapter 3 and will not be developed further. The remainder of this chapter covers how natural resources in their broadest definition are integrated in macroeconomic models and what modeling techniques are used to accomplish this.

The fundamental laws of nature are the first and second law of thermodynamics. Economic modelers have only recently begun to account for these fundamental and irrevocable constraints and to integrate them into behavioral models. The first law states that matter (mass and energy) can neither be created nor destroyed in any physical process. The principle of the preservation of matter was codified in the seventeenth century, but Einstein's famous equivalency law ($E = MC^2$) showed the transformation between energy and matter by fusion and fission. The application of the first law by economists has been called the material balance approach. When applied, all of the inputs and outputs to a production and consumption process are traced; these include waste products, which are not traded in markets and have zero prices. The second law of thermodynamics is also known as entropy. It is a misunderstood and misapplied concept (for a clear explanation, see Commoner 1976). Entropy is a measure of how much energy contained in a system is available to do useful work on some other system. The law states that for any process within a closed system (when all inputs are accounted for), the entropy of unavailable energy associated with the system always increases.

## Economics and Conservation of Energy and Mass

The first law as applied in theoretical and empirical economic models is called the *materials-balance principle* (for example, see Boulding 1966; Ayers and Kneese 1969; Kneese and Bower 1972): the sum of all materials and energy extracted from the natural environment as raw materials must precisely balance the sum of materials and energy returned to the environment as waste flows minus materials that are accumulated as capital stocks and product inventories. In its most-complete form, the approach accounts for all physical materials and energy. In its applied form, selected materials flows only are accounted for. Because all production and consumption activities use natural resources to produce human satisfaction, it could be argued that the materials-balance approach should be incorporated in all macroeconomic models, and to ignore the use of the natural-resource endowment can be justified only in models of the very short run.

When properly modeled, this approach reveals the implicit but unrecognized value that society places on unpriced or improperly priced (market failures) natural resources (measured by shadow prices). The first conclusion to be drawn is obvious from the natural law that it is based upon: externalities and market failures are pervasive rather than exceptions and aberrations of the market economy, which is how they have been treated in traditional economic models.

Maler (1974) presents a complete macromodel using the materials-balance approach, which describes the flows among the environment, production, and consumption (shown in figure 4-1). The environment provides the services of renewable and nonrenewable resources and receives the residuals from production and household wastes. However, people can apply their labor as well as man-made and natural capital to modify those residuals in ways that are more benign and less damaging to the environment by means of environmental management, such as pollution abatement and long-term storage of toxic wastes. Note that the capital accumulation block is made up of man-made and transformed natural materials that are of positive value to people and is not directly linked with the environment block in figure 4-1. This separation emphasizes the distinction between man-made capital (the capital accumulation block) and the environmental endowment (the environmental block). The environmental block represents the stock of nonrenewable and renewable natural resources in their natural state. The interdependency between man-made capital and natural-resource capital is considerably more intimate and complex than depicted in this schematic, and certain of these complexities are discussed in chapter 5. The independence assumed here allows all arrows in figure 4-1 to represent flows of materials and services. These flows are assumed to be infinitely sustainable, which makes the model static, thus neglecting the exhaustibility and depletion of natural resources. Some economists treat natural and man-made capital analogously for both display properties of depreciation (extraction with exhaustion and degradation) and investment (improvement in environmental quality). Maler's model is incomplete in its failure to treat depletion of nonrenewable resources correctly.

Another limitation in Maler's static model is that the materials-balance approach may not be strictly adhered to, for it is not introduced as an explicit constraint in the mathematical version of the schematic shown in figure 4-1. However, the model has more to tell than the stark schematic. Maler constructs a mathematical representation (using an optimization method) of the model with which he proves that if the services of the environment are priced correctly, a general equilibrium exists wherein producers and consumers have no incentive to change behavior in order to increase their welfare, and efficient use of natural and man-made resources prevails. The implication is that the first law and existing institutional limitations in the ownership and pricing of natural resources are not incompatible. It is theoretically possible to derive shadow prices for environmental services, which he has done, and these induce people to act in a socially responsible manner.

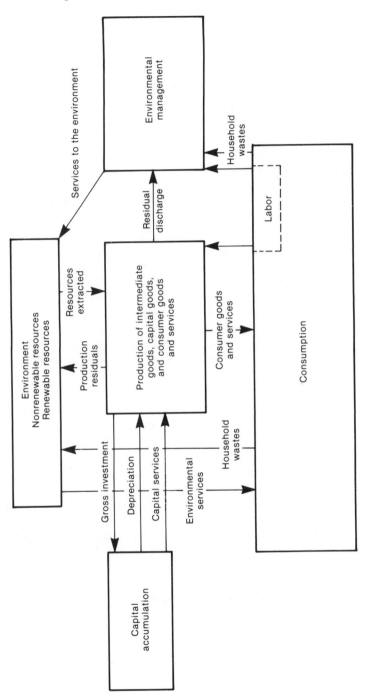

Source: Adopted from Maler (1974).
**Figure 4-1.** General Equilibrium Model of the Environment and Economy

without direct regulation of production and consumption by government. These shadow prices could be achieved by means of taxes and subsidies on conventional production and consumption activities that affect the environment.

Other macromodels have been developed that deal explicitly with the dynamic nature of the economy, environmental interdependence, and the depletion of natural capital. d'Arge and Kogiku (1973) assume a single consumer good is produced and consumed, which produces waste as a by-product. Their original contribution is in integrating both the benefits of consumption and the total accumulation of past wastes (no environmental assimilation is allowed for) to enter into present and future consumer satisfaction. d'Arge and Kogiku derive an optimal dynamic consumption path (optimal control-theory method), which maximizes present and future welfare (an economically efficient solution). The necessary conditions for efficient resource use are that the marginal utility of consumption (its shadow price) equals the marginal disutility of waste output. This implies that consumption rises over time with waste accumulation and terminates in a "final picnic." Although this model is only the first of several such efforts, it reveals the difficulty of analyzing dynamic phenomena, which is required when exhaustibility and the welfare of future generations are accounted for. This, in turn, necessitates highly abstract and simple models in order that analytic solutions can be derived. Furthermore, these macrogrowth models fail to account for the second law or entropy.

The second law of thermodynamics states that for any process in a closed system, the entropy of unavailable energy always increases. This relationship is unidirectional, which makes entropy identifiable with time and provides direction, whereas the first law is symmetrical with respect to the direction of time. In an engineering interpretation, the second law states that the ability of a thermal-energy conversion system to transform heat energy into kinetic energy depends upon temperature differentials and that absolute efficiency is unachievable because the conversion process reduces the temperature differential and degrades the efficiency of the system. Thus all physical and chemical activity tends toward homogeneity in which no work is possible, and all motion is random (most probable). The ultimate of high entropy is heat death for the universe at some time in the distant future when our sun is extinguished.

Another way of describing entropy is by orders. Low entropy implies a high level of order and low probability, and the converse. Some use the term *negentropy* to describe high quality or high order, and this term is applied to natural resources by Ayers (1978). Natural resources can be thought of as a stock of negentropy. The quality of natural resources can be described in terms of the amount of other inputs or work that must be applied to them in order to provide useful work. Negentropy is forever present, but it changes as knowledge improves and as new technologies are developed and applied to production and consumption activities. Currently our nearly exclusive source of energy is fossil fuels, which are irreversibly depleted with use. Over geologic time these are renewable energy sources produced by energy from the sun.

The model incorporating the first law (the materials-balance approach) integrated natural resources and environmental services with an economic model of production and consumption. The discussion of the second law included no mention of economic models based on entropy because its significance to economics has not been settled although some economists have emphasized it (Georgescu-Roegen 1971, 1975). Many economists feel that the economic significance of the second law is reflected in fuel and other prices and so is integrated into existing models. Engineers designing devices that transform and dissipate energy, on the other hand, measure efficiency in terms of the second law, and engineering decisions are economic decisions in that they allocate resources.

Engineers have applied efficiency concepts based on the second law to ever-larger projects and systems and in so doing have become increasingly critical of economic models and distrust markets and prices to allocate resources efficiently. They have pursued an independent path, which has been joined by some economists, of evaluating energy systems by using engineering-efficiency criteria instead of economic criteria.

First law efficiency is generally measured by the ratio of energy transfer to total energy input for the operation of a single process. Ratios for all energy-conversion processes except heat pumps are less than 1.0. For example, it is 0.09 for urban driving and 0.75 to heat domestic water with electricity. A heat pump, essentially an air conditioner in reverse, extracts heat from the environment by using smaller amounts of electrical energy to extract higher-entropy heat from the atmosphere or water and transmit it for space heating (for 110° Fahrenheit, the coefficient of performance ratio is 2.45 and this measure is somewhat different from that for heat processes cited above).

Second law efficiency takes into account the total energy inputs and outputs that are available to carry out useful work in a system. The engineering measure is the ratio of available work of final outputs to the available work of inputs to the process. Heating water with electricity plummets from its 0.75 for first law efficiency to 0.045 for second law efficiency because so little heat from the fuel used to produce electricity ends up warming water. The heat pump falls to 0.202.

The economists' retort is that if the prices of fuel reflect its true opportunity cost and the prices of final output reflect what people are willing to pay, which occurs if there are no market failures, economic and financial evaluation accounts for all inputs, including the cost of designing and building the machine (capital), as well as operating it. The engineering advocates have responded by including the energy inputs used directly and indirectly in producing a final output (Herendeen and Bullard 1974), called *net energy analysis*. Energy input-output methodology is particularly well suited to this task. The two groups have not reconciled their differences, and there is little likelihood they will in the near future. Regardless, both the first and second laws should be considered in any model, and instances where they may reveal existing or potential market failures must be scrutinized closely.

Technological advances have permitted us to shift to higher negentropy energy sources—wood to coal to petroleum. The United States converted from wood-based to coal energy in the late nineteenth century and from coal to petroleum at mid-century. Now the process has reversed itself, for no other source has greater negentropy except the potential for nuclear fusion, and we are rapidly depleting the high-quality natural capital of oil and natural gas. As high-quality, low-entropy energy sources are used up, lower-quality resources, which necessarily involves greater entropy and less efficiency, must be exploited. The DOE forecasts that coal will become the dominant fuel by the end of this century. The distribution of the quality of energy sources and other natural resources as granted in our natural endowment is best described in terms of extraction costs and uncertainty as to their extent and quality (figure 4–2). Although there are disputes among experts as to the precise relationships among the amounts of resource endowments or stocks of various qualities and the certainty of discovering them, there is no doubt that we are going from high quality to lower quality with respect to every exhaustible natural resource. Empirical evidence from past extraction activity supports the inverse relationship between the quality of the resource and the size of the remaining stock. The shape of this function implies that while the total unexploited amount of the resource is large, the highest grades and orders (most certain and accessible, cheapest to extract, and of the highest order) are both limited and diminishing. Entropy and disorder is higher the lower the grade, and this increases the amount of effort and environmental disruption to discover, extract and process these lower-quality resources.

There is a technological race between exhausting high-quality and low-cost resources and discovering and perfecting the technological advances that make lower-quality resources economically exploitable. The race reduces to one between technology or human knowledge and entropy. As Ayers has pointed out, to believe that technology can outpace depletion (entropy) is to imply that "there must be no limit to the amount of negentropy that can be created by intellectual activity" (Ayers 1978, p. 49). While knowledge has been growing at an explosive rate, the ability to convert it into increases in efficiency and productivity gains have been less spectacular. The meager data that are available indicate that new discoveries and

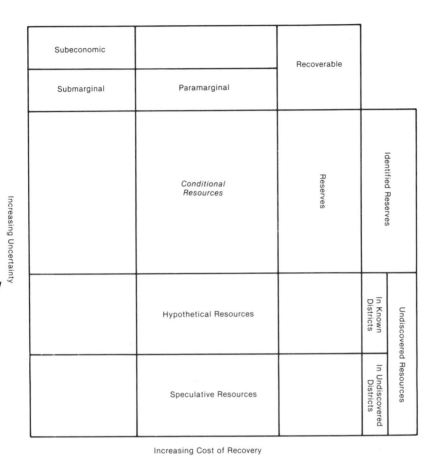

Source: U.S. Geological Survey. 1973. *United States Mineral Resources,* edited by D.A. Brost and W.P. Pratt. U.S. Geological Survey, Professional paper no. 820. Washington, D.C.: Government Printing Office.

**Figure 4–2.** Resource Classification

successful applications are most likely losing the race. It is only the most optimistic person who would contest that advances in usable resource productivity (output per unit increase in resource input) are not without bound.

The fortuitous discovery of new resources and new technologies to exploit them in the past allowed the world to achieve unprecedented economic advances, especially in the Western countries, which first experienced the conversion to higher-negentropy sources of coal and then petroleum (industrial revolution). Unless we discover a way of utilizing nuclear fusion efficiently (sometimes referred to as the backstop technology), we have reached a peak because there is no other energy sources with higher negentropy than fossil fuels. Conservation can slow this process, but a transition to higher-entropy energy sources is inevitable. Renewable energy sources utilize a high-entropy, low-quality resource (solar radiation) and convert it at low efficiencies to usable work. Although the fuel is free, this technology requires far larger total inputs of reproducible and natural capital (energy and materials), thus again revealing that the second law cannot be violated.

The precise shape and character of the quality to size of the stock relationship is unknown (figure 4–3) and subject to speculation. For example, some observers believe that there may be a hump at the right-hand tail of this curve and that we may be on this small hump on the larger hill. If so, we would shortly see a temporary decreasing stock of lower-quality resources as resource use proceeded along the left side of this small hump. The U.S.

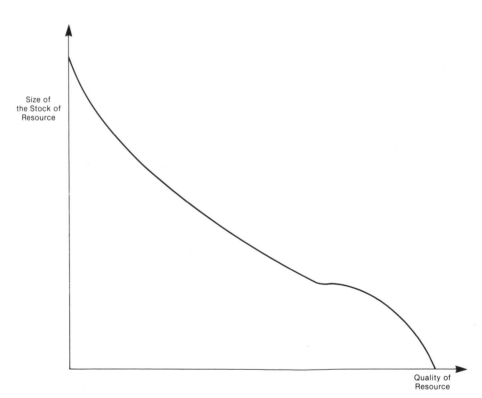

**Figure 4–3.** Quality and Size of Stock of a Natural Resource

Bureau of Mines has developed a scheme that integrates decreasing quality (corresponding to increasing cost) of the resource and increasing uncertainty. This is shown in figure 4-2 along with vertical and horizontal dimension. "Reserves" are both known and economically exploitable, while some "resources" are known but not currently economically feasible, and most are hypothetical or speculative. This two-dimensional schema illustrates why simple quantifications purporting to reflect the stocks of natural resources vary so greatly.

Although this discussion has centered on energy and exhaustible resources, there are obvious implications for renewable natural resources. All resources, natural and human, are governed by the first and second laws. Furthermore, the waste disposal from extraction and production activities involving nonrenewable resources is bound by entropy and has far-reaching implications for renewable natural resources, particularly the air, water, and vegetation. Examples of strip-mining, mine dewatering, clear-cutting (in tropical environments reforestation of hard woods at best takes eighty to one-hundred years, and many believe such woods are a nonrenewable resource), slash-and-burn agriculture creating attendant erosion, oil spills, the atmospheric greenhouse effect of carbon dioxide from fossil-fuel consumption, long-lived toxic residuals of certain chemicals, nuclear wastes, and heavy metals, and many other examples come to mind. All illustrate examples of depleting our environmental capital and the first and second laws.

Critical determinants of people's behavior within the natural laws are the prevailing interest rates, which reveal the value placed on the future vis-a-vis the present in financial markets, and other measures of future expectations. Many believe that we are overly and dangerously myopic by not properly valuing the preferences of future generations (Page 1977). Consequently we may be handing over an inappropriately small stock of human and natural resources for future generations. A perplexing problem is that if mistakes are made in resource use, irreversible changes may take place. Nonrenewable resources can never be recovered (entropy), and renewable resources may be so degraded that they are extinguished, and they are always diminished in quality (entropy). Uncertainty is an even greater problem when irreversibilities are considered because the cause of the damage may be initiated before knowledge of its ultimate impact is known and correctly anticipated.

Risk and uncertainty is measured by known past variation and unknowable future outcomes and possibilities. Human systems and behavior are highly variable and uncertain (wars, revolution, famine, overpopulation, business cycles), and human experience has proven them difficult to predict or to control. Barring human intervention, natural phenomena are remarkably stable in the sense that they are self-correcting and self-regulating.

However, it is clear that we are increasingly affecting the natural order and perhaps making the future more uncertain by disturbing natural systems.

For example, as agriculture has become highly productive, it has also become more specialized into monocultures, and these are dependent on fossil fuels, pesticides, fertilizers, hybrid seeds, irrigation, continued stable weather, and many other factors that we only partially understand. Particularly when one realizes the singular role the United States, Canada, and Argentina play as exporters in the world grain markets, agriculture concentrated into a few species and geographical regions increases risks, but we are uncertain as to how much.

Human work increases entropy, and this increases the demand for energy. Our efforts at environmental management also hasten entropy, and this in turn creates greater demands for natural resources. The natural environment contains enormous diversity, which is inherently stable. Furthermore, we may need environmental services in the future that are hitherto unknown or unused. Consequently future models of the economics of natural resources should include risk and uncertainty, as well as the constraints imposed by the first and second laws of thermodynamics.

In 1977 President Carter directed the Council on Environmental Quality and the Department of State to integrate the work of thirteen governmental agencies and conduct a long-range study of the world's population, environment, and natural resources. *The Global 2000 Report to the President* (1980) was the result of the three-year study, which conceptually and to a limited scale quantitatively integrates models of natural resources, population, and economics in order to forecast likely future conditions. The predictions are gloomy but not so dire as those made by the Club of Rome group in the early 1970s. The study forecasts more people, more pollution, and more degradation of the environment by 2000. It also foresees less economic stability, heated competition over natural resources as poor but resource-rich nations try to exert more control over ownership, a widening gap between the rich and poor nations, and continued loss of cropland and grassland due to overcropping and erosion.

The report is broken into two volumes—one a description of the findings and the other a technical volume describing the individual models and how they were linked. The resources studied and topics considered included technology, food, fisheries, forestry, water, energy, mineral fuels, nonfuel minerals including seabed mining, and the environment. Appendix B of the report summarizes the views of an advisory panel who criticized the report. Their comments are valuable, providing insight into the weakness of economic and natural-resource modeling. The first criticism, which can be ascribed to all modeling, is that the recent past dominates the structure and quantified relationships in the model. Data from the past thirty years used for the *Global 2000* study ignore previous technological transformations and structural changes, such as the shifts in energy from wood to coal and to petroleum. Furthermore, the past thirty years have been characterized by close to ideal climatic conditions for agriculture, which are unlikely to prevail in the future. Severe global perturbations are likely, and a long-term deteriorating trend is possible. Also new and probable technologies were not incorporated into the modeling exercise.

The panel pointed out that the linkages between the component submodels were inadequate. For example, the impact of mineral production on water use was neglected; population projections ignored environmental and health effects; fishery models neglected pollution effects; and nowhere was a total accounting made of required economic resources of capital, labor, and land to produce the forecast levels of GNP. These criticisms mean that the models lack sufficient provisions for various feedback effects among subsectors and fail to account for the laws of nature, as well as economic realities. The panel also found that no consideration had been made of exogenous or unanticipated shocks to the world's economy and the environment. These perturbations included natural (epidemics), technological (toxic leak, nuclear mishaps, practicable nuclear fusion), and social surprises (a cartel of agricultural exporters, breakdown of the world financial markets).

The panel also felt the model should accommodate discontinuities that are nearly certain to arise in the future, for the models relied too heavily on extrapolation in which the future is expected to be a continuation of the past. This is particularly misleading in resource models because the long-term fall in energy prices was reversed in 1973, and the critical threshold of the assimilative capacity of the environment to absorb untreated waste has been achieved in many regions and seems close to being achieved on a worldwide scale. Modeling nonrenewable resources must be a forward-looking endeavor because as depletion occurs, prices will rise, and exhaustion will eventually be reached.

One panel member used a simple mathematical example, taken from Oscar Morgenstern's *The Construction of Economic Data,* to illustrate how sensitive quantitative models are to the completeness and accuracy of data and of estimated numerical relationships. At their heart, most models are systems of simultaneous equations and this example is the simplest: two linear equations in two unknowns ($x$ and $y$). One form was given as:

$$x - y = 1.0$$
$$x - 1.0001y = 0.0.$$

its solution is $x = 1000,001$ and $y = 100,000$. If the coefficient of $y$ in the second equation is reduced to 0.999999:

$$x - y = 0$$

$$x - 0.999999y = 0.0,$$

the solution is changed to $x = -99,999$ and $y = -100,000$, an order of magnitude difference from the newly identical first version. Although this example was established to maximize sensitivity, it illustrates a significant pitfall in quantitative model building of using statistical procedures to estimate hypothesized relationships and then proceeding to trust in their reasonableness and veracity.

One way to test for this problem is to conduct a sensitivity analysis: incrementally changing one variable or relationship at a time and seeing how the solution to the model behaves. A complete sensitivity analysis does just what it says, for it highlights which variables and relationships are critical in a model. This example also illustrates that it is possible for models to become so interdependent and sensitive that they respond only to noise, small random shocks or data inaccuracies and do not describe the actual underlying system. When noise prevails, as the sensitivity of the above example shows, this is not much of a model, for the purpose of modeling is to focus on critical relationships and problems. This is an inherent problem in large-scale modeling efforts.

The panel also pointed out that no single model should be taken at face value and used in isolation. The safest course is to compare several independent modeling efforts. At a minimum, a model and its results should be scrutinized by a panel of outsiders, as was the case with the Global 2000 model, and it should be completely documented. An informal review by those in industry, government, and academia should always be undertaken both during the construction of a model and after the project is complete.

The other criticisms of the *Global 2000* model relate the explicit and implicit assumptions made by the modelers. The panel pointed out that the normative goals that the study team implicitly applied were never elucidated. Modeling involves normative judgments, which become incorporated into the structure as hidden premises that need to be brought forth. Competent and honest modelers recognize the limitations of their models more than any outsider, although outside criticism invariably points out what has been overlooked. Modelers should be encouraged to present information on limitations inherent in the methods used and inadequate or inaccurate data. Their caveats and warnings must be carefully listened to by all users.

Many large-scale energy models have been built and employed in forecasting and policy analysis and in supporting policy positions, ranging from extensive direct regulation and nationalization, total deregulation and reliance on free markets, to "counter" or "adversary" models used by interviewers appearing before federal and state public utility regulators. Manne, Richels, and Weyant (1979) surveyed three medium-term (to 1990) models where price regulations, taxes, and the policies adopted by OPEC affecting oil and natural-gas prices, production, and consumption are highlighted (75 percent of America's energy). Long-term scenarios are estimated (2000 or beyond) in four models where the transition to a postpetroleum world occurs and technology and investment become the variables of interest. They summarized several characteristics for each model: principal policy issue addressed; number of regions considered; modeling methodology; time horizon and time intervals; and pricing energy demands and energy-economy interactions. Their comparison of these efforts provides insight into what models are expected to do and how the model builders proceed.

The models considered were the Project Independence Evaluative System (PIES), originally developed under near-wartime conditions, which includes 2,500 equations and 7,000 variables to provide analytic substance for President Nixon's energy speech in November 1973 and to analyze the effects of policy options. The Kennedy World Oil Model simulates market prices and trade flows for refined oil products on an international scale with OPEC acting like a revenue maximizer. The Baughman-Jaskow Regionalized Energy Model assumes existing technologies for electricity production and simulates regional demand and supply and integrates economic and engineering relationships. In 1976, the model correctly indicated that the Atomic Energy Commission had been substantially overestimating nuclear-power growth. The ALPS model (A Linear Programming System) was constructed by that commission to assess the benefits of alternative electricity production technologies over the long term. BESOM (Brookhaven Energy System Optimization Model) integrated electricity technology with pricing and regulatory policies and other uses of fossil fuels. ETA (Energy Technology Assessment model) is another model of the U.S. energy supply and demand for electricity used to evaluate new energy technologies such as plutonium reprocessing. The ETA-MACRO adaptation integrates it with a model of the entire U.S. economy. The synfuels model (Synthetic Fuels Decision Analysis) is the only model in table 4–1 to account specifically for uncertainty. It was built to analyze the commercial feasibility of synfuels and the impact of various government programs designed to stimulate development of these technologies.

The government policies considered in these seven models are wide-ranging, and no single model is comprehensive enough to include all of them. However, no energy subcomponent can exist in a vacuum because of the substitutability of one energy source (fuel) for another as existing equipment wears out, fuel reserves are depleted, and economic growth takes place. The way modelers handle these interdependencies is to concentrate on the primary questions asked of the model and to simplify the less-impor-

**Table 4-1**
**Seven Representative Studies**

| | Medium-term (to 1990) | | | Long-term (2000 or beyond) | | | |
| | PIES | Kennedy | Baughman-Joskow | ALPS | BESOM | ETA, ETA-MACRO | Synfuels |
| --- | --- | --- | --- | --- | --- | --- | --- |
| Principal policy issues addressed | U.S. dependence on oil imports. Impact of domestic price controls | Pricing policies of OPEC oil cartel | Electric utilities pricing and equipment-ordering policies | Demonstration and commercialization of advanced nuclear reactors | Comprehensive accounting framework for R&D planning | Interrelations between U.S. economic growth, conservation, coal and nuclear energy | Demonstration and commercialization of synfuels technologies |
| Number of regions | U.S. divided into 9 demand regions; with transportation links | Non-communist world divided into 6 regions; with transportation links | U.S. divided into 9 demand regions; no transmission interties between regions | U.S. total | U.S. total | U.S. total | U.S. divided into 8 demand regions; with transportation links |
| Modeling methodology, time horizon and intervals | Interregional equilibrium through iterations between linear programming model of energy supplies and economet- | International equilibrium through quadratic programming model of price-responsive oil demands and supplies in | Year-by-year simulation to 1995, with capacity investment decisions based on energy price projections and load | Linear programming model of U.S. nuclear energy supplies and uranium resource depletion. Covers 120 years from | Linear programming model for energy services delivered in 1985 and 2000. New supply technologies based on engineering | Intertemporal equilibrium through reduced gradient optimization algorithm. Price-responsive energy demands, resource deple- | Interregional and intertemporal equilibrium through recursive network algorithm. Covers 52 years from |

| | | | | | | |
|---|---|---|---|---|---|---|
| | rically estimated model of energy demands in 1985 and 1990 | 1980 | forecasts | 1969 through 2089, subdivided into 35 intervals of unequal length | process analysis | tion and new supply technologies. Covers 75 years from 1975 through 2050, subdivided into 16 intervals of equal length. Sequential resolution of breeder uncertainties | 1973 through 2025, subdivided into 17 intervals of unequal length. Decision tree refers to aggregated version of network model, with sequential resolution of uncertainties between 1985 and 1995 |
| Pricing, energy demands and energy-economy interactions | Demands based on regulated or competitive prices, depending on policy scenario | Cartel-determined Persian Gulf crude oil price. Competitive supplies and demands for crude oil and products elsewhere | Electricity demands based on regulated prices | Fixed demands for nuclear energy | Fixed future demands for "energy services." Interfuel substitution based on engineering process analysis | Demand curves with own- and cross-price elasticities for electric and nonelectric energy. Energy-economy interactions included in ETA-MACRO (but not in ETA) | Fixed future demands for "end uses." Interfuel substitution based on market share price elasticity assumptions |

Source: Manne, Richards, and Weyant (1979).

tant interdependencies, use forecasts made from other models, or interconnect models of various sectors to construct one large model. This last procedure is difficult and expensive and has been attempted only in a limited
number of instances.

The first row of table 4–1 reveals the purpose of these seven models and
the specific policy issues considered. Not all policies and the methods to
achieve them can be addressed simultaneously because of interdependencies
and complexities. The more important policy tools that have been implemented in the recent past include:

*Direct Regulation*

1. Price controls and decontrol.
2. Leasing government-owned land and regulations on leases on private
   lands.
3. Sharing of federal and state lease payments among jurisdictions.
4. Environmental regulations.
5. Siting regulations for mines and synfuel and electric plants.
6. Import quotas, voluntary quotas, fees, and tariffs.
7. Mandated conservation measures (for example, the 55 mph speed
   limit).
8. Mandated technology (for example, the Powerplant and Industrial Fuel
   Use Act).
9. Health and safety regulations.
10. Reclamation regulations on mining firms.

*Indirect Regulation*

1. Government expenditures on research and development.
2. Subsidies for conservation and research and development.
3. Investment tax credits and special depreciation allowances.
4. Tax deductions for depletion (for example, percentage and cost depletion).
5. Tax deductions of state taxes and royalties from federal tax base.
6. Tax depreciation rules.
7. Windfall-profits tax applied to state and Indian tax and lease revenues.
8. Resource taxes (for example, the windfall-profits tax).
9. State severance and other taxes and the investment policies of state permanent funds from resource taxes.
10. Federal deductibility of state resource taxes and lease payments.
11. Federally imposed limitations on state resource tax rates.
12. Effect of OPEC and other international cartels.
13. Alteration of federal grant formulas, particularly the fiscal effort pro-
    visions, which reward states that invoke heavy tax burdens relative to
    private-sector income.

Given these multiple public policies and foreseeable changes in domestic and international economic conditions, an almost infinite number of future scenarios could be conceived of and traced through these and other natural-resource models. Modelers and model users must decide what is likely, what the more important policies are, and what future conditions may occur and simulate these. Row 3 of table 4–1 indicates how each model simulates the effect of future policies and conditions. The uncertainty of knowledge and resource discoveries and the long time spans necessary to implement these by exploratory development, extraction, and construction means that investment must play a primary role in resource models. Furthermore, the depletion of nonrenewable resources means that the past is not a good indicator of the future. These uncertainties, the unreliability of extrapolating from the past, and the prevalence of externalities and public-good attributes place a heavy onus on model builders. Most resource modelers simulate future outcomes by techniques that are able to incorporate changed conditions, technology, and behavior. The most-prevalent methodology (row 3 in table 4–1) is optimization implemented with the specific computational techniques of linear programming, quadratic programming, and gradient methods. The less-frequently employed techniques are econometric and engineering process models.

The lack of detailed information (documentation) and the inconsistency of assumptions and data among models precluded direct comparisons of resource models until two major universities established institutes to accomplish just that. Stanford University established the Energy Model Forum in 1976 to conduct nose-to-nose comparisons among ten models, forecasting fifteen future scenarios using identical data. Massachusetts Institute of Technology formed its Model Verification and Assessment Project to conduct similar activities in 1977. The Stanford comparison includes: the American Gas Association's Total Energy Resource Analysis Model; the Energy Information Administration (DOE) and ICF, Inc., U.S. Energy Outlook Analysis; the Texas Energy Advisory Council/University of Houston Model; the Long-Range Energy Development and Supplies Model at Virginia Polytechnic Institute and State University; the LEAP Gulf Oil and Stanford Research Institute Model; the MIT World Oil Project Model; the National Energy Plan Model at Oak Ridge National Laboratory; the Erickson/Milsaps/Spann Model by the Brookings Institute; the Epple/Hansen Model at Carnegie-Mellon University; and the FOSSIL 2 Model at the Office of Policy and Evaluation of the Department of Energy. These forums should be helpful in future modeling efforts, and documentation of the comparisons should be of interest to those engaged in policymaking.

In 1981 the Energy Modeling Forum at Stanford University used ten energy-simulation models to project the response of world oil supply, demand, and price to various scenarios of OPEC production plans and world economic growth, conservation, and transition to alternative technologies. The simulations provide information on which to base policy decisions. As one example, they analyzed two discrete components of the oil import premium, which occurs because imports make countries vulnerable to oil-exporting countries' economic and political policies, and economic losses would occur should a supply disruption arise. They decomposed this oil import premium into a security premium and a market-power premium, brought about because larger current imports increase the price of energy and support larger future price increases, which are not reflected in today's price. The latter occurs because larger imports increase costs of supply disruptions. They concluded that the total import premium was $8 to $24 per barrel in 1981. This implied that any policy that would reduce imports at a cost less than $8 per barrel is clearly justifiable on economic-efficiency grounds, whereas any program costing more than $24 per barrel would be a wasteful use of resources.

Although large-scale models were instrumental in formulating the U.S. national energy plans, their usefulness and impact on policy has been questioned. The U.S. General Accounting Office (1979) after reviewing the DOE's tax-policy analysis efforts concluded that the agency had made little or no contribution to the adminstration and probable effects of tax policy or even analyzed it. In other words the agency had not utilized the extensive work to model energy undertaken by government agencies and private institutions.

Conceptual models are intuitive and unique to their creators. They rely on elementary analysis and relationships that can be carried around in one's head integrated with the output of other models, data, and expert opinions. One such modeler is Lovins (1980) whose criticisms and analysis of the Western world's energy policies have been widely and critically recognized. He focuses on the evolution of what is technologically feasible and how energy policy can be used to direct the world away from a hard energy path to a soft energy path. He defines the hard path as one that assumes that energy consumption will continue to grow but at a somewhat diminishing rate, and energy technologies will be large scale, sophisticated, and capital intensive, encompassing central electric power plants (coal and nuclear) and huge synfuels plants, and transportation will continue to be provided by heavy and relatively inefficient automobiles. The soft energy path, which he foresees as being feasible, concentrates on a rapid transformation to renewable sources of energy (solar, wind, water), transformed by highly dispersed facilities using known and evolving technologies and enormous progress in conservation, which all lead to a large absolute decrease in energy consumption and waste. He foresees virtually all oil and natural gas being used as feedstock for fertilizers and chemicals and electric power used exclusively for electric motors and lighting. Lovins argues that the West is following a hard energy path, that social institutions are unimaginative and inflexible, and that government tax, subsidy, and regulatory policy overwhelmingly supports the hard path, making the soft path economically unattractive. He arrived at this analysis by means of a conceptual model incorporating the work of others and a large number of rather elementary calculations utilizing the first and second laws applied to entire energy systems rather than to components. One example of his analysis is heating domestic hot water using electricity, which can be shown as:

> coal or nuclear fuel →capital cost of plant →transmission
> lines cost and loss →cost and conversion efficiency to heat
> water to 120° →consumption

compared to a solar technology:

> sunlight →cost and efficiency of on-site collectors and
> storage →consumption.

By his calculations of both the economics and overall engineering efficiencies (including building the machines), solar wins hands down, for this as well as for virtually all space heating and cooling. The feasibility of Lovin's approach was tested by applying it to California in a study funded by the DOE (Craig and Levine 1979). Although most states have conducted energy studies, California is by far the most advanced, and this application shows that enormous energy savings are possible without infringing upon the California life-style.

Lovins has applied his conceptual model to evaluating forecasts of energy consumption made by others and himself. He has found an interesting relationship among how those forecasts have changed over time. He places the total energy consumption forecast for the United States into four categories ranging from low to high—"Beyond the Pale, Heresy, Conventional Wisdom, and Superstition"—as the columns of a table and the year in which the forecast was made—1972, 1974, 1976, and 1978—for the rows. He has found sufficient forecasts of future total energy use in 2000 to fill up the table and finds that the diagonal is roughly constant at $124 \times 10^5$ Btus (or quads) per year. This illustrates that forecasts that had previously been thought of as wildly optimistic ("Beyond the Pale") evolve to become the accepted and eventually conservative view. He reports ( *Washington Post,* November 24, 1980) that a study by Sant shows that if a nationwide least-cost energy strategy had been followed from 1968 to 1978 (in retrospect), a net dollar savings of 17 percent could have been realized and that 25 percent less oil, 34 percent less coal, and 43 percent less electricity would have been used. A draft study by Sawhill shows that a least-cost strategy from 1980 to 2000, assuming that GNP increases by two-thirds, reduces energy use by 25 percent and nonrenewable fuel consumption by nearly 50 percent.

**Elements and Techniques of Models**

A model is an abstraction and simplification. It is only by reducing the complexity of the real world, ignoring the periphery and concentrating on the core, that it becomes possible to comprehend how things work. Thus, the heart of a model is explaining the abstractions. This process should produce hypotheses and predictions that are testable under either experimental conditions (rare in social science models) or with data collected from past events when controlled experiments prove to be impossible or too expensive to undertake. The social sciences and economic fall almost entirely into the latter category, making model testing and validation important and difficult, particularly for natural resources because of their special characteristics. The reasons for constructing models are to enable us to understand the world around us and how our behavior affects it. This knowledge in turn supports problem solving and helps underwrite private and public (collective) decisions and policy.

Models accomplish these goals in a number of ways. The building blocks are theories (abstractions), data, and techniques. Theories allow for specifying relationships, and the implications of theory tell the direction and rough magnitudes of what to expect in those relationships. Data collection and experimentation permit testing relationships and quantifying them mathematically. Modeling techniques enable the researcher to employ information and data to test the hypotheses developed from theory and to simulate likely future scenarios and conditions.

In a sense, any abstraction of reality is a model, no matter how simple. Logical thought and classification schemes are models, as is a diagram or a graphic, a written or a verbal description. Qualitative models, while providing insight, are not emphasized in economics because the measurability of both man-made and natural resources creates an imperative for quantifiable models. In quantifiable models, exogenous inputs are assumed to be determined outside the model. Once specified, the inner workings and relationships within the model structure (a combination of the theoretical model and the modeling techniques) determine the predicted values for the endogenous variables. There are two fundamental paradigms of how the exogenous variables, which include all forms of natural and man-made constraints, determine the endogenous variables: optimization and explanations.

The paradigm of optimization is most widely used in economics. Sometimes referred to as economizing, people and nature are assumed to act as if they were optimizing something. Consumers are assumed to optimize their own or their family's welfare, subject to constraints on time and feasible alternatives given education, prevailing wage rates, and so forth. The entrepreneur and owner of resources is assumed to maximize wealth and profits.

Collective action and government bureaucracy are depicted as ensuring the efficient use of resources or seeking the goals of various interest groups by using public policy.

The optimization paradigm is used in two ways: first to analyze how people choose and second to analyze how resources should be employed. The former is self-explanatory and results in predicted market equilibrium and collective decisions, while the latter, referred to previously as economic efficiency, requires some clarification. The economic definition for the efficient use of resources is when there is no reallocation of resources that would produce greater satisfaction for one or more individuals without diminishing the satisfaction of any other individual. The allocation of resources that corresponds to this efficiency maximum can be calculated in an economic model that contains sufficient information.

One of the significant insights of twentieth-century economists is that efficient resource allocation can be achieved in the marketplace, where people make voluntary and selfish choices and exchanges. If a special set of circumstances prevails—the most important being sufficient competition so that no individual or group of individuals can affect prices and no unnegotiated externalities or public goods exist—prices determined in the marketplace serve to allocate resources efficiently. When these conditions do not prevail, there is said to be a market failure. However, with an optimization model, it is possible to derive prices artificially, which if imposed in the marketplace would have people acting in a way that produces efficiency, and thus these models simulate market behavior. When a market failure occurs, these artificially derived prices deviate from market prices. They are called *shadow prices.*

The second class of model is a descriptive one. In a descriptive model, no optimization is presumed, but the model is constructed to duplicate observed behavior. If the model explains past data or predicts future events more accurately than do competing models, it becomes the accepted explanatory model. There are several characteristics relating to theoretic models that need to be reviewed. Time enters dynamic models and is treated explicitly or is ignored in static models by assuming that flows per unit time persist ad infinitum (static models where time is treated as a constant). While static modeling is an acceptable simplification in conventional economics where only human activities are of interest and nature is ignored, it is necessary in models involving natural resources. Time is obviously critical in the use and exhaustion of a nonrenewable resource. The passage of time and the rate of extraction determine how much has been removed from the earth's crust. The laws of nature regulate the growth rate of renewable resources so that time becomes a critical element.

Models run a wide range, from those that are highly abstract to those that are realistic. At the abstract end of the spectrum are models based on general observation and imagination; these are theoretical and data independent. They are intended to generate theorems, postulates, and limiting cases, which are dependent on highly abstract and artificial assumptions unlikely to be observed in the real world. The bulk of economic models, especially in resource economics, are such simplified models, and these frequently fail to produce implications that can be tested directly.

At the other end of the spectrum are data-dependent or empirical models. In these, theory often plays a secondary role to relationships and statistical techniques that explain data. Charges of "ad hocery" and pure empiricism are often made of these efforts, and these models are most prevalent in multidisciplinary quantitative modeling efforts of large-scale phenomena. The difficulty with large-scale, computer-based models is that their quantitatively precise output and forecasts may fail to predict the future accurately because of their dependency on past data. They also may fail to lend insight into understanding or the implications of policy. The inherent complexity of large data-dependent models is that the uninitiated and sometimes the modeler may place too much confidence in the solutions, which are usually printed out to several decimal places of accuracy by the computer, but the underlying structure or core of the model is sometimes never understood. On occasion these models produce counterintuitive results, and they often produce inaccurate forecasts. The complexity of these models, which may entail thousands of relationships (the ALPS model in table 4–1 consisted of 4,000 relationships) and variables, often makes analytic solutions impossible, so that multiple simulations and approximations are run on computers in order to derive results. Because so many variables are involved, frequently it is difficult to interpret meaningful results when there is such a flood of information. This means that not even the model builders understand why the results may have occurred. Consequently the models may not help the analyst understand the problem of interest, and users of such models should be skeptical of their capabilities.

On the other hand, abstract models are usually solved analytically, and the results can be traced through the model and understood. Models without data are frequently deterministic and produce one solution for each specification of the exogenous variables. Uncertainty can be introduced into abstract models by random variables with known statistical characteristics, while data-dependent models are intrinsically probabilistic. The general nature of relationships among the variables may be specified by theory, but quantified relationships rest on data. Probabilistic models possess statistical distributions whose characteristics, such as average and standard deviation or standard error, are statistical measures of their accuracy. A common example is weather forecasts reported with probabilities. Some forecasters give the odds or chance that it will rain tomorrow. Deterministic models have only one outcome for each set of values of exogenous variables.

Another distinction among models is the time spans they are meant to describe—ranging from short term to long term. Obviously these definitions are flexible, but among economic models short-term is defined to be when the majority of variables and relationships remain constant. This typically means that the capital stock, such as plant and equipment and natural-resource endowment, is constant, but its rate of utilization is a variable, along with price of outputs. The long run occurs when more relationships and variables are free to change. In conventional models, this is when the capital stock and technology can change, deterioration and obsolescence occurs, and investments are made. Natural resources involve a close interdependence between stocks and flows. Flows are what is taken out or added and affect the size and quality of the stock, whether one considers a nonrenewable resource such as iron ore or a renewable one such as a fishery or forest. Thus models of natural resources must be long-run models that consider time explicitly if they are to be relevant.

Long-run models describe trends where temporary deviations from these are ignored and are assumed to be self-correcting. This requires historical data. Short-term models concentrate on smaller deviations and disequilibrium and therefore require more accurate, contemporary data. Short-term models are more suitable for predictions, for they are calibrated to recent data and initialized with the most recent observations. Their predictive power, however, deteriorates rapidly with the passage of time. Long-term models do not forecast deviations but are used to make projections about the more-distant future. In view of the numerous factors that determine future events, some of which are explicitly accounted for in the model and others which are not, long-run models are best viewed as tracing out the implications of certain conditions that may exist in the future. They serve best in "what if" exercises.

## Modeling Techniques

The explosion of economic, mathematical, engineering, and natural science knowledge in the twentieth century has given rise to a large number of ways in which models of social and scientific phenomena can be specified and quantified. Models of economic behavior and integrated natural phenomena, however, use a limited number of techniques. The person who uses the output of a model to make policy recommendations or to predict future implications of policy needs to know both the theoretical structure of the model and a minimal description of the techniques used to quantify the model.

Approaches to constructing operational and empirical models integrating economics and physical sciences have evolved almost exclusively since

World War II. The techniques are most easily described by progressing from those that are transparent and most readily comprehensible to those that are more esoteric. Judgmental models or consensus forecasts and evaluation are based on the premise that asking the experts and those best informed will capture the essence of a problem. Case studies are detailed examinations of one particular example or incident from which some basis for making generalizations may be possible. This approach was taken in describing and analyzing regional competition over energy resources in the United States and Canada. Engineering models integrate natural laws and knowledge of engineering production processes. Sometimes these are integrated with models of economic behavior. Input-output analysis abstracts from engineering models by empirically describing flows of inputs and outputs into many production processes and products simultaneously. Optimization models rely on mathematical techniques and derive both abstract and quantifiable implications and simulations of the "what-if" variety (the assumption of economizing was discussed previously). Statistical methods rely on mathematical statistics to test and quantitatively test implications and hypotheses derived from theoretical models. Simulation models are more eclectic than any of the above and may rely on some or all of the previous techniques. Many operational models are not designated as simulation models but involve one or more techniques; these are hybrid models. They vary so greatly from application to application that they cannot be described as a technique.

## Judgmental Models

The premise of judgmental models is that experts have assimilated the necessary knowledge and information from the literature, their experience, other models, and theories and can process it both to predict and to analyze policy options. The technique boils down to asking the experts. Individual problem-solving ability and planning horizons vary, and thus the expert problem solver appears to be mentally guided by large numbers of patterns and sources of data and information.

Informed individuals may be a source of valuable insights about the future and the past. Much is made in the popular literature of predictions made by experts that have proved wrong. Nevertheless, forecasting by judgmental means remains in wide use and is perceived to be a useful technique by those in private industry, government, and academia.

Expert opinion can be solicited by direct, personal, one-to-one dialogue or interview, by group sessions or committees, and by questionnaires or remote conferencing. The delphi method is an iterative questionnaire procedure that is widely used to elicit information. It involves a group (such as a panel of experts) in a remote structured conference procedure using iterative questionnaires while maintaining individual anonymity. Initial responses to questions relating to the likelihood of future events and various scenarios are collected, tabulated, and returned to the participants along with a new questionnaire. This procedure allows the experts to find out the opinion of others, and in many cases this process converges to a consensus forecast or opinion.

*Case Studies*

One cannot say a great deal about the case-study technique because it produces a model only in the most general sense. In a case study a historical period, product, process, firm, or other institution is examined and described. In this process certain relationships, tendencies, and specifications may be brought to light. Some of these may be unique to the thing being examined, while others may be generalizable; however, this can be determined only from other corroborating information. The uniqueness of each case study and a lack of a methodology mean that the technique is best viewed as an informal method for verifying hypotheses derived from abstract models and for eliciting information and stimulating ideas that may be helpful in formulating and empirically estimating models using other techniques.

*Engineering Models*

Engineering modeling stresses physical criteria, production processes and methods, and engineering parameters, and it may include economic factors. Thus these models incorporate natural laws, and engineering data and formulas can be used as submodels in larger efforts that incorporate economic relationships and choice.

   Alternative choices are essential in evaluating policies. This is an inherent limitation of all models that are incapable of describing alternative technologies and allocations of natural and man-made resources. In addition, engineering models can be used with various optimization and simulation models, which often go beyond strictly economic considerations to provide a firmer base in physical reality. Engineering analysis can also be used with simulation and systems models, which differ from other types of models in that they incorporate feedback loops, which can forecast the direction as well as size of anticipated future changes and interaction among variables. Most scientific and engineering relationships have well-found and well-developed mathematical concepts and are often more readily treated analytically than are the softer issues in more empirically based models. As is the case with all other modeling techniques, however, engineering analysis has difficulty in addressing many judgmental issues such as the resolution of social and political problems.

Inherent weaknesses of the engineering approach are that it assumes technical feasibility directly to reality, and this must be proved through experience, particularly in total life-cycle evaluations. Second, it fails to evaluate political, social, and environmental as well as purely economic factors. Nor does it address alternative processes or functional substitutions except with great difficulty. The model technique does not permit easy inclusion of quantum changes, such as substitution of solar for conventional energy.

As they currently exist, engineering models have forecasting value mainly for the short-term future (one to three years) and to a limited extent for the intermediate term (three to five years). This stems largely from lack of ability to predict quantum jumps in technology, as well as limited availability of data on new processes under development.

*Input-Output Method*

Although the origins of input-output analysis can be traced to the eighteenth century, it was not until World War II that it was made operational by the economist and planner Wassily Leontief. The fundamental premise of the technique is that production and consumption can be described as interdependent and simultaneous flows of services. The recipe analogy perhaps best describes the technique. Producing a cake requires a certain number of eggs and an amount of flour, butter, shortening, flavorings, and services such as electricity or natural gas, labor, time in the oven, and cooling time. Each output modeled (the cake) requires the services of a number of input services and qualities. Each of these is described by an input-output coefficient, which is the amount of input per unit of output. Coefficients can be derived for a large number of inputs and outputs, and a production process can be described in one step or a number of steps. These relationships are interdependent and simultaneous when the model is transformed from one of describing the input requirement for each per unit of output to all the direct and indirect services of inputs necessary to get a unit of final output. For example, the flour in the case required grain, which required land, fertilizer, transportation, a tractor, and a farmer, and each of these required other inputs such as steel and petroleum. The input-output model is able to quantify all inputs required to produce a given level and mix of outputs, and these models can run into the thousands of variables. Its analytic and predictive power stems from its ability to model large numbers of outputs and inputs simultaneously.

It is apparent why input-output became such a valuable tool during World War II; it enabled planners to anticipate the total material and personnel requirements necessary to achieve a certain level of net outputs. The model is still widely used. One of its strengths is the capability of intertwining dollar flows and physical flows. In a seminal work, Ayers and Kneese (1969) integrated economic inputs and outputs with physical flows of services from natural resources and returns of wastes to the environment to derive their materials-balance approach to modeling.

The strength of input-output analysis is its ability to integrate a large amount of highly disaggregated economic and engineering data, simultaneously and consistently. Because of this, the technique is widely used, but it is not without its drawbacks. Each input-output coefficient is determined by the technology existing at the time the data were collected. Therefore not only is technology embedded when economic data are used to estimate them (as opposed to a physical relationship); it depends on prevailing prices since dollar flows are measured, and the technology is a mix of that which was in place at the time. Thus, relative prices are assumed to be fixed, and technology characteristics are an unknown mix. The former makes the model work for short-term forecasting only when relative prices are quite stable, and the latter makes it inappropriate for long-term forecasting because the capital stock deteriorates and is replaced with new investment, which incorporates new technology and alters the mix. Fixes have been developed to reduce both drawbacks, but the user must be aware of these limitations.

*Optimization Techniques*

In practical applications, particularly where large uncertainties exist or objectives are complex, there has been considerable criticism of the oversimplification necessary to apply mathematical optimization techniques. Some of this criticism is deserved; in particular, the problem of data availability plagues this form of analysis, whose major advantage is its ability to include complex technical and economic interrelationships and its capability of being able to trace how the model functions. However, alternative techniques do not handle such problems well either.

Solutions determined by optimization techniques can provide useful insights into the feasible limits of, say, cost minimization or profit maximization under idealized circumstances. While such solutions may not be practical, they do provide a well-characterized benchmark against which practical compromises may be gauged.

*Statistical Techniques*

Mathematical statistics and probability possess a long and noble history. The classical hypothesis-testing and Bayesian approaches are well developed. Modelers use, and misuse, statistics extensively to estimate the parameters of quantifiable relationships, as well as to test hypotheses. There are two branches to the application of statistics to modeling: time-series analysis (extrapolation) and econometrics. In extrapolation, dynamic processes are described using well-developed statistical techniques and highly simplified economic hypotheses, which boil down to assuming the future will be a continuation of the past. The relationships among variables are dictated by the statistical techniques, and the data are used to estimate numerical quantities for the parameters. The econometricians pride themselves on the fact that data are not used to specify the relationships among variables in models, which instead come from economic theories.

Extrapolative or pure time-series forecasting techniques use the historic behavior of a variable to predict its future. The distinguishing feature of these techniques is the forecasting function, which depends only on time. Usually the variables of interest are observed at discrete, equally spaced intervals, and some systematic pattern is identified. This pattern is then forecast to continue. The simplest example of an extrapolative technique is linear-trend analysis—fitting a straight line to historic data and projecting the continuation of the fitted trend. However, much more sophisticated techniques can be used to estimate a variety of nonlinear trends, as well as cyclical deviations from these trends. For extrapolative techniques to be useful, historic relationships must be relatively stable, and the future must be like the past, a possibility that becomes increasingly unrealistic as the forecasting period lengthens. Therefore, extrapolative techniques are often more appropriate for short-term than for long-term forecasting.

Econometrics may be viewed as a unification of three disciplines; statistics, economic theory, and mathematics. Econometrics is a technique that attempts, through statistical methods, to establish quantitative relationships between economic and other variables. As such, econometric modeling is a two-step process. Initially a functional relationship between economic variables is constructed, based upon economic theory and physical laws of nature. Then the parameters of the equation are estimated with statistical and mathematical tools, and the significance and validity of the assumed structural relationships are tested. Once a model proves satisfactory, it may be used to study past behavior or to predict future behavior.

The use of such models to study past behavior and to predict future behavior relies upon a major assumption: that the structure of the system under consideration neither has changed nor will change significantly. Because econometric estimates are based upon historical data, a valid econometric model will necessarily reflect the structural relationships that existed during the historical period from which the data are taken. As long as the prevailing structure can be assumed to be consistent with that upon which the model is based, the tools of the econometrician can be used with confidence. However, if indications of major structural shifts in system behavior occur, the econometrician's estimates must be considered with more caution. This assumption limits the capabilities of econometric models in analyzing natural resources because future discovery and depletion will not follow past behavior for nonrenewable resources and is unlikely to follow it for renewable resources. Furthermore, technological change is particularly difficult to incorporate into econometric models.

Natural resources are used primarily as intermediate inputs to the production of final goods. Therefore the demand for materials is derived—that is, it is induced by the demand for the products that are produced with those materials. In modeling substitution among natural-resource materials, the characteristics of materials used in production must be accounted for in economic and physical terms. The econometric approach to modeling this technology is to estimate production functions that show the quantity of output that can be obtained from given input quantities and how the level of output changes as the quantities of inputs change. With the neoclassical production function that economists frequently employ, substitution possibilities are assumed to be smooth and continuous. A neoclassical production function can therefore be thought of as a smooth approximation to an engineering production function with a large number of production processes or technologies. Moreover, the modeler must specify the mathematical form of the production function and estimate its parameters from data unsuited for this purpose. Both of those facts constrain the capabilities of this technique. If a major shift in technology may occur in the future, econometrics can be used to summarize the extent of the shift, although it is hard pressed to predict that such a shift will occur.

Great care must be taken if an econometric model is used to forecast outside the historical range of the data. Dramatic variations in observed data may be indicators of major structural upheavals, which could invalidate the model developed. Similarly these variations may also indicate that the model structure was poorly or incorrectly specified. Incorporating engineering and other information directly into the econometric analysis can greatly improve the usefulness of econometrics in such applications.

Econometrics and extrapolation are based on probability theory. Thus the endogenous variables forecast and analyzed by the techniques are assigned probable values, as well as the likely distribution of values. This provides a powerful level for the analyst to judge the strength and robustness of the model. The user of such models should always be informed of the accuracy of the model in explaining past data.

*Simulation*

A simulation model is not always entirely distinguishable from other modeling techniques, for it may incorporate parts of all the other techniques. To distinguish the differences from other modeling approaches—and the differences in practice are ones of degree, not in kind—it is useful to contrast the simulation approach to the other causal modeling methodologies considered—econometrics and optimization. An econometric model can be defined as one in which a relation between economic variables is hypothesized, and statistical procedures are applied to determine whether the hypothesized interdependence can be accepted. The completed model thus describes what has occurred in the past, and when variables determined outside the model are specified, it can predict what is likely to occur in the future. A process optimization model, on the other hand, is one in which optimum behavior is assumed to occur. It predicts that the best course of action will be taken. Optimization models ascribe and attribute rational economic decision making to the situation being modeled and can be either statistically or dynamically specified. In its simplest form, a simulation model is nothing more than a hypothesis of interrelationships among variables, typically dynamically specified, in that the time behavior of the interrelations is revealed by simulation. Thus, a simulation model can be distinguished most clearly from the other causal modeling approaches as one not requiring hypothesis testing in the statistical sense or attribution of rational economic decision making to the actors being modeled (Forrester 1971). Typically a simulation model will interconnect submodels that capture generally accepted behavior in the small in an attempt to simulate overall performance in the large.

*Selecting Models and Modeling Techniques*

The most important questions the user of a model must ask are, What do I intend to use the model for? To whom will it be necessary to present the implications of the model? Because models are abstractions of reality, they are not meant to depict all the facts and nuances; rather they are designed to concentrate on certain core characteristics. When a model is selected, it must be one that allows the fundamental questions the user has to be answered. For example, if one were interested in analyzing how technological change affects the use of a certain natural resource, an input-output model would be inappropriate because technology is frozen, and it is static by construction.

Another key determinant in the selection process is the trade-off made between abstraction and reality. A model that is a useful pedogogical tool in the classroom might be inappropriate for presenting the technical staff of an operating firm in the industry modeled. This means the user must be supplied with documentation. A technician who wishes to employ a model for some purpose or replicate it with different data needs to have complete documentation. Regrettably, most models are inadequately and poorly documented, and it is often quicker and easier to start from scratch than to try to make a poorly documented model usable. Model users must be given sufficient documentation so that they understand the inherent limitations of the model and technique. A professionally competent and honest modeler will always specify the assumptions they are making, the source and limitations of the data, and all of the uncertainties and caveats that they have detected or might foresee in the model. A devious and dishonest modeler does not reveal these things and can produce just about any result that a naive or unscrupulous user may specify.

The user must be conversant with the model and modeler. All modelers assume who their audience and users will be, and the most thorough and honest modeler may have assumed the wrong audience. For example, if a sophisticated user was envisioned, then assumptions and limitations that that user knows are implicit in the technique or data used will not be spelled out.

Finally, the user and modeler should communicate. This will prevent some serious unintended mishaps and benefit both the modeler and the user. Experienced modelers inevitably conclude after reflecting on their most-recent product that the model could have been better, and its predictions or analyses have many limitations that they see only in retrospect. The most positive thing usually concluded at the end of one of these reflections is that both the modeler and user learned much more than they had known previously about what they were modeling. If there is no communication between the two, then the most valuable result of modeling is lost.

The criteria for selecting a method to forecast empirically and analyze natural resources and economics for both the expert and the naive user are laid out in table 4-2. The rankings (low, medium, and high) indicate the relative strengths and weaknesses of each technique, and the interpretation as to whether low means the technique is desirable or less desirable depends upon the specific criteria.

These criteria comprise the questions that a potential user should be asking, for there are fundamental differences among the techniques, and no single one is superior in all respects or for all uses. The most fundamental question is what the analysis and results will be used for and who will be using it and for how long. Use of the selection criteria in table 4-2 should result in the user's being able to address these considerations.

Applications of these eight methods are to forecast future trends and events or to understand and analyze past occurrences. The purpose of the

**Table 4-2**
**Criteria for Selection of Modeling Techniques**

| | Judgmental | Case Studies | Engineering | Input-Output | Optimization | Econometrics | Simulation |
|---|---|---|---|---|---|---|---|
| Application desired | | | | | | | |
|   Forecasting | High | — | Low | — | Low | Medium | Low |
|   Analysis | Low | Medium | High | — | High | Medium | High |
| Budget and time constraints | Medium | High | Medium | Medium | Medium | Medium to low | Medium |
| Sensitivity to change in | | | | | | | |
|   Technology | Medium | Medium | High | Medium | High | Medium | High |
|   Economic factors and government policy | Medium | Low | Medium | Medium | Low | High | Medium |
| Transparency | | | | | | | |
|   To naive user | High | High | High | High | Medium | Low | Low |
|   To expert user | Low | High | Medium | Medium | Low | Medium | Medium |
| Ability to validate | | | | | | | |
|   Internal to method | Medium | Medium | Medium | Low | Low | High | Low |
|   External to method | Low | Low | Low | Medium | Medium | High | Medium |
| Level of aggregation | Low to high | Low | Low | Medium to high | Medium to high | High | Medium to high |

former intent is obvious; the purpose of the latter is to conduct policy analysis. Questions relating to hypothetical changes in various factors—such as new technologies, changes in prices, government regulations, and tax policy—can be posed and their probable implications traced as they affect the model. Some techniques are more able to conduct these what-if questions than others. Clearly the success of any particular application depends on the quality of the specific model and the data employed to estimate it. Model building is a way to abstract systematically from the complexities of the real world and to stress the core relationships that are thought to describe that reality. Each modeling technique imposes both explicit and implicit assumptions and restrictions on the model builder, in addition to those abstractions he or she controls directly when specifying a model. The criticality of the technique-related assumptions surfaces in the application desired and in the transparency criteria. In forecasting, one makes assumptions about the future state of the world and attempts to trace the effects of those implications; hence the further into the future one is forecasting, the less meaningful past experience becomes. In forecasting with extrapolative techniques, the analyst makes the assumption that past trends will continue, and consequently the method is ranked medium for short-term forecasts of less than five years (denoted in table 4–2) and low for forecasts of greater length. The methods involved in case studies are primarily ad hoc and depend entirely on past behavior. Therefore they are not amenable for forecasting. In input-output analysis the economy is assumed to remain in long-term equilibrium and technology is rigidly defined, implying the technique is inappropriate for forecasting. As a result, it is given a blank in table 4–2. Econometric estimates rely on past data but allow the investigator to extract information about a wide variety of relationships, some or all of which may continue into the future. This ability earns it a medium rank. In the cases of optimization, simulation, and engineering methods, the limitations include restrictive implicit assumptions and failure to consider the effects of key variables, which may cause change in the future; these earn a low rank. Judgmental techniques produce forecasts based on informed expert opinion, and accurate forecasts dependent on the quality of the chosen experts or, equally important, on the current state of thinking within the industry or discipline. It earns a high rank, for if specialists in the real world have not formed opinions about the future that are likely to be realized, then forecasting is an empty box altogether.

Alternative outcomes produced by different what-ifs and sensitivity of these results to changes in related variables is the contribution analysis to make in addition to understanding. Techniques that accommodate a wide variety of assumptions about technology, economic conditions, and government regulatory and fiscal policies and allow for discontinuities from the past and judgments about the future are most productive in this respect.

Optimization, simulation, and engineering approaches rank high because each incorporate technological and other relationships directly. Econometric models rank medium because the estimated relationships among variables rely on the past and thus are less able to accommodate structural changes or values for variables out of the range of past observations. Input-output methods can trace through implications of certain assumed changes but in themselves are not suited to analysis. Judgmental models are ranked low unless the questions posed to the participants specifically include the what-if questions. When this is the case, its ranking would advance to medium but not high because subsequent what-if questions entail another replication of the method.

Constraints on the time available to produce results and budget vary directly and the rankings in table 4-2 are self-explanatory. The question of the technique to reflect changes in technology and economic factors, including government policy, differs from analysis because these changes may be posed hypothetically, may be assumed to follow recent behavior, and may be dictated to ranges for outside historical experience. Clearly a method must explicitly consider technology in order to be sensitive to changes in it. Consequently optimization, simulation, and engineering rank high. Case studies where frequently the technology is invariant in a study are ranked low. Econometrics where technological change is sometimes implicitly built into the model and less often described explicitly must be ranked as medium. In judgmental methods, technological change must be posited and responses as to its effect elicited. This additional complexity places it medium. In extrapolation, technological trends are assumed to continue as they did in the past, earning it a low ranking with respect to technological or economic changes. Although most input-output models imply that technology is frozen, it is possible to account for technological change, which nudges it to medium.

Econometric methods invariably include and, in fact, stress economic relationships and are thus responsive to economic changes. Simulation may include economic factors, giving the respective high and medium rankings. In all other techniques, the roles of prices and economics equilibrium are usually ignored or implicitly assumed to be constant, thus making them unresponsive to economic variables. However, it is possible to incorporate assumed economic changes in both judgmental and engineering techniques, which would raise their classification to medium. When one wishes to trace through the effects of changes in demand or economic factors other than price, input-output indicates the primary and secondary effects in a detailed way, giving it a medium.

Transparency is the property that the structure of the relationship among variables can be clearly understood, and the effect of changes in variables on forecasts and simulations is logical and consistent. In order to be transparent, the assumptions and premises that underlie the method, data, and relationships should be made explicit, and their implications should be intuitively plausible. Although the methods may involve sophisticated statistical or mathematical methods, some may be more easily explained to naive nontechnical users than to others. Furthermore, some methods may not be transparent even to experts because of their complexity, particularly in how clearly the model and use of hte method are described in technical documentation. Although econometrics and input-output techniques are well understood, it is possible to introduce unnoticed assumptions, either by accident or by design, which may deceive an expert, earning these techniques a medium. Simulation and the engineering approaches are ad hoc techniques, which means confusion is possible, placing them in the same category. In judgmental techniques no one, not even the investigators, knows what is in the minds of the respondents, and therefore the technique is ranked low. The methods of extrapolation, case studies, and optimization are explicit and have been replicated so many times that deception is unlikely, placing them high. Transparency to the layperson depends on how logical and straightforward the technique appears to be when explained in nontechnical terms. Extrapolation, case studies, input-output, judgmental, and engineering approaches can be explained in a few sentences, which earn them high rankings. Optimization is complex but comprehensible after a paragraph or two, so it gets a medium. Both econometrics and simulation most likely can be explained only by means of black box analogies and are associated with a mystifying jargon, which earn them a low ranking.

The ability to validate the output of a model is next. Of course, there is no way to guarantee the accuracy of forecasts or sensitivity analysis. However, some methods explicitly account for variability of past data, and this provides a means of measuring how accurate they are in explaining past events. Although other techniques fail to check for accuracy internally, the structure of the model and its output is quantified in a manner that allows using past data to check for the accuracy of predictions. External validation is possible for all techniques by means of review by panels of experts. Internally derived validation occurs for the statistically based methods of extrapolation and econometrics, which gives them a high rank; however, a unique or limited data base diminishes the value of any statistical internal or external test. Because history and analysis occur coincidentally in case studies, it is given a medium. If iterative methods such as delphi are used in judgmental models, the coincidence of initial responses and the speed of convergence to consensus or a stable diversity indicate the confidence experts have in their judgments; it earns a medium. All others are ranked low. The ability to use external information and data to validate model output is potentially high for all methods; however, I chose to limit this criterion to formal statistical methods of validation. In this case only econometrics ranks high because numerous formal tests of validation exist, some of which may be applied to extrapolation (medium rank). The quantifiable outputs of optimization and input-output and simulation make them susceptible to external validation, which earns them a medium. Judgmental, engineering, and case studies are ranked low, either because they fail to produce quantifiable outputs or because the outputs may be in a form that makes them difficult to test.

The final criterion that might be employed for selection is the level of aggregation that the technique is most suitable for. Extrapolation and econometrics depend on plentiful, accurate data and a wide range for the variables being observed. Furthermore, the abstract behavior assumed in economics and specified in econometric models is more likely to be revealed at an industry or greater level of aggregation for cross-sectional data and in relatively long trends for time-series data, thus requiring a high level of aggregation. Conversely case studies and engineering models most frequently apply to a single situation or technology and can take many unique and detailed factors into consideration, making them most suitable for individual firms and the lowest level of aggregation. Judgmental models are unique in that they are suitable for all levels of aggregation; optimization,

**Table 4–3**
**Comparing Human and Computer Capabilities**

| Human Superiority | Computer Superiority |
| --- | --- |
| Filter incoming information and concentrate on what is of interest or is important | Input, store, and retrieve large amounts of information accurately and quickly |
| Establish goals and criteria and implement them in a computer program | Compare, manipulate, and calculate quantifiable information according to an established procedure or program |
| Respond and improvise to unanticipated conditions and events | Monitor and identify prespecified conditions from a large body of data |
| Make decisions drawing on past experiences using analytic and intuitive capabilities | Make rapid and consistent responses according to a prespecified program |
| Reason objectively and subjectively and generalize from complex and seemingly unrelated events | Carry out variable tasks and programs simultaneously |
| Recognize gross inconsistencies and errors | Check for internal consistency of data according to a specified procedure |
| Handle unique and low-probability situations and abstract from inconsistent and conflicting data | Trace the implications of many different conditions and simulate many possibilities |

input-output, and simulation, while nearly as flexible, are classified as being most applicable for medium to high levels of aggregation.

A final point should be emphasized. The techniques were considered individually in table 4-2. However, judgment and feedback from practitioners and experts will enhance any of the other seven techniques. Forecasting and analysis are both art and science and requires simplification and abstraction. Human judgmental inputs can be used effectively to identify defects in the models themselves and in the forecasts and simulations undertaken with them. The blind application of a single technique is ill advised and at best should be used to stimulate thought and discussion among those who are affected and those who are making decisions.

All of the modeling techniques just described, except in the simplest of applications and except for judgmental or consensus techniques and case studies, rely on computers. Although the computer imposes no technique or assumptions and, given the low cost and high speeds of modern machines, few limitations on the analyst, it can overwhelm the modeler. Because the computer can manipulate enormous quantities of information rapidly, the modeler may lose control and lose sight of the problem under investigation, ending up inputting and outputting enormous amounts of useless information. If modelers, users, and advisers to policymakers are to avoid becoming duped by the computer, they must understand its capabilities and limitations. One way in which to accomplish this is to compare with with the human being for tasks that one or the other accomplished better. This comparison is shown in table 4-3.

# 5

# Modeling Natural-Resource Supply and Demand

Microeconomic models of natural-resource extraction and consumption focus on how individual decisions by the consumer, resource owner, managers and owners of extractive firms, and laborers interact. In market-based economies, these interdependencies determine the allocation of resources and prices. Public policy established by direct and indirect regulation is analyzed by how it affects private markets. It is bottom-up modeling because market behavior is found by summing the decisions made by individuals. The complex interconnections between the environment, defined by natural endowments and physical laws, economics, and the larger social order are described by linking behavior and markets together. Macroeconomic models proceed from the top down, where aggregated indexes and variables are analyzed and individual behavior is lost in aggregates. In this chapter the microeconomic models reviewed concentrate on the behavior of the firm because most resource-related taxation and regulation falls on the firm.

The foundation of microeconomic models is the preference of the individual as consumer, as owner of labor, capital, land, and natural resources, and as entrepreneur constrained by resource endowments and technology. In contrast, macroeconomic models deal in aggregated variables, which obscure the behavior of individuals. While aggregation is useful in describing how the overall economy functions, the process averages over the multitude of commodities and markets, and thereby valuable information is lost. Because regulatory policy and taxes are applied to natural resources nonuniformly, their effects on each resource must be traced separately, and so a microeconomic model becomes the required method.

The focus in microeconomic models is how the consumer and producer choose. The consumer is depicted as maximizing preferences within a context of alternative sources of income, prices, and expectations about the future. The producer is depicted as maximizing profit (or their present value) for every product produced and sold within a context of knowledge of the technology of production and expected market conditions and prices. The individual decides what and how much to consume and how to sell his or her services and the services of his or her capital, land, and natural resources. The producer decides what and how much to produce and when and how much to invest. Whenever consumers and producers act as if their individual decisions have little or no effect on prices, they are called *price takers.* When this situation prevails, aggregating over consumers to construct demand relationships and aggregating over producers to develop supply relationships is possible. The interaction of supply and demand is represented in market where voluntary exchanges take place. Each market is said to be in equilibrium when no individual has an incentive to alter present decisions, which means that the amount consumed equals the amount supplied. Otherwise instability and disequilibrium would prevail. Flexible prices are the primary and usually the sole means that bring markets into equilibrium.

Once any of the variables describing income, consumer tastes, technology of production, prices of substitute and complementary commodities, or other variables that alter the supply and demand relationships change, the market being described is thrown into disequilibrium because individuals have reason to change their behavior. This situation (*disequilibrium*) will be replaced by a new equilibrium with newly established prices. The net changes brought about by a change in equilibrium is called *comparative statics* by economists. Models in which the time path of prices, consumption, production, and other variables can be traced are called *dynamic models.* Thus microeconomic models allow economists to analyze the quantity consumed and produced and prices of individual commodities or several commodities when they are interrelated.

Because individual behavior is simulated, micromodels are capable of revealing the likely effects of taxes and regulations affecting each separate renewable and nonrenewable natural resource. This is an important advantage for although the laws of nature are universal, the characteristics of natural resources vary widely among locations. Meteorological, geologic, and other conditions and our knowledge determine the costs of locating, developing, and using natural resources. Past knowledge and the productivity of current and future research and development determine the technical feasibility of using various materials. The demand for goods and services that fulfill human wants and the alternatives that are available at different prices determine what is produced and consumed and what materials and energy sources are employed in the process and thus determine the economic practicality of various feasible alternatives. In microeconomic models how markets develop and how relative prices affect decisions and the allocation of resources are the core concepts. Natural materials make up but a small component of most finished products, and there are numerous manufacturing steps from the raw material stage to the finished product. The demand for natural resources is thus derived indirectly from the demand for the final goods and services. Thus all of the production technologies from extraction to the final commodity play a significant role in determining resource markets.

## Technology of Production

Economists have created a generalized picture of the firm whose role is to transform inputs into outputs, with the entrepreneur's objective being to maximize profits. Ayers and Kneese (1969) have expanded the concept of the firm to how the various production and consumption processes of the economy affect the environment, and all macromodels explicitly or implicitly include an aggregate and simplified rendition of the production process. However, it is in micromodels that the role of technology and the alternative of production are emphasized. The economist makes the convenient assumption that all feasible technologies are known with certainty and are available to entrepreneurs. As technological progress occurs, new and more-efficient techniques become available. Since alternatives are available, the entrepreneur must decide not only what and how much to produce but also what methods to use and which technologies to invest in. The goal of profit maximization implies an optimization process whose dual and simultaneous solution is how to use inputs and technology efficiently. The dual is to minimize cost for every level of production. Thus the entrepreneur is modeled as sorting through all feasible technologies and by examining prices of inputs and outputs selects the process(es) that are most inexpensive for the chosen level of production. However, what is critical and elusive is how accurately technology is depicted in models and, more particularly, how technology constrains the substitutability among inputs and outputs. The neoclassical model specifies not only how many alternative technologies are available but also how easily one input is substituted for another. For example, in automobile production, the costs of gasoline and consumers' preferences for lighter, more-fuel-efficient designs have led to the substitution of aluminum, fiberglass, carbon fibers, plastic, andother materials for steel; however it is constrained by the characteristics of the materials and the economics.

Substitutability in production means that more than one production technology or process that is efficient in an engineering sense exists. Thus the entrepreneur faces many alternatives to choose from, and the character of these choices and the relative prices of inputs determine the ability to substitute. Although we frequently think of technology as being fixed, with the analogy between making steel or any other commodity and cooking with a recipe showing fixed input combinations, this is false. Although only a few specific technologies (recipes) may be in use at any particular time, technological change and past knowledge mean there are other ways to produce steel, although they may not be profitable techniques at the present so are not in use. However, should the relative prices of inputs change, entrepreneurs will respond by changing technology when doing so increases profit, and because investment occurs in the long run, changes will be greater than over the short run. These responses occur in both theoretical models and in the real world.

For example, the response by industry to rising fuel prices has been dramatic since 1973. Initially energy usage continued to rise with population and economic growth at approximately the same rates as it had in the past, although the 1974–1975 recession brought a slowdown in the growth of both. However, as businesspersons realized that high energy prices were not transient and as old equipment wore out and new expansion was undertaken, a reevaluation of technology took place. Labor (by different methods of utilization) and man-made capital (by new machinery, insulation, and other adjustments too numerous to mention) were substituted for fuels. In the short run there are fewer opportunities to make such adjustments, but with time they grow. The result has been decline in the use of energy per dollar of GNP produced in most Western countries (Lovins 1980; Yergin and Stogaugh 1980), reversing a trend of several centuries. These can be called scarcity-induced innovations to energy-using technologies (Solow 1974a). These innovations would not have been predicted from a naive extrapolation of past data on the ratio of energy use to GNP, one more example of how reliance on modeling past data may mislead those making policy for the future. In fact, oil use and imports to the United States hit an apogee in 1979, and imports fell by 20 percent in 1980 due in large part to industry conservation. From 1973 to 1980 electricity use per unit of output declined 14 percent.

Efforts have been made to estimate the degree of substitutability on both the microlevel and macrolevel (Kopp and Smith 1980, Jorgenson 1970, Humphrey and Moroney 1975). Because of its immediate relevance, most work has concentrated on the substitution (measured by the elasticity of substitution) between reproducible capital and natural resources and between man-made capital and energy by means of quantified models of the production process. Kopp and Smith (1980) find that such estimates depend critically on the level of aggregation of technological processes and natural-resource measures, the mathematical specification of models, and the data used in estimating. For example, data range from engineering-based descriptions of steel-making processes (Kopp and Smith 1980) to aggregates representing all manufacturing (for example, Humphrey and Moroney 1975). Kopp and Smith (1980) point out that the errors induced by aggregating multiple technologies, products, and firms distort estimated elasticity of substitution so that they may not reflect the elasticities at the microlevel. However, the two authors conclude that the neoclassical (conventional economic) model of the firm accurately characterizes true production relationships derived from engineering-based process-analysis models of iron and steel production, which includes basic oxygen, open hearth, and electric arc technologies. Furthermore, the true models incorporate residual discharge constraints, which are consistent with the physical laws governing materials transformation (the first law). Their estimates indicate that if these relationships are ignored when model building, measures of input substitution are distorted.

The evidence on input substitution at the microlevel implies that substitution is possible and that a fixed-recipe technology does not prevail. Although the various estimates are diverse, one must conclude that substitution is possible and constrained by the laws of nature and human knowledge. Most researchers find the elasticity of substitution estimates (the percentage change in the ratio of reproducible capital to natural resources with respect to a 1 percent change in the ratio of their prices) are less than one.

Of course, this work on production technology ignores the ability of consumers to substitute. Changes in consumer behavior may occur to a far greater degree in the long run than in production, out of both choice and necessity. Automobiles can achieve 50 to 60 miles per gallon with current technology, homes and business can be insulated, and less energy- and resource-intense activities and technologies can replace existing ones. For example, in 1980 the stock of automobiles in the United States averaged 6.3 years old and delivered an average 13.1 miles per gallon. As older cars are scrapped and new automobiles with greater efficiency replace them, these averages will change. The potential efficiency gain is large.

## Microeconomic Models of Natural Resources

In order to understand the basic microeconomic models of resource industries, it is necessary to know something about capital and investment. A capital stock is defined at a specific point in time, a static concept. However, capital stocks change over time as investment and depreciation occur for man-made capital and as extraction and growth occur for natural resources. Gross investment consists of the amount necessary to replace depreciated capital plus net increases, while net investment equals the change in capital stock. Thus investment has a time decision. The current rate of return on a capital stock is the services that it yields; this includes production time for a machine, interest and profits for financial wealth, the services of natural species growth and harvest for a renewable resource, and extraction for a nonrenewable resource.

Individual behavior is predicted in most microeconomic models by assuming that people choose so as to maximize their preferences. Efficient or Pareto optimal resource allocation is found by solving the optimization problem for society. This exercise is called *welfare economics*. The optimization problem can be solved only if there is an objective or target specified. Economists use the target of satisfying human wants. One difficulty with this standard definition of welfare in dynamic models is that welfare of present and future generations must be accounted for (Page 1977). Once the objective is specified, the economic welfare problem becomes an analytic one of finding the policies that maximize the object function over time, subject to the initial endowments and the laws of nature.

A powerful and general way to solve this problem of dynamic allocation in an abstract model is to employ optimal control theory (an optimization technique). The theory indicates the optimal time path for individual decisions or public policies. The theory is a straightforward application of mathematical tools to select the best time path for the decision or control variables from all feasible paths. Applying the theory to specific models can become complex, however, and in all but the simplest cases insoluble. When this occurs, researchers take a somewhat different and less general approach. They specify numerical relationships that seem to be reasonably representative of the theoretical relationships and the real world. They proceed to run the model on a computer, or simulate it. After the invariable juggling and adjustments are made so that everything appears to be operating within the bounds of reason, the simulation exercises' output is interpreted as an approximation of the more-general but unavailable theoretical result (a simulation technique).

The value of an analytically solvable model lies in its generalized characteristics (the solutions are qualitative and are expressed as relationships that would apply to any specific quantified relationship) and the insight that the conditions give the researcher and policy analyst. A solvable and workable analytic model is understandable and interpretable, and it produces predictions that can be tested empirically. Another advantage to the analytic approach is that the mathematical process of optimization inevitably produces an artificial variable, which can be assigned an interpretation. In economic models these artificial variables are called *shadow prices,* and they represent the value that society (via consumers' preferences) places on the commodity whose supply is constrained by the initial endowment and laws of nature.

The mathematics of optimization ensures that a shadow price is created. This shadow price embodies a converse statement of the original optimization problem. For example, the problem to maximize the preferences of present and future generations by using capital optimally subject to the initial endowment produces shadow prices that reveal the value of capital to society. The converse or dual to this problem is to minimize the capital necessary to provide this level of welfare (a maximum one). As the mathematical process sorts through all possible solutions to both the maximization and minimization problem, it turns out that the solution to the original problem (the primal) and its dual converge. The shadow price then is an analogue of the maximum welfare, and it is interpreted by economists as a set of prices that correspond to economic efficiency (the term *Pareto optimality* can be used interchangeably). When actual market prices or prices predicted from market behavioral models differ from the shadow price, this is evidence that a market failure will occur. Conversely, if regulatory and fiscal (taxes and expenditures) policies result in market prices equal to shadow prices, this is evidence that resources are being allocated efficiently, and an optimizing problem can be formulated to solve for this condition.

**Optimal Extraction of Nonrenewable Resources**

The optimum extraction of nonrenewable resources over time can be solved by maximizing the welfare of present and future generations subject to the initial natural-resource endowment (natural capital stock), which is depleted as it is consumed. The solution to this problem was first shown by Hotelling (1931), and his basic results, with numerous variations, have been reproduced by many since (for a review of the literature, see Church 1981; Peterson and Fisher 1977). The necessary conditions for an optimum show that the rate of extraction should increase until the value placed on a unit of labor effort necessary to extract a unit of the resource equals the value (shadow price) society places on the resource. This plausible result is equivalent to the price of the extracted resource equaling the cost of reproducible (man-made) capital and labor in extracting each unit plus the scarcity value (a shadow price) of a unit of natural capital left in the ground if it were extracted in some future time period. This latter concept is the shadow price of the resource in situ and has been labeled *user cost* or *scarcity value*. It is a hypothetical measure of the current cost of the future profit (net social value) sacrificed when the resource is extracted now rather than in the future.

Because the extraction of a nonrenewable resource of known quantity is purely a matter of allocating a limited stock over time, consumption deferred today is available in the future. However, ownership of the stock is similar to ownership of any other capital; the reason not to consume it today is that it will produce future output or generate future profit. This implies that the value of the resource in place must increase at a rate commensurate with other investments. In a world of riskless certainty, this is "the" interest rate or, equivalently, the rate of return on capital. This implies that the scarcity price of the resource will rise over time, and the rate of extraction will continually fall because less is demanded at higher prices, finally approaching zero as long as the amount demanded is solely a function of price. Hotelling (1931) showed that if resources in situ were privately owned and their location and quality known and the future certain, individual profit maximization would result in the same rate of extraction as the socially optimal one, and the price of the unextracted resource would rise at the rate of interest. This result demonstrates that as long as property rights to the resource are clearly assigned to individuals in the private sector, the allocation of the resource stock over time by profit-maximizing owners equals the socially efficient rate.

However, the cost of extracting the resource may rise over time due to more-difficult removal as the stock is depleted and lower-quality ores are mined. For example, both effects arise in oil extraction. As the resource is removed, the pressures from natural gas decrease, requiring secondary and eventually tertiary recovery methods and, further, depending on the porosity of the rock, movement of the oil is impaired as the stock at any single location is depleted. It can be shown that the market price of the extracted resource at any point in time equals the incremental cost of extracting the lowest-quality reserve plus the user cost or scarcity value per unit. If the marginal cost of extraction is rising and the decreased stock of the remaining reserve increases recovery costs, both the market-determined and the socially efficient percentage price increase of the resource in situ equals the rate of interest minus the increase of the ratio of the incremental labor cost of extracting another unit to the incremental capital cost (see Herfindahl and Kneese 1974). Other cases are possible depending on the assumed present and future conditions, but the pattern of an increasing price, decreasing extraction rate time path remains (Jacobson 1979).

The market price of the extracted ore will increase at a weighted average of the interest rate plus the percentage increase in the cost of extraction. Schulze (1974) shows that improvements in extraction technology that reduce extraction costs may swamp the interest rate and mean that resource prices decrease over time. The impact of multiple quality ore grades has been considered by Herfindahl (1974), Solow (1976), Schulze (1974), and Conrad and Hool (1980), and it is both socially optimal and most profitable to extract the highest-grade, lowest-cost resources first. Schulze (1974) and others have considered the effects of recycling (possible only for nonfuel minerals), and competitive markets were found to allocate resources efficiently. The assumptions underlying these models and their predictions for price and output are rigid and unrealistic. However, empirically testing the accuracy of the predictions determines whether the model is worthwhile.

## Empirical Tests of Resource Prices

The theory of capital and the abstract models of exhaustible and renewable resources indicate that the price of resources in situ should increase at the market rate of interest (when extraction costs are constant), the extraction rate of nonrenewable resources should diminish over time, and the price of extracted resources should increase proportionally to a weighted average of the interest rate plus the increase in extractive costs. The extraction rate of renewable resources should be steady for ones where the common-property problem does not prevail (forests are an example). For common-property resources (for example, fisheries) new entrants should initially increase extraction, depressing prices below the social value, until the resource stock is diminished, at which time extraction will slow, prices will rise, and extinction may occur. How closely do these predictions correspond to experience?

The 1952 report of the President's Materials Policy Commission (Pauley Commission) concluded that, in general, prices of natural resources dropped in this century, and there were no signs of general exhaustion from then to 1975. The 1963 study by Barnett and Morse (1963) was the most exhaustive up to that time. They analyzed price and cost trends between 1870 and 1957 for a number of natural resources and found no evidence to support increasing real (inflation adjusted) prices (both absolute prices and prices relative to labor) except for forest products, which had increased in price. They hypothesized that technological advances had permitted the mining of lower-grade ores, which had increased effective resources. They suggested that physical depletion may be a preferred measure of resource scarcity to price movements and hypothesized that it was conceivable that market failures may have caused resources to be underpriced and overconsumed during the period studied. It should be pointed out that the abstract model assumed fixed reserves whose quantity and quality is known with certainty, whereas experience points to rapidly increasing resource stocks as technology advances and quality falls.

Another factor is that as technology changes and as relative resource prices increase, substitution of other materials becomes both feasible and more economically attractive. Also absolute and relative price increases provide added incentives for investment in exploration, development, and recycling. Furthermore, noncompetitive elements and government regulation and taxation may mean that market prices fail to reveal the cost of newly discovered resources, thus accounting for deviations of reality from predictions premised on these models.

Hotelling (1931) and others have considered monopoly power as a source of market failures. The general case implies that the profit-maximizing monopolist will extract more slowly than competitie firms, and prices will be higher, so the monopolist is a conservationist. The Hotelling model shows that if for any reason prices rise more slowly than the optimal time path, resources will be extracted at a faster rate than for maximum efficiency, and conversely. One cause may occur when market interest rates differ from the socially optimal rate of interest, an aberration that Hotelling and many others have considered. Hanson (1977) shows that if less than the optimal savings is occurring in an economy, resource prices will rise faster than interest rates, and this is inefficient. When externalities occur (for example, free disposal of toxic or contaminated mine tailings and water), the resource owners' costs are inappropriately low, and their marginal extraction rate is too rapid. Then the market price is less than optimal (Cummings and Schulze 1977). Schulze (1974) derives a tax on extraction that makes extractive firms operate at the socially correct level of output and that will result in the correct price for the resource both in and out of the ground.

As exhaustion approaches and the price becomes very high, there is a strong incentive to find substitute materials and technologies. This possibility also introduces uncertainties that Dasgupta and Heal (1974) maintain are not properly accounted for in market interest rates. A future technology that makes an alternative resource available almost without limit but at a higher cost than the current resources is called a *backstop technology*. Examples include nuclear fusion and mining of deep sea bed and seawater. This uncertain technology reverses the conventional time path of scarcity prices from low to high (Heal 1976).

Solow (1974b) has shown that any positive discount rate coupled with technological limitations on the substitutability of man-made for natural capital favors the present over future generations. The favoritism is so extensive that over time per-capita consumption declines asymptotically to zero. If substitution is more easily accomplished, a steady-state level of consumption is possible if a zero discount rate is used, and when the resource base is fixed, a constant per-capita income is possible until ultimate exhaustion. However, Solow (1978) has also stated that he believes that a reduced natural-resource base is not especially detrimental to overall economic activity. Rosenberg's (1971) historical analysis of economic growth and technological change led him to a similarly optimistic conclusion. He pictured technological changes as continuously expanding the effective resource base. Based on historical experience, he saw no reason why future growth of technology will not make it possible to shift dependence from scarce to abundant resources. One way to explain these differences is the implicit time frame considered, and even here the patterns are not consistent. Some observers are pessimistic about the near term and optimistic about the distant future as grand new technologies evolve. Others hold the reverse view.

The empirical evidence as well as a number of more exhaustive studies led the eminent economist Houthaker to state, "The ancient concern about the depletion of natural resources no longer rests on any firm theoretical basis" (1976, p. 5). Solow (1978) concludes that aggregate economic activity is insensitive to a narrowing in the resource base. However, others less sanguine about the validity of the model of capital dispute this data. Solow (1974b) speculates that one needs to look at both resource prices and the capital value of the resource in place. If resource prices have fallen over time, this means that the return for owning resources in place has fallen. This effect is accounted for in capital markets by a fall in the price of the asset itself (not the flow of extraction, which has been measured by all researchers) in order for the value of the asset in place for a new buyer or one searching for it and anticipating a new discovery to realize a competitive return.

Peterson and Maxwell (1979) cite the fact that prices of metals discovered and utilized in the past have leveled off or have started to climb (copper may have hit a minimum in 1930) versus newer metals whose prices are declining because of rapid technological advances. In an empirical study of oil and natural gas, Norgaard (1975) considers factors that increase extraction costs for newly drilled wells, such as the declining success rate, increased depth, and analyzing and developing more-difficult and less-productive formations, independently of technological advances. These factors would have produced a 233 percent cost increase from 1939 to 1968 in the United States. Actual costs increased only 64 percent in real terms, and if geologic quality had been held constant, well-drilling costs would have decreased between 53 and 87 percent during the period. The difference are attributable to technological change.

Using sophisticated econometric techniques, V.K. Smith (1979, 1980a) has carried out both theoretical and empirical studies of prices of nonrenewable resources. He analyzed the prices of twelve minerals and fuels and three aggregate price indexes for the period 1900 to 1973 to determine how closely they paralleled movements in five different interest-rate series, which reflected different degrees of liquidity and risk. The results, while not entirely consistent with the theoretical model of capital, suggest that "minerals where developed markets have existed for the majority of the time period were more likely to be consistent with the model." Price fluctuations for oil, natural gas, and coal were correlated with changes in short-term interest rates standing in conflict with the Barnett and Morse conclusions. A relationship was also found for pig iron, copper, lead, and zinc but not for bauxite, manganese, tungsten, and molybdenum. However, the statistical fits were not good enough to use the findings for forecasting future prices.

Regardless of the outcomes of studies of natural-resource prices, costs, reserves, and annual production, the relevance of the theoretical model for policymaking is questionable. The purpose of policy is to ensure the present and future efficient use of natural resources. The theoretical model of capital assumes that the future is known with certainty. This includes the extent and quality of all natural resources, future costs, prices, interest rates, and demand. In order for correct market prices to prevail (those that utilize resources efficiently), not only must externalities be accounted for with taxes and regulation, which make market prices equal to correct shadow prices, but there must be complete and well-ordered markets to exchange property rights in current and future production.

Markets for current output are called *spot markets,* and they exist for all economic commodities. However, free goods, including the assimilative capacity of the air, land, and water, and use of an access to common property, are unpriced and not exchanged. Either these goods need to be allocated and priced directly—they are not because technical and institutional barriers prevent ownership and exchange—or their scarcity value must be included in the prices of the production of priced goods and services that utilize these services. If not, market failures occur.

Furthermore, unpriced and priced commodities must be traded in futures markets. When property rights to the future use of resources are exchanged and prices are established, information concerning the future is generated and can be evaluated and acted upon. These future prices determine the allocation of resources over time. However, futures markets exist only for a limited number of commodities (copper, uranium, oil, gold, plywood, pork bellies, timber, and orange juice) and not for all future time periods as assumed in theory (future contracts are limited in time).

Another difficulty lies in the distinction between long- and short-term models. Barnett and Morse (1963) sought to identify the long term, whereas other studies have focused on the short term where fluctuation in price and output is wider because of the effects of the business cycle, interest rates, and all other variables affecting investors' and speculators' expectations. Natural-resource-policy-oriented models should concentrate on long-term effects. Since critical natural resources are unpriced and not all futures markets exist, many economists believe that market failures prevail. If this is true, then analyzing past data provides little guidance for the future, and what we think we know about resource availability may be severely biased by inappropriate past data (Smith 1980b).

Another problem with theoretical models is the lack of knowledge about technology and technological change. Economists usually assume certain general properties of production relations, with specifics given to them by physical scientists and engineers. This has created enormous information and communication gaps. The ability to substitute one natural resource for another and to substitute man-made capital for natural-resource capital is critical to the future of humanity and to the correct specification of macromodels and micromodels. This area is relatively unexplored. Before long-run policies are put in place, these uncertainties need to be reduced.

## Theory of Renewable Resources

Although biologists and economists have developed theories of renewable resources over the past one hundred years, it has only been recently that the problem has been clearly conceived. The theory of renewable natural resources is a special case of capital theory. A fishery, forest, agricultural system, and underground aquifer are similar to the theory of the mine except that renewable resources are capable of regeneration and recharge. The rate of depletion for the mine case becomes the rate of extraction of harvest minus the rate of natural recharge or growth. A good deal is known about the growth and regeneration in some, primarily agricultural and biological systems. The species stock (population) grows to a naturally stable maximum where overcrowding and competition for space, food supplies, and predators ultimately limit the population. The growth rate in achieving this maximum stock is not constant. Initially it grows rapidly and at an increasing rate in percentage terms, but eventually the growth rate tapers off to a decreasing rate, falling to zero at the maximum population. The relationship between the stock and growth rates is not as clearly understood in cases of hydrology and the assimilative capacity of the environment because of the complex interdependencies that are present. Research currently underway should provide some insight into the regeneration and optimal use of these resources.

When we harvest from the species stock or for that matter harvest from any natural source that takes more than one year to grow to a usable yield, the economic question is when to harvest. How much is harvested affects future resource stock, as is the case of nonrenewable resources. At one extreme, too rapid and complete a harvest will reduce yields in future years and may extinguish the species (for example, many believe that sperm whale overhunting has them threatened with extinction). But if the yield is too small, we are forgoing benefits.

If the relationship between the growth rate, the size of the capital (species) stock, and the rate of extraction are known, the problem can be solved analytically with the optimal-control model of capital. The biologists' view and the naive observers' view is that harvests should be regulated so that the species stock is maintained at a level corresponding to the maximum sustainable yield. However, if a single individual owns the forest or the fishery, this is not what that person would do. That person's goal is to maximize present and future profits. Since owning the natural-resource stock (perhaps uncaught fish) is like owning any other asset, the financial yield from this ownership must yield the rate of interest (in the absence of risk). This means that present extraction and profit are worth more than future profits because the current profits could be invested elsewhere and earn the current rate of interest. Only when the interest rate is zero would an owner maintain the stock at the maximum sustainable yield. Positive interest rates tilt the focus to the present. The owner will extract at a somewhat slower rate, and the profit-maximizing stock will be somewhat larger; this rate will be stable as long as expectations are realized. The tilt occurs because the price of the unextracted resource in situ is increasing at the rate of interest. Harvesting uses up resources that must be purchased now, but it harvest is delayed, the future costs are lower because of a positive interest rate. Also with delay, the stock is larger and the effort necessary for capture is less (effort will be lower). But delaying too much will increase current prices and reduce future prices as the harvest would be shifted into the future. The net result is that the optimal level of extraction is generally less than the maximum sustainable yield. It can also be shown that if expected future prices for the extracted resource are lower than the current price and if the effort is easy or resources necessary for harvest are low, the opposite case will occur; the rate of extraction will be so rapid as to reduce the stock to a size below that necessary for maximum regeneration in the absence of harvest. The case may be so extreme that the species stock is reduced to an unsustainable level and may be extinguished.

The potential extinction of the species is one possible market failure. It would be caused by incorrect or myopic perceptions of present versus future prices, interest rates, and costs of harvest or capture. These potential failures exist for all capital stocks. Unique to many renewable resources is that if the stock is reduced to a critical level, the resource may be irreversibly lost, and property rights to them are not always clearly assigned, or if assigned, they are unenforceable for technical and social reasons, and these characteristics lead to market failure. The owner of a forest or agricultural system can exclude nonowners from harvesting her or his resource. In this case, it can be shown that profit maximization corresponds to the socially optimal use of resources under certainty (efficiency or Pareto optimality). However, for fisheries, the assimilative capacity of the environment and solitude in wilderness areas, control of entry and use is impossible, extremely expensive, or, for historical and social reasons, not practiced. In such cases users have no incentive to value how much others value the resource because the user does not have to pay those individuals or society for the use of the resource. The result is overextraction and overcrowding because each individual user does not account for how his or her presence and use affects others, and the rule of capture defines ownership, thus encouraging more-rapid use (see Hardin 1968).

Where the resource or property is privately owned and entry controlable, each user would be charged for the cost of the resource and the costs imposed on others because profit-maximization motives would make the owner charge such prices. However, with a common property, entry is open, or the user fee is nominal and less than the social cost of another user. In the case of a fishery, free entry means that fishers consider only their private costs (harvest costs) and not the effect their removal of the species has on other fishers (increasing fishing effort and lowering productivity), the size of the stock, or the rate of its growth. It is easily shown that over-fishing results (see Herfindahl and Kneese 1974; Peterson and Fisher 1977). The same situation occurs for communal-owned forests and hunting grounds, in underground and surface waters that are interconnected, and oil and natural-gas reserves that several surface leases have access to. When surface land is held in multiple ownership, the incentive is to drill and extract subsurface material as fast as possible. This not only results in too-rapid extraction, because the one who extracts it owns it, but in the case of oil reduces the total reserve and total recovery. Oil developers have gone so far as to slant drill into other subsurface reserves. The result is a too-rapid exhaustion and in some cases (for example, for certain animals) extinction. Fisher and Peterson (1976) apply the same analysis to claims taking on public lands. Another example is the boom in U.S. offshore fishing starting in 1977 when the United States declared a two-hundred-mile economic zone and began restricting foreign vessels but permitted entry of U.S.-owned fleets.

The economic solution of the model of renewable resources produces a shadow price for the scarcity value of the resource analogous to the one produced for extractive resources. When the renewable resource is owned, the profit-maximizing owner implicitly takes its value in situ into account, for extraction today reduces the amount that can be extracted in the future. When the resource is a common property, the rule of capture prevails, and no one takes the shadow price into account. Users measure their own effort only, additional users enter the industry and overuse results. Thus economists have devised a method to calculate scarcity value for fish; the assimilative capacity of air, water, and land for waste dumping as, for example, in pollution from power plants; sparks from passing steam locomotives landing in a farmer's fields; and hundreds of other examples. Were these charges assessed to users, an optimal allocation of resources would have resulted because the fees would make them act as if the resources were privately owned (Kneese and Herfindahl 1974).

It can also be shown that if all affected parties could be assembled, they would voluntarily agree to a system of user changes for common-property use or any other externality (although those paying the charges would have to be compensated with lumpt-sum subsidies). The reason is that market failure produces an inefficient use of resources. If resources are allocated optimally (efficiently), total real economic output (satisfaction of wants) is greater, and theoretically no one would have to be made worse off and some people could be made better off. The critical word is *theoretically*. Charges, subsidies, and lump-sum transfers would have to be negotiated, and for large-scale externalities and common-property problems (the common-property phenomenon is basically a large-scale externality), the number of participants would be unmanageable.

Three problems arise with the negotiated solution. The first is that if exclusion were difficult and expensive, those benefiting from an improvement could refuse to pay and not reveal their true preferences so that the correct computation could be made. This is the free-rider problem. The second is that if unanimous agreement were required, a few individuals would hold out and not agree in order to force others to pay them off. This strategic behavior, similar to competition for rents, may result in a failure to reach agreement and to implement collective action. The third problem is that negotiations among a large number of people are difficult, time-consuming, and use resources. It may be that in many cases it is easier to disagree than to agree, so no bargain is struck. For those reasons, a majority of economists advocate a less than unanimity rule and use of government's coercive power in order to implement solutions. Other economists steadfastly adhere to the position that private negotiations among the affected parties will achieve an optimal solution. They maintain that government policy and social institutions need by changes only so that property rights are clearly assigned and that no artificial impediemtns stand in the way of private agreements.

The role of the interest rate is critical in both private and public use of natural resources. Many economists and others believe that a deviation of market interest rates (employed by private owners) and socially correct interest rates (called the *rate-of-time preference,* which is necessary for the efficient use of a resource) is likely, and this is a reason that markets fail. Because natural resources are long-lived, their use involves many—in the case of some key attributes of the environment, all past, present, and future generations. The rate-of-time preference or social-discount rate is how society evaluates present vis-a-vis future generations (Georgescu—Roegen 1975). If a welfare measure (GNP is commonly used but is inappropriate because of externalities) is simply added for all generations, the rate-of-time preference is assumed to equal zero. But if the rate is greater than zero, this implies that the welfare of future generations is discounted (assumes a lower value).

The reason for discounting and having a positive rate-of-time preference is that technological progress and the net accumulation of capital produces economic growth (net per capita), giving people more in the future. By making these investments, the current generation is sacrificing for the good of the future generations, and this is a reason to discount the future. Consequently some economists suggest that the appropriate rate of discount should be the long-term sustainable growth rate for the economy as a whole or the regeneration or agricultural productivity rate for projects involving renewable natural resources. A major problem with such an approach is that future technological advances and prosperity are uncertain, and the definition of capital should include both natural and man-made resources.

The uncertainty aspect of the future is yet another basis for discounting the future, as is the observation that people act as if they prefer the present to the future, and this preference should be acknowledged. The philosophic basis for the last reason is that the present generations will take appropriate care of future generations, for this is the world for our offspring (see Page 1977). The retort to this proposition is that only the future generations can speak for themselves, but obviously this information is impossible to ascertain. Rawls (1971) takes a normative solution of ensuring that no one is made better off unless those worse off are made better off. His notion of equity implies a zero social-rate-of-time preference, as well as being open to some absurd implications (see Solow 1974b).

Ecologists and environmentalists point out that the relatively high discount rates (interest rates) evidenced in the financial marketplace are inappropriate for resource consumption, and investment based on them will be too little and may doom future generations. This brings up another difficulty: should use and depletion of resources be measured in prices, which are determined in markets made up of the present population and its income distribution (the future generations cannot bid against present generations), or by physical rates of depletion and use, which are impossible to reconcile among different renewable and exhaustible resources? Although answers to these questions are a necessary prerequisite to the formation of natural-resource policy, they have not been resolved. Thus we move on without an answer or an optimal policy to a brief review of how taxes are thought to affect resource use and prices.

## Taxes and Natural Resources

The primary purpose of taxes is to raise revenue. If government expenditures produce greater benefits than the welfare loss created by the tax, society is better off. The second purpose of taxes is to redistribute income. When the tax structure is not strictly proportional to income after taking the shifting and incidence effects into consideration, relative incomes are altered, and the tax burden is not shared equally. The redistribution brought about directly by taxes and expenditures and indirectly by regulation reflects both the purposeful and unintentioned policies of federal, state, and local government. The final purpose of tax policy is that it is an indirect means to regulate resource allocation. Tax rates and provisions can be developed that either encourage or discourage activities and decisions undertaken by consumers, business, labor, and virtually any other subsector in the economy.

Economists are in near-unanimous agreement that, ignoring for the moment the second and third purposes, taxes should be designed in a way that minimizes their distorting effects on privately made decisions and agreements. This goal is called *tax neutrality*. However, when market failures are present, most professional economists agree that tax policy should be designed to maximize social welfare and, correspondingly, minimize the loss of economic rents to owners of production inputs and to consumers. The professional attitude among most economists is to disavow knowing that the "correct" distribution of income should be and therefore stating that it is a social and moral problem. They say only that their models can predict the effect of taxes and regulation on resource use and incomes under various conditions.

We have specified a number of instances when markets unencumbered by taxes, regulation, or any other form of government interference fail to allocate natural resources efficiently. In such cases, taxes and regulations that are designed to affect prices and resource use may be a desirable policy, and most economists would agree to them. In all other cases, the goal of taxation advocated by most is that the tax not affect the market-determined allocation of resources (tax neutrality).

When markets fail, taxation may be an appropriate policy to effect efficient resource use. We have identified a number of such instances. One results when market interest rates and the social-rate-of-time preference are unequal. When this occurs, natural resources—in fact all capital—are extracted and consumed inefficiently over time. The question of how well private markets reflect the true social discount rate or even what that rate is or what it should be is not fully resolved. Furthermore, these questions involve both efficiency and equity among different generations, which involve basic philosophical questions, and all capital vis-a-vis consumption is affected. One must conclude that these questions go beyond tax policy considered here. A second instance of market failure is monopoly and other noncompetitive behavior. Monopoly is not limited to resource industries, nor is it amenable to solution by tax policy in a pragmatic world.

It has been argued that externalities and the associated use of common resources (as in interdependent water and petroleum-bearing formations and renewable resources such as the assimilative capacity of the environment and access to fisheries and public lands) are a pervasive problem. In many instances taxes and fees are an appropriate policy (see Kneese and Herfindahl 1974). Both could be formulated to change users appropriately, whereas previously the resource was free or imperfectly priced.

Although the distinction between the short and long run was made previously, it needs to be applied to how taxes affect the economy. Economists define the short run to occur when some inputs into the production process are fixed. In most analyses, it is assumed that the capital stock of reproducible capital is the constant input, because to change it requires investment of resources and time. Constant capital constrains technology to utilize existing plant and equipment either more or less intensively. This means that business's primary decision is how much to produce and attempt to market from fixed plant and equipment. When natural resources are involved, the decision is how rapidly to extract (deplete) the resource stock.

It is possible to predict how business chooses from the theory of capital developed previously. Economic theory shows that the rational entrepreneur will expand output as long as the expected revenues from sales of additional output (marginal revenue) exceed expected costs (marginal costs). Marginal cost to the owner of natural resources is the sum of extraction costs plus the scarcity value or user cost of depletion of the resource when the resource is owned. If the operation is unable to cover costs that vary with the level of output (generally all costs except the cost of capital, which must be paid regardless of output), the business will chose to shut down.

In the long run all inputs are variable. This means business makes investment decisions about expanding existing plant and equipment and developing new sites, both of which may involve new technologies, and allowing existing sites to deteriorate and shut down. In the extractive-resource industries, investment and its implementation takes longer than in most other industries. The process of exploration, discovery, and development of a major new oil field may take ten years or more and as much as five years before a major coal strip mine goes into full production. Thus, the definition of the long run has no fixed chronological counterpart. Another factor that is characteristic of natural-resource industries is the high risk associated with investment. Exploration obviously is a probabilistic venture, although large firms are able to diversify sufficiently so that risk is reduced to levels commensurate with other industries (see Church 1981). A societal risk that is becoming increasingly acknowledged is that of new technology and the chance that the assimilative capacity of the environment may be permanently and irreversibly damaged.

When investment can take place, this means that capital is mobile. Because investment takes place in the long run, the dislocational effects of taxes are more pronounced in the long run because the entrepreneur can decide to change location by not replacing depreciating capital and investing elsewhere. A factor that makes natural-resource firms unique is the critical role that the quality of inputs plays. The characteristics of each specific reserve and the ways in which it is extracted, processed, used in the production of commodities, embodied in commodities, and consumed all affect production costs and the volume and quality of by-product discharges. In mining, a critical decision is at which ore grade to cease extraction. Lower-quality that are bypassed and remain in situ may never be recoverable, whereas ores found in old mine tailings and virgin low-concentration reserves may be recovered economically in the future. Taxes that affect ore quality (the ore cut-off grade) affect total recovery of the resource stock, and analogous arguments can be applied to other renewable and nonrenewable resources.

Taxes are levied on virtually everything that is countable. However, ultimately people bear the burden of taxes, so an important role for the economic analyst of taxes is to determine who ultimately pays the tax (called *tax incidence*) and how taxes affect the allocation of resources. As we have learned, all taxes except those falling on economic rents affect decisions. Tax-induced behavioral changes are revealed as pretax and posttax changes in resource allocation and prices. Any tax that creates distortions in the allocation of resources also ends up dissipating economic rents.

Tax-induced changes in prices are used to measure how taxes alter the distribution of income (tax burdens). To the extent that consumers bear the burden through increased prices, the uses of income are said to be affected. A tax lowers consumers' welfare to the degree that they consume the taxed item. Owners of natural resources, land, capital, and labor bear the tax burden when the prices of reproducible and nonreproducible capital and wages are affected and the sources of income are reduced. Taxes falling on transactions for commodities, or any other tax base, are ultimately traceable to either the uses or sources of income, and it is the task of the tax-incidence analysis to ascertain these affects.

When a tax affects the pretax allocation of resources, a tax-induced distortion is said to occur. When the tax corrects for an externality or other market failure, the distortion enhances society's welfare by ensuring that resources are used efficiently. Whenever a distortion disturbs a previous situation of efficiency, the distortion reduces welfare. Economists since the nineteenth century have been devising and fine tuning methods on how to measure these distortions (see, for example, Kneese and Herfindahl 1974; Atkinson and Stiglitz 1979; Harberger 1955).

It is possible to estimate the social costs of tax-induced distortions. Perhaps the best-known advocate who argues for the efficacy of this approach in public-policy analysis is Arnold Harberger (1964, 1974a, 1974b). The technique is described most easily in a diagram. In figure 5–1 price $(P)$ is depicted on the vertical axis, and the flow of a good or service over time $(Q)$ is shown on the horizontal axis. Consumer behavior is revealed by the ubiquitous demand curve, labeled *DD,* which depicts the law of demand (an inverse relationship between price and quantity). It is also known as the *willingness-to-pay function* because consumer behavior involves voluntary exchanges and the demand curve measures this willingness

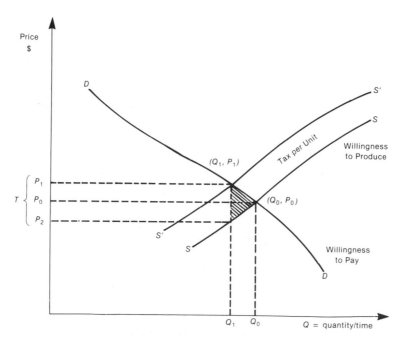

**Figure 5-1.** Effect of a Tax on Price and Output

in dollar quantities. The behavior of business is revealed by the equally famous law of supply, labeled *SS*. It depicts a positive relationship between price and quantity, which results from technological constraints and profit-maximizing behavior. It is also known as the *willingness to produce function,* for it reveals voluntary behavior. Market equilibrium occurs $(Q_0P_0)$ when the amount supplied equals the amount demanded, and the only such point achieved with price acting as an allocating mechanism is at point $Q_0P_0$. This corresponds to the maximum number of voluntary exchanges and the maximum net social value for the good $Q$ (measured by the area under demand, *DD,* and above supply, *SS*).

When a tax is levied on consumers or producers, costs or gross prices (with the tax) are affected, and market equilibrium is reestablished. In the example in figure 5-1, a tax of $T$ per unit is levied on the commodity $Q$. This drives a wedge between what consumers pay and what producers receive. This difference ($T$) is shown by shifting the supply curve upward by the amount of the tax ($S'S'$) because the net or after-tax price to business determines production decisions, while consumers face the gross price with the tax. The new equilibrium occurs at $(Q_1P_1)$ where consumers pay $P_1$ and producers receive $P_1$, net after taxes ($P_1 - P_2 = T$). When less is produced

($Q_1$), scarce resources are released, which are assumed to be employed elsewhere in the economy. The supply curve depicts the value of the next-best alternative use for inputs used or released (opportunity cost) as the production of $Q$ increases or decreases. Consumers value the commodity not produced and consumed because of increased taxes and lowered consumption ($Q_0 - Q_1$), by the area under the demand curve. The difference between the value consumers placed on these forgone commodities (willingness to pay) and the opportunity cost of production (amount produced in the next-best employment for resources released) is depicted as the vertically lined triangle in figure 5-1. This triangle can be estimated quantitatively if the demand and supply functions and the tax rate are known. It measures welfare loss or the net social loss due to the tax-induced distortion in resource allocation (a reduction to $Q_1$ from $Q_0$). This net welfare loss is also known as excess burden because it exceeds the amount of tax revenues ($T \times Q_1$) and the value (opportunity cost) of resources released from producing less $Q$ (the area under supply from $Q_1$ to $Q_0$).

This diagram depicts a partial equilibrium model; as such it is oversimplified because it fails to account accurately for what happens in the rest of the economy. The tax revenue collected ($T \times Q_1$) may be spent in a way that benefits consumers more or less than alternative uses of the inputs. In balanced-budget tax incidence, this effect is neutralized by assuming government spends the tax revenue in precisely the same manner that consumers would have.

The tax-induced shift in resource allocation shown in figure 5-1 results in tax shifting. When equilibrium is reestablished, prices have changed because of altered resource allocation. The relative change in prices from a pretax to a posttax situation measures the actual burden of the tax levied on producers (supply) or consumer (demand). In the example, the gross price to the consumer increases ($P_1 - P_0 = a$) and the net price to the producer decreases ($P_0 - P_2 = b$). These relative price changes show the percentage of the burden falling on consumers [$a/(a + b)$] and on firms [$b/(a + b)$]. The relative burdens depend on the properties of the demand and supply curves, and their relationship quantifies who ultimately pays for the tax.

In general equilibrium models of tax shifting and incidence, the burden to each group and sector of the economy is measured by tax-induced price changes. The tax burden can fall only on persons, and so tax burden analysis traces the effects of taxes on transactions (such as sales taxes), incomes, and commodities to persons who are affected. This is measured by individuals' uses of income (tax-induced changes in prices of final consumption, called *forward shifting*) or sources of income (tax-induced changes in payments for the factors of production, which are labor, capital, land, and natural resources, called *backward shifting*). The example in figure 5-1 is a partial equilibrium model and is unable to trace the tax burden back to the factors of production used by the firm. The distribution of the tax burden among factors of production depends on technology and economic markets. In most cases, tax policy induces resource reallocations, which inevitably result in tax shifting. However, taxes on economic rents are one exception. By definition, a tax on economic rent cannot be shifted onto others and consequently produces no distortion or excess burden. In its broadest definition, economic rent is a payment for a commodity or a factor of production in excess of what is required to secure use of that scarce resource from its owner. Another way of defining economic rent is the difference between market price and opportunity cost. Since the latter indicates how valuable a resource is in its next-best employment, payment above that level is not required in order to induce it into its most-productive role. The public sector may socialize economic rents by means of taxes or regulation, and in private markets individuals capture rents by means of negotiation, lawsuits, and other activities that affect property rights.

Subnational units of government are intent upon serving regional and local interest groups because these residents are the voters. The overall objectives of state and local government policymakers have not been clearly or unambiguously characterized in the professional literature. Furthermore, the taxation of natural resources is uniquely amenable to differential policies among taxing jurisdictions because the resource is immobile. The situation of one jurisdiction containing a large body of reserves, which for analytical convenience are assumed to be exported in their entirety, and the effect of subnational taxes can be analyzed by means of expanding figure 5-1. The demand curve for the resource ($DD$) and the supply ($SS$) for all producers except those in the jurisdiction introducing a tax policy resemble those developed for figure 5-1 and are shown in panel A of figure 5-2. The supply curve ($S$) is drawn to indicate that producers with resources in this jurisdiction possess high-quality/low-cost reserves, which are less expensive to extract than in certain parts of the rest of the world. Demand for this jurisdiction ($D_{net}$) is derived from panel A; it is the difference between world supply and demand at all prices below the intersection of world supply and demand without this jurisdiction's contribution. From the standpoint of the taxing jurisdiction, all of the revenue in panel B in the area above $P_0$ and the demand curve ($D_{net}$) represents potential economic rent, which initially is going to consumers in other jurisdictions.

Should the jurisdiction impose a per-unit tax on the resource extracted, it increases production costs and may be depicted as shifting the supply curve upward by the amount of the tax ($S + T$) in panel B. This change is identical to the tax effect shown in figure 5-1. In the case of a zero tax, producers in the jurisdiction produce $Q_0$ at price $P_0$, and capture the portion of the market (exports) denoted as $D$ in panel A. Producers in other jurisdictions have the portion $E$ of the total market. However, the imposition of a

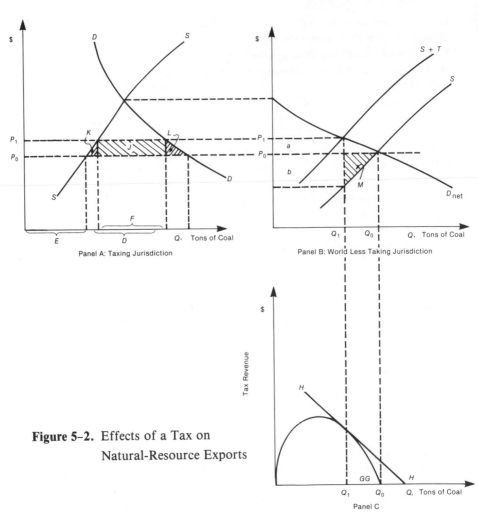

**Figure 5–2.** Effects of a Tax on
                   Natural-Resource Exports

tax ($T$) by this one jurisdiction results in market prices increasing to
$P_1$ and output in the jurisdiction falling to $Q_1$, which means that their exports account for $F$ of the world market (panel A). The tax-policy alternatives available to the taxing jurisdiction are depicted in panel C. The
horizontal axis depicts the amount of the resource extracted and lines up
with panel B. The vertical axis depicts tax revenue ($T \times Q$). The curve $GG$
shows the feasible tax revenues available to the jurisdiction at different tax
rates and the output that corresponds to those tax rates. Tax revenue must
equal zero at a zero tax rate (at $Q_0$ in Panel C) and at a tax rate so high that
in-jurisdiction producers cease to operate. Consequently the alternative tax

revenues-output combination has a maximum. Panel C is useful in analyzing the options available to tax policymakers. Producing at higher levels of output creates benefits to the jurisdictions and its residents, as well as to those who are directly employed, many of whom may be in-migrants. Payrolls and local expenditures have indirect effects, which create secondary economic activity, such as jobs and incomes that depend on the extent and characteristics of the local market. This economic activity also results in government revenues from sales, income, and other taxes. These effects can be characterized as the benefits of development, which are offset by the associated costs of environmental damage, boom towns, and required public expenditures.

Tax revenues derived directly from resource extraction may be employed to mitigate these costs as well to provide public services and to allow for reductions in other taxes. Policymakers and the public may be thought of as possessing relative preferences for these conflicting objectives of resource development versus tax exploitation. The implied rate of trade-off between the two objectives is depicted as $HH$ in panel C. If the goal were to maximize tax revenues, the preferred tax rate would correspond to the peak of $GG$. Some observers have hypothesized that the goal in some resource-rich states is to maximize tax exporting, but tax exporting occurs when both nonresident owners of productive resources and firms and consumers bear the burden of a tax. The share of the burden shifted to nonresident consumers is depicted in panel B by the difference between the pretax and the posttax price (distance $a$). The portion of the tax falling on resources and inputs to the extractive firm (capital and labor) is shown as distance $b$. This portion of the tax is shifted to labor, owners of extractive firms, and owners of resources. It is necessary to know the technology of production and the supply of these factors in order to analyze relative tax shifting and tax exporting to nonresident resource and capital owners.

Another effect of tax shifting is to cause prices for the extracted resources from all jurisdictions to rise (to $P_1$). This price increase benefits producers in other areas and may stimulate tax increases as other policymakers see the potential revenue. The portion of the tax burden exported by the jurisdiction to consumers is labeled $J$. However, since consumers pay more for a smaller amount of the resource, which comes from all jurisdictions (assuming inelastic demand), even a tax that results in a small fractional price change may burden consumers by the entire tax revenue raised in the taxing jurisdiction. This result occurs if demand and supply in all regions have identical price elasticities. If so, market shares are unaltered by a tax in one jurisdiction regardless of how small a portion of the tax rate is forward shifted. This outcome implies that other jurisdictions benefit from the tax because their output expands, prices rise, and the value of thier resources increases commensurately. It follows that other resource-rich areas may not only be encouraged to tax but would be expected to encourage tax increases by their neighbors and competitors.

The concern expressed by energy-consuming states over bearing the burden of taxes on fuels exported from producing states is simplistic. Figure 5–2 reveals that exporting the tax burden to consumers and nonresident owners involves more factors than observing trade flows. However, to the extent that forward shifting does occur, its impact on consumers is amplified to the entire amount produced and consumed. This poses a legitimate concern to consuming regions, which was expressed in the *Commonwealth Edison* v. *Montana* Supreme Court decision over the 30 percent coal severance tax. The Court held the tax to be constitutional, saying that tax limitations would have to come from the legislative branch.

The tax depicted in figure 5–2 produces excess burdens, which exceed the tax revenues raised, and these correspond to the tax-engendered welfare losses described in figure 5–1. The first such net loss occurs because producers in other jurisdictions expand output and thereby use up scarce resources. The triangle in panel A labeled $K$ depicts the net loss due to the fact that labor and man-made capital could have been used more efficiently in other activities, and the higher-cost natural resource is extracted before it would have been in the nontax situation. Triangle $L$ depicts the net loss to consumers who sacrifice consumer surplus that would have been created in the nontax situation. The final component is the net profits or producer surplus lost by owners of extractive firms in the taxing jurisdiction because of curtailed output; it is labeled $M$ in panel B. The magnitude of these three components depends on the properties of the demand and supply functions, wherein the more price elastic they are (that is, responsive to changes in prices), the greater the excess burden engendered by a tax. The goal of economic efficiency is achieved when excess tax burdens are eliminated or, as a second best, are minimized. However, this efficiency criterion of welfare economics would only be operative, if at all, at the national government level. The objective of subnational-jurisdiction tax policymakers is a parochial evaluation of the benefits from using taxes to socialize resource income versus stimulating economic development by maintaining low taxes. Even if economic development were the sole objective in some jurisdictions, and this would imply zero total taxes, the incentive to support high taxes in other jurisdictions remains.

Should the federal government step in and mandate that the efficiency goal prevail, the steps necessary to implement that goal in the presence of existing taxes could not be easily ascertained. For one, taxes falling on true economic rents are not resource distorting and thus would have to be identified and left unaffected. Second, the policy would have to focus on how to reduce or eliminate excess burdens. However, tax effects are interdependent. For example, the excess burden of a tax increase in one region is offset partially when output is shifted to other regions where taxes were previously in place. The effect is to counter prevailing tax distortions and the attendent excess burdens. Harberger (1964) develops a measure of net welfare loss to account for these interdependencies. In its simplest for it is:

$$- \tfrac{1}{2} \sum_i T_i \, \Delta \, Q_i,$$

where $\Delta Q_i$ is the tax induced change in region $i$ and $T_i$ is the previous tax in effect on commodity $i$. This is summed over all affected regions. The $\frac{1}{2}$ comes from approximating the welfare loss triangle and the minus $(-)$ comes from measuring welfare loss by a positive number. However, this measure may not be easy to construct in practice.

Another way in which to analyze the incentive for subnational jurisdictions to impose taxes or to benefit from the effects of others is to test for the existence of market power. When a jurisdiction or group of jurisdictions acting together affects prices, they possess market power and forward shift their tax burdens. Possessing a large share of the market or possessing significantly higher-quality, lower-cost resource stock is a prerequisite to market power. This can be seen in figure 5-2 as either the net demand curve ($D_{net}$) in panel B shifted up and to the right or the supply curve ($S$ other) shifted down and to the left. The comparable term *market dominance* has been used for examples of the resource industry by Gillis and McLure (1975) who analyzed the potential for bauxite producers to export tax burdens.

There are certain resources in which significant quantities are consumed and used in the industry's jurisdictions, such as natural gas in Texas and Louisiana. In such cases the analysis shown in figure 5-2 is inappropriate. When significant consumption takes place within the jurisdiction, the amount exported is a residual. Demand and supply of the resource within the jurisdiction is depicted in panel A of figure 5-3. The demand curve ($D$) is for in-jurisdiction use and supply is for total production. Panel B illustrates the demand outside the jurisdiction (or net demand derived similarly to that in panel B, figure 5-2), and the supply ($S_{net}$) is the difference between the supply and demand curves in panel A. The situation formulated in figure 5-3 shows that output is sold both in-state and out-of-state at the same price, which implies that transportation costs are assumed to be zero. Should the jurisdiction decide to invoke a tax on the resources, it would have to be at a uniform rate on interstate and intrastate sales so that the commerce clause of the U.S. Constitution not be violated. The tax on the extracted resource shifts the supply curve ($S + T$) upward in both panel A and in panel B. As a consequence, the exported resource falls from $Q_0$ to $Q_1$ (panel B). The burden of the tax falls on both in-jurisdiction and out-of-jurisdiction consumers and on producers (owners of resources and capital) according to the proportions $a/T$ and $b/T$ ($T = a + b$) shown in panel A.

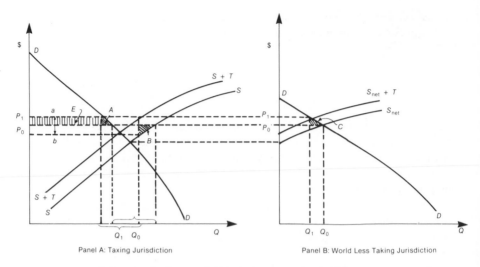

**Figure 5–3.** Effects of a Tax within and out of Jurisdiction Consumption

However, a significant portion of consumers reside in the jurisdiction, and the total burden they bear is denoted by the vertically lined area in panel A(E). Out-of-jurisdiction consumers pay the diagonally lined segment of total tax revenue, with the remainder falling on owners of extractive firms and resources (assuming that labor is perfectly mobile). The net loss to society engendered by the tax is made up of the loss in consumer surplus to residents of the jurisdiction (A in panel A), the loss of net producer surplus to firms (B in panel A, figure 5–3), and the loss of consumer surplus to nonresidents (C in panel B). As in previous cases, all of these magnitudes depend on the properties of the demand and supply functions. However, it is apparent that when a portion of the resource is consumed or used in manufacturing or other production within the state, it is more likely that the burden is internalized significantly. As the number of suppliers from other jurisdictions grows, the demand for the exported portion of the product becomes more price elastic (price responsive). This reduces the portion of the tax forward shifted to consumers and places it on producers. Under these conditions, there is less incentive to impose taxes, which explains why natural-gas taxes in Texas, where approximately two-thirds of output is consumed in-state, are relatively low.

In the foregoing analysis, time was assumed to be frozen or, alternatively, could be considered as repeating a fixed increment continuously into the future. While this analytic convenience is accepted for infinitely reproducible commodities, it is less acceptable for resources that are fixed and ultimately exhaustible. Taxes have been shown to distort the rate of extraction from known reserves, the quality break-point where material is either extracted or left in the ground (ore cutoff grade), and the level of investment in exploration and development. While the static assumption made in figures 5-1, 5-2, and 5-3 fails to capture the entire spectrum of resource dislocations and distortions created by taxation, much of this is included in the supply curves as depicted. The error becomes significant in two cases. The first is that accumulated past extraction has depleted the resource to the point that exhaustion is sufficiently close to affect resource prices significantly. Except for conventionally extracted fuels, the specter of imminent exhaustion is not, in general, present because of the large resource stocks of reduced quality, technological change, and substitution of other materials justifiable at somewhat higher costs. The second occurs when the ore cutoff is increased as a result of a tax, and the bypassed material becomes irretrievable. This loss occurs in coal mining when overburden is replaced or underground ceilings collapse.

Readers should also recall the discussion in chapter 3 of the interaction between taxes and regulation. Regulation can be analyzed as a tax or a subsidy (a negative tax) for both its income-allocative effects and distorting effects. Although in the remainder of this chapter tax effects are analyzed, readers should bear in mind the parallels with regulation as a means of government control.

Another useful way to describe the effects of taxes on the allocation of natural resources and the incomes of owners of inputs into production processes (natural resources, land, capital, and labor) is separating out the capitalization and mobility effects. The former reveals how the market value of capital stocks is affected by a tax and the effect is primarily restricted to the commodity being taxed. The portion of a tax that stays put and is not shifted to others is capitalized. If the item being taxed provides useful services for more than one year, the price that reflects the tax burden is ownership of the underlying asset. For example, property taxes are applied to both land and real improvements as well as personal property in some jurisdictions. Although the tax is paid annually or semiannually and is a flow, the portion that stays put is reflected in reduced prices of land and improvements. When alternative locations are available and new investment is mobile, a property tax that reduces net income to the owners is partially capitalized (fully capitalized if immobility is absolute) by a reduced market value for the property. Tax capitalization occurs for all long-lived resources (natural resources, land, and capital), and it is true for labor, but only in the sense that wages decline. Taxes falling on economic rents are capitalized, and no shifting is possible.

In order for taxes to be shifted, there must be tax-induced reallocations of resources. This is called the *mobility effect,* for displaced resources escape the tax by changes in use. There are several ways in which this occurs. The most obvious one is by individuals' and firms' moving operations to jurisdictions where taxes are nonexistent or lower. The term *mobility* as applied to changes in location is obvious. Other ways to mitigate taxes are to substitute materials that are taxed more lightly, to change technology to those that use the resource more efficiently, and finally for consumers to alter demand by buying fewer commodities containing the taxed material. As these four measures of mobility become more prevalent, a tax is shifted to a greater extent. Because natural resources are highly immobile, it is believed that tax capitalization of in situ resource prices is where the bulk of tax burdens occurs (Gillis and McLure 1975; Church 1981; U.S. General Accounting Office 1981a).

## Tax Effects on Nonrenewable Resources

The effects on various taxes on the extraction on nonrenewable resources are summarized briefly. (For a more-complete analysis, see Church 1981; Burness 1976; Conrad and Hool 1980.) Taxes on extraction of nonrenewable natural resources are called *severance taxes,* and taxes on their sale are called *excise, processing,* and other names. They may be levied on the quantity, quality, and value of the natural resource at various stages of processing. Any tax on output creates a distortion in the long- and short-run extraction rate, except one whose rate is increasing exponentially over time.

A conventional excise tax affects the cost of extraction and processing to the firm. The response of the profit-maximizing firm in the short run is to slow the rate of extraction and defer it to the future because prices will be higher, and the cost of extraction is delayed until the future. However a variable rate can either speed up or slow the extraction rate (Conrad and Hool 1980; Burness 1976). The tax will cause high grading (shifting to a higher-quality ore cutoff grade) and may so burden marginally profitable mines that it causes them to shut down. Thus the tax is sometimes called a *conservative tax.* In the long run, a tax that affects costs, like this one, will discourage investment and reduce output and discovery of new reserves. In this case, more of the tax will be shifted to consumers, and there is an incentive to relocate to a jurisdiction with lower taxes.

If the tax rate on output corresponds to the rising price of the resource in situ, there is no incentive for the owner to alter the rate of extraction, and resource owners will bear the tax burden. The effect of the tax will be the same as a proportional tax on the value of the deposit in situ and will lower the asset value of the resource (capitalized). However, in the long run, less investment will take place and high grading may occur, both of which introduce distortions, and the tax burden will be shared among consumers and resource owners due to this mobility effect.

Property taxes are leveled on the value of the resource in situ, the value of related plant and equipment (reproducible capital), and a host of combinations and formulas based on these factors, as well as the level of extraction. A property tax on reserves can be mitigated by mining rapidly in the short run (increasing the extraction rate and lowering prices) and by investing less in the long run (ultimately reducing the extraction rate and raising prices). However, the tax also provides an incentive to lower the ore cutoff grade when accurately applied and thus increases reserves and the total amount extracted. Property taxes based on formulas related to output act like a tax on sales and should be interpreted as such. Taxes on plant and equipment have no effect in the short run but discourage investment in the long run.

Perhaps the most-complex tax levied on the extractive firm is the corporate profit and resource profits (net proceeds) tax. When the corporate-profit tax rate is constant (a proportional rate on profits), it has no short-run effect. The effects of a progressive rate structure depend on the time path of resource prices and costs (Conrad and Hool 1980). However, in the long run, it is a tax on both economic rents and on the return that is necessary to provide business incentive to invest and allocate capital. To the extent that it falls on economic rent, it has no distorting effect, and the burden falls on the owner (this is equivalent to a tax on royalty payments). To the extent that it falls on the necessary return on capital, it discourages investment, and its burden is shared by owners and consumers and the rate of extraction is lowered. However, a tax on royalties is usually levied as a percentage of the value of extraction and thus has the same effect as a sales tax. The U.S. tax code treats capital-gains income separately and favorably. A tax on capital gains has no distorting effect as long as an interest deduction is allowed for the amount of reproducible capital tied up in ownership of reproducible and natural capital. Interest is usually deductible only for borrowed capital and not for equity (ownership interests). This distorts the financing decision, and the tax then acts to discourage investment of equity capital.

The depletion allowance of the corporate income tax acts like a negative severance tax (that is, a subsidy for its lower after-tax costs), so that the effect is to accelerate depletion and economic investment, producing lower prices and greater current output at the expense of future generations. Cost depletion is analogous to a negative tax per unit of output (providing an incentive to lower the ore cutoff grade), whereas percentage depletion is analogous to an ad valorem severance tax on the value of output.

A true depletion allowance would account for the fact that a resource in situ is appreciating in value, and timing of the depletion allowance occurs only when extraction takes place. However, the replacement for the previously discovered resource will be more expensive and increases the true cost of depletion. A corporate-profits tax with a constant rate over time, with taxation of capital gains realized on the appreciated value of the resource in situ, and a constant depletion rate based on the value of the unextracted resource would be neutral with respect to the rate of extraction and investment. The effect of the capital-gains tax would be to compensate for what the depletion rate gives up by being based on the current value of the unextracted resource. Expensing rather than amortizing exploration and development investments encourages investment, and when coupled with other provisions of the U.S. personal and corporate tax code, it encourages riskier investment than would otherwise occur.

Although economic rent is clearly defined in economic thoery, it is nearly impossible to measure empirically and harder to tax. A necessary return to a factor of production in order to ensure its services and the higher return that constitutes economic rent depends upon the expectations and preferences of business. Those receiving economic rents have an incentive to allocate part or all of those rents in order to secure ownership and control. And others have an incentive to expend funds and engage in collective action that transfers economic rents to them, up to the point where expenditures are just short of their expected gain in rents. Consequently everyone has a personal incentive to conceal the existence and extent of rents and to fight for those that are thought to exist. Furthermore, once economic rents are established, taking them away means reducing those persons' real income (capitalization). However, there is a tax that falls solely on rents to natural resources. For example, Emerson (1980) simulated the effectiveness of a corporate income tax, property tax, production sharing (used by some foreign nations), a resource rent tax, a royalty, and various hybrids in their ability to capture rents without creating distortions. A complex combination of a progressive tax on resource rents with a safeguard tapering provision was best, but it was impractical and not perfect.

Economic rents, property rights, and the regulation, taxing, and spending power of government are inexorably interdependent. Since no tax is completely effective in singling out economic rents, a more-efficient way to secure natural-resource-related rents may be to redefine property rights. When government is the resource owner, as in commonwealth countries and many other foreign countries and on U.S. federal and state lands and offshore regions, the problem is one of devising an effective means to farm out exploration, development, and production or conduct it with nationalized firms and capture the economic rents. Lack of knowledge and the uncertainty inherent in resource development make this a difficult task. Teisberg (1980) simulated how effective federal leasing policies are in this respect. He derived a model of how a competitive firm would make profit-maximizing exploration and development decisions after it had secured property rights to a nonrenewable resource. He used the model to test various alternatives and assumed the current federal tax structure was in place. He concluded that the exploration date would be earlier if the royalty rate were lower, the depletion rate were greater, the corporate-tax rate were higher, or exploration costs were smaller. The development data would be earlier if the size of the expected reserve was greater, extraction costs were smaller, the royalty (depletion) rate was smaller (larger), or the tax rate was greater. He derived a combined tax rate, exploration and development deduction rate, and royalty rate that is neutral with respect to exploration and development timing. This is significant because in the absence of market failures, government as owner should strive to capture rents without creating distortions in the allocation of resources. He also analyzes the effect of the requirement for due diligence, which is part of U.S. leasing policy. He shows that a correct royalty rate protects submarginal deposits from being forced into premature development by the requirement. This rate varies over time unless the market price of the resource increases exponentially, in which case the royalty is constant. He also shows that if the 50 percent of income-maximum-depletion deduction is binding, then an optimal royalty rate requires a fixed (one time) lease bonus prior to exploration. Competitive bonus bidding is current federal policy for most offshore oil and gas leases. Teisberg derives numerical estimates for optimal royalty rates by taking the estimated price path of oil at 2 percent per year in real terms and coal at 0.7 percent annually. If the real interest rate is 6 to 8 percent, then the optimal royalty rate on oil is 25 to 33 percent and 9 to 11 percent on coal if the depletion rate is not a binding constraint on the firm's decisions. Otherwise the rates should be 25 to 33 percent for oil, 16 to 20 percent for coal, and 35 to 40 percent for shale oil. Except for the oil rate, those royalty rates are in line with recent U.S. policy for coal, oil shale, natural gas, sulfur, and phosphates, although Teisberg notes that when high prices prevail under the bonus-bidding system on top of a fixed royalty, this may indicate that access to the resources is too limited, and this causes some distortion.

Many others have pointed out that competitive bonus bidding compared to royalty rate bids shift all risk to the private sector and lower government's share. Percentage royalties and production sharing both result in risk sharing and increase goverment's take. Foreign governments are particularly concerned about collusion and are distrustful of competitive bidding for leases as a means of capturing economic rents, and this may explain their preferences for nationalized industries and production sharing where either the resource or cash payments constitute the royalty.

**Taxation of Renewable Resources**

Tax effects of renewable natural resources are similar in some ways to those regarding nonrenewable resources. Developed agriculture and row crops are different because harvests are annual, and they are taxed much as any firm using reproducible capital. However, slow-growing and slow-rejuvenating resources such as forests, fisheries, and the unpriced assimilative properties of the environment present special difficulties because the rate of extraction and the quality of the resource are affected by taxes. The tax effects have in large part been covered in the nonrenewable-resource discussion.

The two primary issues in agriculture revolve around tax-induced problems of liquidity and taxing agricultural land on its income-producing basis or the highest and best use. Farmland and, to a lesser extent, grazing land have been increasing in market price at rates far exceeding those that are reflective of farm incomes, for a large number of reasons. One is conversion to residential and industrial land uses. When tax policy causes premature conversion, and at some future date it is discovered that converted farmland would have been better maintained in its previous state and is now irreversibly lost, then tax policy creates undesirable distortions. The U.S. soil-conservation service estimated that between 1967 and 1975 85 million acres of farmland was irreversibly converted to urban and water-storage uses in the United States. It is estimated that 35,000 acres are lost each week, and some people believe this is the result of myopic decisions and the interplay of government tax, housing, highway construction, and expenditure policies. However, this topic goes beyond the intent of this discussion.

Tax policy has adverse effects when it prevents those who wish to remain farmers from doing so. The primary culprits are property taxes and inheritance taxes, which are geared to the market value of the land as opposed to its ability to produce agricultural income. Recent changes in the inheritance tax permit farms to be valued on their income-producing capabilities and not on inflated market value. This, coupled with provisions for deferred tax payments, have eliminated part of the problem. The property tax has the same effect in that farm income may be insufficient to pay taxes based on market value for the land in its highest and best use. This creates the liquidity problem. Many states provide special property-tax relief for agricultural land (Clark 1979), and the U.S. tax code is particularly advantageous for farmers in a number of respects.

Forestry is similar to other natural resources in that the harvest decision affects the stock of the resource and so has long-range effects. A good deal of confusion in the literature on forestry taxation prevails over determining the effects of various taxes, particularly in how they affect the date of harvest and total yield. The tax bases most widely used and considered in the theoretical literature are a property tax on the value of the timber, a property tax on the site productivity (related to differential economic rent) that exempts the timber (all the former are paid annually), a tax on output or yield, and the income tax (those latter taxes are paid at harvest). A property tax on the value of standing timber is widely used, but valuing timber is difficult and expensive, and the tax has been accused of being discriminatory because of the capital-intensive character of the industry. Since forestry is more capital intensive than other manufacturing, it distorts economic choice by inducing early harvest, and it favors low capital-intensive forestry techniques, all of which distort resource use. However, this effect is not exclusive to forests, for the property-tax burden falls more heavily on all capital-intensive industries, and these include most nonrenewable natural resources.

Advocates for and against exemption or special treatment of timber have battled for years (for a recent example see Pasour and Holley 1976; Trestrial 1969 and 1980). The debate over whether property taxes do distort harvest away from the culmination of mean annual incremental growth is in error. Although the tax distorts because it promotes premature cutting, the optimal harvest date determined from the model of a renewable resource as capital occurs before full growth. Waiting until maturity implies a zero interest rate, but the exact optimum solution remains in contention (Comolli 1981).

Nevertheless, some conclusions about the effects of taxes are possible. A property tax on the potential income from the land that exempts the crop growing on the land falls on economic rent, stimulates the most-intensive use of the land, and is not discriminatory to marginal lands for if administered accurately, it effectively isolates the fertility and proximity to market differences (economic rents). This tax does not distort the harvest date, and it encourages the restocking and rapid development of cut-over areas. However, the tax may be difficult to assess, and the rate must be much higher than for a conventional property tax (Gaffney 1978 and 1980). The tax would also stimulate the conversion to other land uses at the time when economic rents were higher in these uses, and the tax would have to be universally applied to the site value of all land for whatever uses to prevent distortions. A tax on timber yield (stumpage) defers revenues and for smaller jurisdictions may result in unstable revenue flows. The tax provides incentives to deferring the harvest date (as the severance tax does for exhaustible resources) and leaves restocking to nature. This is discriminatory to higher-quality sites on which shorter growing cycles occur and to species that mature more rapidly and thus creates a distortion as with any output or income-based tax (high grading). With this tax, local government shares risk with the landowner. Gaffney (1980) concludes that if the share of sales revenue attributable to the input of land is no greater than 50 percent, an excise or severance tax reduces average annual output and raises prices more than a conventional property tax does.

Income taxes can take on various forms, but basically they resemble taxes on output (stumpage or yield); however, the bias against short growing cycles and higher-quality land is less than for a pure output-based tax.

The federal tax treatment is to expense costs of holding the forest prior to harvest except for the forgone cost of equity capital, which is particularly significant because forestry lands are largely held with small debt. Restocking costs are capitalized over the growing cycle. Gaffney (1978) demonstrates that this treatment of expenses is the reverse of that called for with a neutral tax. The capital-gains tax provision in the federal tax code benefits the forest owner.

Another way that government captures forest rents is by selling stumpage from public lands. The management of federal and state lands and the multiple-use concept has come under sustained theoretical and political (the "sagebrush rebellion") criticism. Evidence of mismanagement was shown by Bert (1979) by evaluating the net return to owners of private forests who have been alleged to cut more rapidly than is socially desirable. By assuming that they know what is best for themselves (profit maximizers), he determines that private owners act as if their real (after removing inflation) return on investment is 5 percent, half of which comes from the growth of the timber and the other half from its price appreciation. This rate is not less than the rate for equally risky manufacturing and thus does represent too-rapid harvest and restocking. However, leases on federal lands allow for much longer growing cycles, which is consistent with the assertions of many economists that the government acts as if real interest rates are close to zero. Bert concludes that appealing to values other than timber yield is unfounded, for there are no uses sufficiently valuable to justify such slow harvesting (except, of course, unique species, national parks, and some others).

The taxation of fisheries is analogous to the taxation of other slow-growing and nonrenewable resources. The unique attribute of fisheries is their common property and free access, which induces too-rapid extraction. In some cases this has resulted in species extinction and resulting wasted capital tied up in unused fishing fleets. The political solution to this distorted resource use has been protracted and complex, and frequently it has resulted in direct regulation and, for a far lesser degree, taxes on extraction (calculated on the unpriced scarcity value of the fish). The regulations include extended economic zones in which fleets are excluded or regulated (the United States extended its zone to two-hundred miles in 1976), restrictions on boat size, number of fishers, fishing methods (for example, mesh size of nets and type of lines), size of the fleet, and minimum fish size.

Resource economists advocate a two-part fishery tax as the optimal one (Peterson and Fisher 1977). The first would be a tax based on extraction equal to user cost of reducing the stock of fish (scarcity value). The second would be a tax to preserve economic rents to fishing fleets by preventing entry of new boats, which occurs as long as profits are higher than in alternative occupations. The reason that such entry is nonoptimal in fishing is that each additional boat obtains an average yield and realizes average cost. The individual boat imposes an externality on other boats by creating crowding, which increases the costs (or effort) to others, and the new entrant does not pay for this effect. A tax on crowding—perhaps a license fee for new craft—could internalize this cost and prevent the dissipation of rents. However, the efficient use of resources requires that investment proceed up to the point where the incremental cost of an additional boat equals incremental revenues. This would occur at smaller fleet size.

# Bibliography

Ackerman, Bruce A., and Hassler, William T. 1981. *Clean Coal/Dirty Air.* New Haven: Yale University Press.

Adams, F. Gerard, and Behrman, Jere R., eds. 1978. *Econometric Modeling of World Commodity Policy.* Lexington, Mass.: Lexington Books, D.C. Heath and Company.

Allain, R. 1979. *Capital Investment Models of the Oil and Gas Industry.* New York: Arno Press.

Allen, Brenda J. 1979. *The Integrating Model of the Project Independence System.* Vol. 6: *Data Documentation.* Washington, D.C.: U.S. Department of Energy.

Anderson, Robert C. 1976. "Federal Mineral Policy: The General Mining Law of 1872." *Natural Resources Journal* 16 (July).

Atkinson, Anthony B. and Stiglitz, Joseph E. 1979. *Lectures on Public Economics.* New York: McGraw-Hill Book Co.

Ayers, Robert V. 1976. "A Taxonomy of Environmental Models." In W.R. Ott, ed., Proceedings of Conference on Environmental Modeling and Simulation. Washington, D.C.: Environmental Protection Agency.

———. 1978. *Resources, Environment and Economics.* New York: Wiley.

Ayers, Robert V., and Kneese, A.V. 1969. "Production, Consumption and Externalities." *American Economic Review* 59 (June).

Ayers, Robert V.; Noble, S.; and Overly, D. 1971. "Effects of Technology Change on, and Environmental Implications of, an I-O Analysis for the U.S., 1967-2020." International Research and Technology Report 219-R/I. [Washington, D.C.]

Bamrick, Susan. 1979. *Resources Rent Taxes.* Melbourne, Australia: Committee for Economic Development of Australia.

Barnett, H.J., and Morse, C. 1963. *Scarcity and Growth: The Economics of Natural Resource Availability.* Baltimore: Johns Hopkins University Press.

Barzel, Yoram. 1969. "Two Propositions on the Optimum Level of Producing Collective Goods." *Public Choice,* 6 (Spring):31-38.

———. 1974. "A Theory of Rationing by Waiting." *Journal of Law and Economics* 17 (April):73-96.

Beigie, Carl E., and Hero, Alfred O. 1980. *Natural Resources in US-Canadian Relations.* Boulder, Colo.: Westview Press.

Bentick, B.L. 1979. "The Impact of Taxation and Valuation Practices on the Timing and Efficiency of Land Use." *Journal of Political Economics* 87.

Bert, Peter. 1979. "The Economics of Timber: A Renewable Resource in the Long Run." *Bell Journal of Economics* 10 (Autumn):447–462.

Blackstone, Sandra L. 1980. "Mineral Severance Taxes in the Western States: An Economic and Legal Analysis of State Tax Policies." Ph.D. dissertations, Colorado School of Mines.

Boadway, Robin, and Flatters, Frank. 1981. "Efficiency, Equity and the Allocation of Resource Rents in a Federal State: The Case of Canada." Paper to the 1981 Taxation, Resources and Economic Development conference, Cambridge, Mass.

Bohi, D.R., and Russell, M. 1979. *Limiting Oil Imports.* Baltimore: Johns Hopkins University Press.

Boulding, K.E. 1966. "The Economics of the Coming Spaceship Earth." In *Environmental Quality in a Growing Economy,* edited by H. Barell. Baltimore: Johns Hopkins University Press.

Bradley, Paul G. 1976. "Governments and Mineral Resource Earnings: Taxation with Over-Simplification?" In A. Scott, ed., *Natural Resource Revenues: A Test of Federalism.* Vancouver, B.C.: University of British Columbia Press.

Brannon, Gerard K. 1975a. "Existing Tax Differentials and Subsidies Relating to the Energy Industries." In M. Brannon, ed., *Studies in Energy Tax Policy.* Cambridge, Mass.: Ballinger, 1975.

———. 1975b. "U.S. Taxes on Energy Resources." *American Economic Review* 65:396–404.

———. 1978. "Taxation and the Political Economy of the Energy 'Crisis.' " *Natural Resources Journal* 18:825–843.

———. 1979. "Tax Policy and Producer Incentives in the Energy Crisis." *Growth and Change* 10 (Spring):28–36.

———., ed. 1975c. *Studies in Energy Tax Policy.* Cambridge, Mass.: Ballinger.

Brewer, G.D. 1973. *Politicians, Bureaucrats, and the Consultants—A Critique of Urban Problem Solving.* New York: Basic Books.

Breyer, S. 1979. "Taxes as a Substitute for Regulation." *Growth and Change* 10:39–52.

Brown, G.M. 1974. "An Optimal Program for Managing Common Property Resources with Congestion Externalities." *Journal of Political Economy* 82 (January–February).

Brown, R.D. 1970. "Round Three for the Taxation of Mining Income." *Canadian Tax Journal* 18 (September–October).

Buchanan, James. 1968. *The Demand and Supply of Public Goods.* Chicago: Rand McNally.

Burness, H.S. 1976. "On the Taxation of Nonreplenishable Natural Resources." *Journal of Environmental Economics and Management* 3 (December):289–311.

Burness, Stuart; Cummings, Ronald; Morris, Glen; and Paik, Inja. 1980. "Thermodynamic and Economic Concepts as Related to Resource-Use Policies." *Land Economics,* 56 (February):1-9.

Burns, R.M. 1976. *Conflict and Its Resolution in the Administration of Mineral Resources in Canada.* Kingston, Ontario: Center for Resource Studies, Queens University.

Burt, O.R. 1964. "Optimal Use of Resources over Time." *Management Science* 11 (September):80-93.

Campbell, Harry F. 1976. "Rent vs. Revenue Maximization as an Objective of Environmental Managment." In A. Scott, ed., *Natural Resource Revenues: A Test of Federalism.* Vancouver, B.C.: University of British Columbia Press.

Campbell, Harry F.; Gainer, W.D.; and Scott, Anthony. 1976. "Resource Rent: How Much and for Whom?" In A. Scott, ed., *Natural Resource Revenues: A Test of Federalism.* Vancouver, B.C.: University of British Columbia Press.

Carson, Richard S. 1978. "The Impact of Taxes on Energy Needs." *Canadian Business Review* 5 (Spring):10-15.

Carter, Kenneth Letil, (chairman), et al. 1967. *Report of the (Canadian) Royal Commission on Taxation,* including "The Taxation of Mineral Extraction," by M.W. Bucovetsky, and "Taxation of the Mining Industry in Canada," by D.Y. Timbrell. Ottawa: Queen's Printer.

Chambers, Winston G., and Reid, John S. 1979. "Resource Management in the Conflict of Canadian Federalism." *AIME Council of Economics, Proceedings,* pp. 43-46.

Cherry, Kid. 1979. "State Mineral Development Policy in Wisconsin." *AIME Council of Economics, Proceedings,* pp. 117-120.

Cheung, Steven N.S. 1974. "A Theory of Price Control." *Journal of Law and Economics* 17 (April):53-72.

Chisholm, A.H. 1975. "Income Taxes and Investment Decisions: The Long-Life Appreciating Asset Case." *Economic Inquiry* 13:565-578.

Chung, Pham; Church, Albert; and Kury, Channing. 1980. "Taxation of Electricity Generation: The Economic Efficiency and Equity Bases for Regionalism within the Federal System." *Natural Resources Journal* 20 (October):878-885.

Church, Albert M. 1978. "Conflicting Federal, State and Local Interest—Trends in State and Local Energy Taxation—Coal and Copper—A Case in Point." *National Tax Journal* 31 (September):269-279.

———. 1980. "State Taxation of Coal—Revealed Preferences of Economic Development versus Tax Exploitation of a Natural Resource." *Western Tax Review* 1 (May).

———. 1981. *Taxation of Non-Renewable Natural Resources.* Lexington, Mass.: Lexington Books, D.C. Heath and Company.

Church, Albert M.; Clark, Joel P.; Foley, Patricia T.; and Zimmerman, Martin B. 1980. *The Economic Effects of State and Federal Tax Structures on the Exploitation of Mineral Resources. Final Report to the National Science Foundation,* Albuquerque, N.M.: University of New Mexico Press.

Church, Albert M., and Folsom, Roger. 1978. "Optimal Taxation of Natural Resources by the State of New Mexico." Unpublished paper for the New Mexico Energy Institute.

Church, Albert M.; Zimmerman, Martin B.; Foley, Patricia, T.; and Clark, Joel P. "The Effects of Taxation on the United States Copper and Coal Industries." *Materials and Society.* Forthcoming.

Church, Albert M., ed. 1977. *Non-Renewable Resource Taxation in the Western States.* Monograph 77-2. Cambridge, Mass.: Lincoln Institute of Land Policy.

Ciriacy-Wantrup, S.V. 1952. *Resource Conservation: Economics and Policies.* Berkeley: University of California Press.

Clark, C.W. 1973. "Profit Maximization and the Extinction of Animal Species." *Journal of Political Economy* 81 (July–August).

Clark, Jon. 1979. *Conserving the Nation's Farmland.* Northeast-Midwest Institute. Washington, D.C.

Coal Severance Taxes. 1980. *Hearings before the Subcommittee on Energy and Power.* 96th Congress. HR 6654, HR 7163 (bills to amend the Powerplant and Industrial Fuel Act of 1978).

Cole, S., et al. 1973. *Models of Doom: A Critique of Limits to Growth.* New York: Universe Books.

Coleman, James S. 1970. "The Benefits of Coalition." *Public Choice* 8 (Spring):45–61.

Commoner, Barry. 1976. *The Poverty of Power.* New York: Alfred A. Knopf.

Comolli, P.M. 1981. "Principles and Policy in Forestry Economics." *Bell Journal of Economics* 12 (Spring):300–309.

Conrad, Robert F. 1980. "Mining Taxation: A Numerical Introduction." *National Tax Journal* 33 (December):443–450.

Conrad, Robert F., and Hool, R. Bryce. 1980. *Taxation of Mineral Resources.* Lexington, Mass.: Lexington Books, D.C. Heath and Company.

Corina, Giovanni Andrea, and Mayorya-Alba, Eleodoro. 1980. "The Energy Constraint in the 1980s and the Scope for Import Substitution in Western Europe." *Journal of Policy Modeling* 2 (May):205–227.

Corrigan, R., and Stansfield, R.L. 1980. "Rising Energy Prices—What's Good for Some States Is Bad for Others." *National Tax Journal* 12: 468–547.

Courchene, Thomas J. 1976. "Equalization Payments and Energy Royalities." In A. Scott, ed., *Natural Resource Revenues: A Test of Federalism.* Vancouver, B.C.: University of British Columbia Press.

Cox, J.C., and Wright, A.W. 1975. "The Cost-Effectiveness of Federal Tax Subsidies for Petroleum Reserves." In G.M Brannon, ed., *Studies in Energy Tax Policy.* Cambridge, Mass.: Ballinger Publishing Co.

————. 1976. "The Determinants of Investment in Petroleum Reserves and Their Implications for Public Policy." *American Economic Review* 66: 153–167.

Craig, Paul P., and Levine, M.D. 1979. "Distributed Energy Systems in California's Future: Issues in Transition." Berkeley, Calif.: Lawrence Berkeley Laboratory, January 16.

Crutchfield, J., and Zellner, A. 1962. "Economic Aspects of the Pacific Habitat Fishery." *Fishing Industrial Research* (April).

Cuciti, Peggy, and Galper, Harvey. 1981. "State Energy Revenues—A Potential Intergovernmental Problem." Paper to 1981 Taxation, Resources and Economic Development Conference, Cambridge, Mass. and study available from Agency and Intergovernmental Relations.

Cummings, Ronald G.; with Burness, H. Stuart, and Norton, Roger D. 1980. "The Proposed Waste Isolation Pilot Project and Impacts in the State of New Mexico: A Socio-Economic Analysis." Draft report to the New Mexico Energy and Minerals Department. December.

Cummings, Ronald G., and Burt, O.R. 1969. "The Economics of Production from Natural Resources." *American Economic Review* 59.

Cummings, Ronald G., and Mehr, Arthur F. 1977. "Investments for Infrastructure in Boomtowns." *Natural Resources Journal* 17 (April).

Cummings, Ronald G., and Schultze, W.D. 1978. "Optimal Investment Strategy for Boomtowns: A Theoretical Analysis." *American Economic Review* (June).

————. 1977. "Ramsey, Resources and the Conservation of Mass Energy." Paper presented at the Conference on Natural Resources Pricing, Trail Lake, Wyoming, August, 1977.

Cummings, Ronald G.; Schulze, W.D.; and Mehr, A.F. 1978. "Optimal Municipal Investment in Boomtowns: An Empirical Analysis." *Journal of Environmental Economics and Management* 5:252–267.

d'Arge, Ralph C., and Kogiku, J.C. 1973. "Economic Growth of the Environment." *Review of Economic Studies* 40 (January).

Dasgupta, P.S., and Heal, G. 1974. "The Optimal Depletion of Exhaustible Resources." *Review of Economic Studies,* symposium on the Economics of Exhaustible Resources.

Daugherty, Arthur B. 1980. "Preserving Farmland through Federal Income Tax Incentives." *National Tax Journal* 33 (March):111–114.

Davenport, C. 1978. "The Role of Taxation in the Regulation of Energy Production and Consumption (1978 Energy Act—A Case in Point)." *Economic Journal* 5:308–323.

Davidson, P.; Falk, L.; and Lee, H. 1975. "The Relations of Economic Rents and Price Incentives to Oil and Gas Supplies." In Gerard M. Brannon, ed., *Studies in Energy Tax Policy,* pp. 115–173. Cambridge, Mass.: Ballinger.

Davis, Ronnie J. 1970. "On the Incidence of Income Distribution." *Public Choice* 8 (Spring):63–74.

Denise, Paul A., and Ervin, Osbine L. 1979. "Energy Resources and the Legal Community: A Secondary Analysis of Impact and Policy Options." In Edward J. Miller and Robert P. Wolensky, eds., *The Small City and Regional Community.* Stevens Point, Wis.: Foundation Press.

Denver Research Institute. 1979. *Socioeconomic Impacts of Western Energy Resource Development.* Washington, D.C.: Council on Environmental Quality.

Devarajan, Shantayanan, and Fisher, Anthony C. 1981. "Hotelling's 'Economics of Exhaustible Resources' Fifty Years Later." *Journal of Economic Literature* 18 (March):65–73.

De Young, John H., Jr. 1978. "Measuring the Economic Effects of Tax Laws on Mineral Exploration." *Proceedings of the Council of Economics.* Denver, Colo.: American Institute of Mining and Engineering.

Duerr, William A. 1960. *Fundamentals of Forestry Economics.* New York: McGraw-Hill.

Dumars, Charles T., Brown, F. Lee; and Browde, Michael B. 1979. "Legal Issues on the State Taxation of Energy Development." Report made to the New Mexico Energy Institute.

Eaton, A. Kenneth. 1966. *Essays on Taxation.* Toronto: Canadian Tax Foundation.

Emerson, Craig. 1980. "Taxing Natural Resource Projects." *Natural Resources Forum* 4 (April):123–145.

Erickson, E.W.; Milsaps, S.W.; and Spann, R.M. 1974. "Oil Supply and Tax Incentives." *Brookings Papers on Economic Activity* 2:449–478.

Fairchild, Fred R., and Assoc. 1935. *Forest Taxation in the United States.* U.S.D.A. Misc. Pub. 218. Washington, D.C.: GPO.

Fisher, Anthony C., and Peterson, Frederick M. 1976. "The Environment in Economics: A Survey." *Journal of Economic Literature* 14.

Foley, Patricia T., and Clark, Joel P. In press. "The Effects of State Taxation on the United States Copper Supply." *Land Economics,*

Forrester, J.W. 1971. *World Dynamics.* N.p.: Wright Allen Press.

Foster, Edward. 1981. "The Treatment of Rents in Cost-Benefit Analysis."

*American Economic Review* 71 (March):171–178.

Fowler, Pete H.S. 1979. "Reconciling the Conflicts between Objectives of Owner, Developer and the Public in Mineral Ventures." In American Institute of Mining and Petroleum Engineers Council of Economics, *Proceedings.*

Freeman, David S. 1974. *Energy: The New Era.* New York: Vintage Books.

French, David. 1980. "The Economics of Renewable Energy Systems for Developing Countries." *Natural Resources Forum* 4 (January):19–42.

Friedman, Milton. 1980. "Our New Hidden Taxes." *Newsweek,* April 14, p. 90.

Fromm, G.; Hamilton, W.L. and Hamilton, D.E. 1974. "Federally Supported Mathematical Models: Survey and Analysis." Washington, D.C.: National Science Foundation.

Furubota, Erick G., and Pejovich, Svetozar. 1972. "Property Rights and Economic Theory: A Survey of Recent Literature." *Journal of Economic Literature* 10 (December):1137–1162.

Gaffney, Mason. 1967. "Tax-Induced Slow Turnover of Capital." *Western Economic Journal* 5:308–323.

———. 1977. "Intergovernmental Competition for Energy Reserves: The Public Interest." *Proceedings* of the 76th Annual Conference of the National Tax Association, St. Louis, Mo.

———. 1978. *An Overview of Forest Taxation: Pros and Cons of Alternative Forest Taxes.* Blacksburg, Va.: Forest Taxation Symposium, Virginia Polytechnic Institute.

———. 1980. "Alternative Ways of Taxing Forests." In *State Taxation of Forest and Land Resources: Symposium Proceedings.* Cambridge, Mass.: Lincoln Institute of Land Policy.

———, ed. 1967. *Extractive Resources and Taxation.* Madison: University of Wisconsin Press.

Georgescu-Roegen, N. 1971. *The Entropy Law and the Economic Process.* Cambridge: Harvard University Press.

———. 1975. "Energy and Economic Myths." *Southern Economic Journal* 41 (January):347–381.

Gilbert, Richard J. 1977. "Resource Extraction with Differential Information." *American Economic Review* 67 (February):250–254.

Gillis, S. Malcolm, and McLure, Charles E., Jr. 1975. "Taxation of Natural Resources—Incidence of World Taxes on Natural Resources with Special Reference to Bauxite." *American Economic Review* 65 (May).

Gillis, Malcolm. 1979. "Severance Taxes on Energy Resources in the United States—A Tale of Two Minerals." *Growth and Change* 10 (January): 55–70.

Gokturk, S. Sadik. 1980. "A Generalization of the Economic Theory of

Clubs." *American Economist* 24 (Spring):18–23.

Goldman, Marshall I. 1980. *The Enigma of Soviet Petroleum*. London: Allen and Unwin.

Gordon, H.S. 1954. "The Economic Theory of a Common Property Resource." *Journal of Political Economy* 62.

Greenberger, Martin; Grenson, Matthew A.; and Crissey, Brian L. 1976. *Models in the Policy Process*. New York: Russell Sage Foundation.

Greene, Kenneth V., and Parliament, Thomas J. "Political Externalities and the Welfare Losses from Consolidation." *National Tax Journal* 33 (June):209–218.

Griffin, James M., and Steele, Henry B. 1980. *Energy Economics and Policy*. New York: Academic Press.

Griffin, Keynon N., and Shelton, Robert B. 1978. "Coal Severance Tax in the Rocky Mountain States." *Policy Studies Journal* 7 (Autumn).

Haefele, Edwin T. 1971. "A Utility Theory of Representative Government." *American Economic Review* (June).

Hanson, Donald A. 1977. "Second Best Pricing Policies for an Exhaustible Resource." *American Economic Review* 67 (February):351–354.

Harberger, Arnold C. 1955. "The Taxation of Mineral Industries." Federal Tax Policy for Economic Growth and Stability. Washington, D.C.: Joint Committee on the Economic Report.

———. 1964. "Taxation, Resource Allocation and Welfare." In *The Role of Direct and Indirect Taxes in the Federal Reserve System*. Princeton, N.J.: Princeton University Press.

———. 1974a. *Project Evaluation*. Chicago: University of Chicago Press.

———. 1974b. *Taxation and Welfare*. Boston: Little, Brown.

Hardin, G. 1968. "The Tragedy of the Common." *Science* 1962: 1243–1248.

Harold, M. Hochman, and Peterson, George E. 1974. *Redistribution Through Public Choice*. New York: Columbia University Press.

Hayden, R.L., and Watt, G.L. 1975. "A Description of Potential Socioeconomic Impacts from Energy-Related Development on Campbell County, Wyoming." Washington, D.C.: U.S. Department of the Interior.

Hayes, Lynton R. 1980. *Energy, Economic Growth and Regionalism in the West*. Albuquerque, N.M.: University of New Mexico Press.

Heal, Geoffrey M. 1976. "The Relationship between Price and Extraction Cost for a Resource with a Backstop Technology." *Bell Journal of Economics* 7 (Autumn):371–378.

———. 1980. "The Relationship between Interest and Metal Price Movements." *Review of Economics and Statistics* 47 (January):161–181.

Heal, Geoffrey M., and Barrow, Michael M. 1979. "Empirical Investigation of the Long-Term Movement of Resource Prices: A Preliminary

Report." Paper presented at the Resources for the Future/Electric Power Research Institute workshop on Natural Resource Price Movements, Washington, D.C.

Hellerstein, Walter. 1978. "Constitutional Constraints on the State and Local Taxation of Energy Resources." *National Tax Journal* 31 (September):245–256.

————. 1981. "Legal Constraints on State Taxation of Natural Resources in the American Federal System." Paper to 1981 Taxation, Resources, and Economic Development Conference, Cambridge, Mass.

Herendeen, R., and Bullard, C. 1974. "Energy Cost of Goods and Services, 1963 and 1967." Urbana, Ill.: University of Illinois, Center for Advanced Computation.

Herfindahl, Orris C., and Kneese, Allen V. 1974. *Economic Theory of Natural Resources.* Columbus, Ohio: Charles E. Merrill.

Hogan, Timothy D., and Shelton, Robert B. 1973. "Interstate Tax Exportation and States Fiscal Structures." *National Tax Journal* 26 (October).

Hogan, William W.; Sweeney, James L.; and Wagner, Michael H. 1978. "Energy Policy Models in the National Energy Outlook." *TIMS Studies in Energy Policy,* in *Management Sciences* 10.

Hotelling, H. 1931. "The Economics of Exhaustible Resources." *Journal of Political Economy* 39 (April).

Houthaker, H.S. 1976. "The Economics of Nonrenewable Resources." Paper No. 493. Cambridge: Harvard Research Institute.

Hubert, M.K. 1969. "Energy Resources." In *Resources and Man,* by the Committee on Resources and Man of the National Academy of Sciences. San Francisco: W.H. Freeman.

Humphrey, D.B., and Moroney, J.R. 1975. "Substitution among Capital, Labor and Natural Resource Products in American Manufacturing." *Journal of Political Economy* 83 (February).

Jacobson, Lawrence R. 1979. "Optimal Investment and Extraction for a Depletable Resource." Ph.D. dissertation, Stanford University.

Jorgenson, D.W. 1970. "The Role of Energy in the U.S. Economy." *National Tax Journal* 31:209–220.

Kahn, H.; Brown, W.; and Martel, L. 1976. *The Next 200 Years: A Scenario for America and the World.* New York: Morrow.

Keynes, John Maynard. 1936. *The General Theory of Employment, Interest, and Money.* London: Macmillan.

Klass, Michael W.; Burrows, James C.; and Beggs, Steven D. 1980. *International Mineral Controls and Embargos, Policy Implications for the U.S.* New York: Praeger.

Kneese, Allen V., and Herfindahl, Orris C. 1974. *Economic Theory of Natural Resources.* Columbus, Ohio: Charles E. Merrill.

Kneese, Allen V., and Bower, B., eds. 1972. *Environmental Quality and the Social Sciences: Theoretical and Methodological Studies.* Baltimore: Johns Hopkins University Press.

Kneese, Allen V., and Schultze, C.L. 1975. *Pollution, Prices and Public Policy.* Washington, D.C.: Brookings Institution.

Knight, R., and Davies, B.T. 1978. "Financial Model Studies in Mineral Exploration." *Mining Magazine* (March):195–202.

Kolstad, Charles D., and Wolak, Frank A., Jr. 1981. "Optimal Coal Severance Tax Rates in the Western U.S." Unpublished paper. Los Alamos Scientific Laboratory, LA-UR-81-3275.

Kopp, Raymond J., and Smith, V. Kerry. 1980. "Measuring Factor Substitution with Neoclassical Models: An Experimental Evaluation." *Bell Journal of Economics* 6:631–658.

Kresge, David T. 1980. "Regional Impacts of Federal Energy Development." Paper delivered at the American Economic Association Meetings, September.

Krueger, Anne O. 1974. "The Political Economy of the Rent-Seeking Society." *American Economic Review* 64 (June):291–303.

Krutilla, J.V., and Fisher, A.C. 1978. *Economic and Fiscal Impacts of Coal Development, Northern Great Plains.* Baltimore: Johns Hopkins University Press.

Kuznets, S. 1946. *National Income, A Summary of Findings.* New York: National Bureau of Economic Research.

Labys, Walter C. 1980. *Market Structure, Bargaining Power, and Resource Price Formation.* Lexington, Mass.: Lexington Books, D.C. Heath and Company.

Labys, Walter C., and Afrusrabi, H. 1980. "Long Run Disequilibrium Adjustments in the U.S. Copper Market." Working paper. Morgantown, W.Va.: Department of Mineral, Energy, and Resource Economics, West Virginia University.

Larkin, J.; McDermott, J.; Simon, D.P.; and Simon, H.A. 1980. "Expert and Novice Performance in Solving Physics Problems." *Science,* June 20, pp. 1335–1342.

Lederman, W.R. 1976. "The Constitution: A Basis for Bargaining." In Scott, A., ed., *Natural Resource Revenues: A Test of Federalism.* Vancouver, B.C., Canada: University of British Columbia Press.

Ledyard, J., and Moses, L.N. 1976. "Dynamics of Land Use: The Case of Forestry." In R.E. Grieson, ed., *Public and Urban Economics.* Lexington, Mass.: Lexington Books, D.C. Heath and Company.

Leistritz, Larry F., and Murdock, Steven H. 1981. *The Socioeconomic Impact of Resource Development.* Boulder, Colo.: Westview Books.

Leith, J. Clark. 1976. "Ontario Mining Profits Tax: An Evaluation." In A. Scott, ed., *Natural Resource Revenues: A Test of Federalism.* Vancouver, B.C.: University of British Columbia Press.

Leontief, Wassily, et al. 1977. *The Future of the World Economy: A United Nations Study*. New York: Oxford University Press.

Libecap, Gary D., and Johnson, Ronald N. 1979. "Property Rights, Nineteenth-Century Federal Timber Policy, and the Conservation Movement." *Journal of Economic History* 29 (March):129–142.

Lichtenberg, A.J., and Norgaard, R.B. 1974. "Energy Policy and Taxation of Oil and Gas Income." *Natural Resources Journal* 14:501–518.

"Limits on State Severance Taxes on Coal Recommended." 1980. *Public Utilities* 105 (April).

Link, Arthur A. 1978. "Political Constraints and North Dakota's Coal Severance Tax." *National Tax Journal* 31 (September).

Linstone, H., and Turoff, M., eds. 1975. *The Delphi Method*. Reading, Mass.: Addison-Wesley.

Little, Dennis L. 1981. *Renewable Natural Resources*. Boulder, Colo.: Westview Press.

Lockner, A.O. 1965. "The Economic Effect of the Severance Tax on Decisions of the Mining Firm." *Natural Resources Journal* 4:468–485.

Long, Stephen C.M. 1976. "Coal Taxation in the Western States: The Need for a Regional Tax Policy." *Natural Resources Journal* 16 (April): 415–442.

Lovins, Emory. 1980. "Soft Energy Paths." *Sunpaper* 5 (October–December):11–24.

Loye, D. 1978. *The Knowable Future*. N.p.: Wiley-Interscience.

MacAvoy, Paul W., and Pindyck, Robert S. 1973. "Alternative Regulatory Policies for Dealing with the Natural Gas Shortage." *Bell Journal of Economics* 4 (Autumn).

MacDonald, S. 1970. "Distinctive Tax Treatment of Income from Oil and Gas Production." *Natural Resources Journal* 10:97–112.

McLure, Charles E., Jr. 1969. "The Inter-Regional Incidence of General Regional Taxes." *Public Finance* 24.

———. 1978. "Economic Constraints on State and Local Taxation of Energy Resources." *National Tax Journal* 31 (September):257–262.

———. 1980. "Administrative Considerations in the Design of Regional Tax Incentives." *National Tax Journal* 33 (June):177–188.

———. 1981. "Tax Exporting and the Commerce Clause: Reflections on *Commonwealth Edison*." Paper to the 1981 Taxation, Resources and Economic Development Conference, Cambridge, Mass.

Maler, Karl Goren. 1974. *Environmental Economics—A Theoretical Inquiry*. Baltimore: Johns Hopkins University Press.

Manne, Alan S.; Richels, Richard G.; and Weyant, John P. 1979. "Energy Policy Modeling: A Survey." *Operations Research* 27 (January–February):1–36.

Mansfield, E. 1961. "Technological Change and the Rate of Imitation." *Econometrica* 29 (April).

Manvel, A.D. 1975. "A Survey of the Extent of Unneutrality Toward Energy Under State Excise, Property, and Severance Taxation." In Gerard M. Brannon, ed., *Studies in Energy Tax Policy.* Cambridge, Mass.: Ballinger, pp. 41–51.

Marshalla, Robert A. 1978. "An Analysis of 'Cartelized' Market Structures for Nonrenewable Resources." Ph.D. dissertation, Stanford University.

Martin, E. Douglas K. 1978. "Taxation of Petroleum Production—The Canadian Experience—1972 to Date." *National Tax Journal* 31 (September):291–307.

Martin, F. William. 1977. *Energy Supply to the Year 2000: Global and National Studies.* Cambridge: MIT Press.

Mead, Walter J. 1978. "The Use of Taxes, Regulation and Price Controls in the Energy Sector." *National Tax Journal* 31 (September).

Mead, Walter J., and Deacon, Robert T. 1979. "Proposed Windfall Profits Tax on Crude Oil: Some Major Errors in Estimation." *Journal of Energy and Development* 5 (Autumn).

Meadows, D.D.; Meadows, D.L.; Randers, J.; and Behrens, W.W. III. 1972. *The Limits of Growth.* New York: Vintage Books.

Mieszkowski, Peter. 1972. "The Property Tax: An Excise or a Profits Tax?" *Journal of Public Economics* 1 (March).

Mieszkowski, Peter, and Toder, Eric. 1981. "Taxation of Energy Resources: Implications for Intergovernmental Relations and Economic Efficiency." Paper to 1981 Taxation, Resources and Economic Development Conference, Cambridge, Mass.

Moore, A. Milton. 1976. "The Concept of a Nation and Entitlements to Economic Rents." In A. Scott, ed. *Natural Resource Revenues: A Test of Federalism.* Vancouver, B.C.: University of British Columbia Press.

Morgan, W.E., and Olson, D.O. 1979. "The Structure of U.S. Energy Taxes—Federal, State and Local." Unpublished paper presented for the Steering Committee on the Impact of Taxation on Energy Markets, National Research Council, Washington, D.C.

Morse, C. 1973. "Natural Resources as a Constraint on Economic Growth: Discussion." *American Economic Review* 63 (May).

Murdock, S.H., and Leistritz, E.L. 1979. *Energy Development in the Western United States: Impact on Rural Areas.* New York: Praeger.

Musgrave, Richard. 1959. *The Theory of Public Finance.* New York: McGraw-Hill.

National Academy of Sciences. 1980. *Energy Taxation: An Analysis of Selected Taxes.* Washington, D.C.: The Academy.

Nehrig, Richard, and Zycher, Robert. 1976. "Coal Development and Government Regulation in the Northern Great Plains: A Preliminary Report." Santa Monica, Calif.: Rand Corporation.

Nelson, Clarence W. 1969. "Broader Lessons from the History of Lake Superior Iron-ore Taxation." In *Property Taxation U.S.A.,* ed. Richard W. Lindholm, pp. 237-261. Madison: University of Wisconsin Press.

Niemeyer, E. Victor. 1976. "The Effect of Energy Supply on Economic Growth." Ph.D. dissertation, University of Texas, Austin.

Nordhaus, W.D. 1973. "The Allocation of Energy Resources." *Brookings Papers on Economic Activity* 3:527-570.

Norgaard, R.B. 1975. "Resource Scarcity and New Technology in U.S. Petroleum Development." *Natural Resources Journal* 15 (April).

Oates, Wallace E. 1972. *Fiscal Federalism.* New York: Harcourt Brace Jovanovich.

Olson, Mancur, Jr. 1965. *The Logic of Collective Action: Public Goods and the Theory of Groups.* Cambridge: Harvard University Press.

Ontario. Department of Treasury and Economics. 1970. *Ontario Proposals for Tax Reform in Canada,* by Hon. Charles McNaughton. Toronto.

Page, Talbot. 1977. *Conservation and Economic Efficiency.* Baltimore: Johns Hopkins University Press.

Pasour, P.C., Jr., and Holley, D.L. 1976. "An Economic Analysis of the Case Against 'Ad Valorem' Property Taxation in Forestry." *National Tax Journal* 29:155-164.

Peterson, F.M., and Fisher, A.C. 1977. "The Exploitation of Renewable and Nonrenewable Natural Resources." *Economic Journal* 87 (December):681-721.

Phares, D. 1980. *Who Pays State and Local Taxes.* Cambridge, Mass.: Oelgeschlanger, Gunn and Hain.

Pindyck, R.C. 1978. "Optimal Exploration and Production of Nonrenewable Resources." *Journal of Political Economy* 85 (October):841-861.

Posner, R.A. 1971. "Taxation and Regulation." *Bell Journal of Economics* 2 (Spring):22-50.

———. 1975. "The Social Costs of Monopoly and Regulation." *Journal of Political Economy* 83 (August):807-827.

Powrie, T.L. 1976. "Static Redistributive and Welfare Effects of an Export Tax." In A. Scott, ed., *Natural Resource Revenues: A Test of Federalism.* Vancouver, B.C.: University of British Columbia Press.

Randall, A. 1978. "Property Institutions and Economic Behavior." *Journal of Economic Issues* 12 (March):1-21.

Rawls, J. 1971. *A Theory of Justice.* Cambridge: Harvard University Press.

Reece, Douglas K. 1979. "An Analysis of Alternative Bidding Systems for Leasing Offshore Oil." *Bell Journal of Economics* 10 (Autumn): 659-669.

Renshaw, E.F. 1979. "Taxation of Crude Oil, Gasoline, and Related Fuels and Commodities." *Growth and Change* 10:75-89.

Rosenberg, Nathan. 1972. *Technology and American Economic Growth.* New York: Harper and Row.

Russell, Milton and Shelton, Robert B. 1974. "A Model of Regulatory Agency Behavior." *Public Choice* 20 (Winter).

Samuelson, Paul A. 1976. "Economics of Forestry in an Evolving Society." *Economic Inquiry* 14:566–492.

Sandler, Todd M., and Shelton, Robert B. 1972. "Fiscal Federalism, Spillovers and the Export of Taxes." *Kylos* 25 (September).

Sandler, Todd, and Tschirhart, John T. 1980. "The Economic Theory of Clubs: An Evaluative Survey." *Journal of Economic Literature* 18 (December):1481–1521.

Schaefer, M.B. 1957. "Some Considerations of Population Dynamics and Economics in Relation to the Commercial Marine Fisheries." *Journal of Fisheries Resource Board of Canada* 14:669–681.

Schulze, William D. 1974. "The Optimal Use of Non-Renewable Resources: The Theory of Extraction." *Journal of Environmental Economics and Management* 1.

Schulze, William D.; Brookshire, David S.; d'Arge, Ralph C.; and Cummings, Ronald G. 1981. "Local Taxation for Boom-Town and Environmental Effects Resulting from Natural Resource Extraction." Paper to 1981 Taxation, Resources and Economic Development Conference, Cambridge, Mass.

Scott, A. 1953. "Notes on User Cost." *Economic Journal* 63 (June).

———. 1955. "The Fishery: The Objective of Sole Ownership." *Journal of Political Economy* 63 (April).

———. 1976. "Who Should Get Resource Revenues?" In A. Scott, ed. *Natural Resource Revenues: A Test of Federalism.* Vancouver, B.C.: University of British Columbia Press.

———, ed. 1976. *Natural Resource Revenues: A Test of Federalism.* Vancouver, B.C.: University of British Columbia Press.

Shapiro, David L. 1977. "The Application of an Agency Decision-Making Model." *Public Choice* 32 (Winter).

Shelton, R.B., and Morgan, W.E. 1977. "Resource Taxation, Tax Exportation and Regional Energy Policies." *Natural Resources Journal,* 12 (Fall) 261–282.

Slade, Margaret E. 1980. "Empirical Tests of Economic Rent in the U.S. Copper Industry." Washington, D.C.: Federal Trade Commission.

Smiley, Donald V. 1976. "The Political Context of Resource Development in Canada." In A. Scott, ed. *Natural Resource Revenues: A Test of Federalism.* Vancouver, B.C.: University of British Columbia Press.

Smith, V.K. 1968. "Economics of Production from Natural Resources." *American Economic Review* 58 (June).

———. 1980a. *An Econometric Analysis of the Behavior of Natural Resource Prices*. Palo Alto, Calif.: Electric Power Research Institute.

———. 1969. "On Models of Commercial Fishing." *Journal of Political Economy* 77 (March):181–198.

———. 1979. *Scarcity and Growth Reconsidered*. Baltimore: Johns Hopkins University Press.

———. 1980b. "The Evaluation of Natural Resource Adequacy: Elusive Quest or Frontier of Economic Analysis?" *Land Economics* 56 (August).

Solow, Robert M. 1974a. "The Economics of Resources and the Resource of Economics." *American Economic Review* 64 (May).

———. 1974b. "Intergenerational Equity and Exhaustible Resources." *Review of Economic Studies, Symposium on the Economics of Exhaustible Resources.*

———. 1978. "Resources and Economic Growth." *American Economist* 22 (Fall).

Solow, Robert M., and Wan, Frederic Y. 1976. "Extraction Costs in the Theory of Exhaustible Resources." *Bell Journal of Economics* 7 (Autumn):359–370.

Starch, Karl E. 1979. *Taxation, Mining and the Severance Tax*. Washington, D.C.: U.S. Department of the Interior, Bureau of Mines.

Steele, H. 1967. "Natural Resource Taxation: Resource Allocation and Distribution Implications." In Gaffney Mason, ed., *Extractive Resources and Taxation*. Madison: University of Wisconsin Press.

Stewart, Marion B. 1980. "Monopoly and the Intertemporal Production of Durable Extractable Resources." *Quarterly Journal of Economics* 94 (February):99–111.

Stigler, George G. 1971. "The Theory of Economic Regulation." *Bell Journal of Economics* 2 (Spring):3–21.

———. 1974. "Free Riders and Collective Action: An Appendix to Theories of Economic Regulation." *Bell Journal of Economics* 5 (Autumn): 359–365.

Stiglitz, Joseph E. 1975. "The Efficiency of Market Prices in Long Run Allocations in the Oil Industry." In *Studies in Energy Tax Policy*, edited by Gerard M. Brannon, Cambridge, Mass.: Ballinger.

Stinson, Thomas F. 1978. *State Taxation of Mineral Deposits and Production*. Washington, D.C.: U.S. Department of Agriculture.

Stobaugh, Robert, and Yergin, Daniel, eds. 1979. *Energy Future—Report of the Energy Project at the Harvard Business School*. New York: Random House.

Strucker, J.P. 1977. "The Distribution Implications of a Tax on Gasoline." *Policy Analysis* 3:171–186.

Sutherland, Charles F., Jr., and Tedder, Philip L. 1979. "Impacts of Federal Estate Taxation on Investment in Forestry." *Land Economics* 55 (November):510–515.

Tauzin, Billy, Rep. 1979. "Louisiana's First Use Tax." NTA-TIA Proceedings of the 72d Annual Conference. Oklahoma City.

Teisberg, Thomas J. 1980. "Federal Management of Energy and Mineral Resources on Public Lands." *Bell Journal of Economics* 11 (Autumn): 448–465.

Tiebout, C. 1956. "A Pure Theory of Local Expenditure." *Journal of Political Economy* 64 (October):416–424.

Timbrell, D.Y. 1967. *Taxation of the Mining Industry in Canada,* in *Studies of the Royal Commission on Taxation,* no. 9 Ottawa: Queen's Printer.

Trestrail, Richard W. 1969. "Forests and the Property Tax—An Unsound Theory." *National Tax Journal* 22:347–356.

———. 1980. "An Economic Analysis of the Case Against 'Ad Valorem' Property Taxation in Forestries: Comment." *National Tax Journal* 23 (March):117–118.

Tullock, Gordon. 1967. "The Welfare Costs of Tariffs, Monopolies and Theft." *Western Economic Journal* 5 (June):224–232.

Tullock, Gordon, and Tideman, Nicholaus T. 1976. "A New and Superior Process For Making Social Choices." *Journal of Political Economy,* 84 (April):1145–1159.

U.S. Council on Environmental Quality, 1980.

U.S. Department of Energy. 1979a. *National Energy Plan II. A Report to the Congress.* Washington, D.C.: GPO.

———. 1979b. *A Taxonomy of Energy Taxes.* Washington, D.C.: GPO.

U.S. Department of the Treasury. 1978. *Effective Income Tax Rates Paid by the United States Corporations in 1972.* Washington, D.C.: GPO.

U.S. Federal Reserve Bank of Kansas. 1980. *Western Water Resources— Coming Problems and the Policy Alternatives.* Boulder, Colo.: Westview Press.

U.S. General Accounting Office. 1979. *A Review of the Department of Energy's Energy Tax Policy Analysis.* Comptroller General's Report to the Congress of the United States. Washington, D.C.: GPO.

———. 1980a. *Long-Term Economic Planning Needed in Oil- and Gas-Producing States.* Washington, D.C.: GPO.

———. 1980b. *Natural Gas Incremental Pricing: A Complex Program with Uncertain Results and Impacts.* Washington, D.C.: GPO.

———. 1980c. *A Shortfall in Leasing Coal from Federal Lands: What Effect on National Energy Grants?* Washington, D.C.: GPO.

———. 1981a. *Assessing the Impact of Federal and State Taxes on the Domestic Minerals Industry.* Washington, D.C.: GPO.

———. 1981b. *Changes in Natural Gas Prices and Supplies Since Passage of the Natural Gas Policy Act of 1978.* Washington, D.C.: GPO.

————. 1981c. *State Taxation of Minerals.* Washington, D.C.: GPO.

Verleger, Philip K., Jr. 1980. "An Assessment of the Effects of the Windfall Tax on Crude Oil Prices. *Energy Journal* 1 (October):41–58.

Vogely, William, ed. 1975. *Mineral Materials Modeling.* Washington, D.C.: Resources for the Future.

Wetzler, James W. 1980. "Energy Excise Taxes as Substitutes for Income Taxes." *National Tax Journal* 33 (September):321–329.

Weyant, James P. 1979. *Advances in Energy Systems and Technology.* New York: Academic Press.

Whyte, John D. 1981. "A Constitutional Perspective on Federal Provincial Sharing of Revenues From Natural Resources." Paper to 1981 Taxation, Resources and Economic Development Conference, Cambridge, Mass.

Williams, Alan. 1966. "The Optimal Provision of Public Goods in a System of Local Government." *Journal of Political Economy* 74 (February): 18–33.

Wilson, Carol. 1980. *Coal—Bridge to the Future. Report of the World Coal Study.* Cambridge, Mass.: Ballinger.

————, ed. 1977. *Energy: Global Prospects 1985–2000.* Report of the Workshop on Alternative Energy Strategies. New York: McGraw-Hill.

Zakariya, Husan S. 1980. "Sovereignty over Natural Resources and the Search for a New International Economic Order." *Natural Resources Forum* 4 (January):75–84.

Ziemba, W.T.; Schwartz, S.L.; and Koenigsberg, E., eds. 1980. *Energy Policy Modeling, United States and Canadian Experiences.* Vol. 1. Boston: Martinus Nijhoff Publishing.

Ziemba, W.T., and Schwartz, S.L., eds. 1980. *Energy Policy Modeling, United States and Canadian Experiences.* Vol. 2. Boston: Martinus Nijhoff Publishing.

Zimmerman, Martin B. 1979. "Rent and Regulation in Unit Train Rate Determination." *Bell Journal of Economics* 10 (Spring).

————. 1980a. *The U.S. Coal Industry: The Economics of Policy Choice.* Cambridge, Mass.: MIT Press.

————. 1980b. "Western Coal Producing Cartel." Paper presented to the International Association of Energy Economists, Denver. September.

Zimmerman, Martin B., and Ellis, Randall P. 1980. "What Happened to Nuclear Power?" Cambridge, Mass.: MIT Working Paper, MIT EL 80–002WP (January).

# Index

# About the Author

**Albert M. Church** received the B.A. from Colorado College and the Ph.D. from Claremont Graduate School. He has taught at Middlebury College and is currently professor of economics at the University of New Mexico. He is the author of numerous publications in professional journals and of *Computers and Statistics in the Appraisal Process* (with R. Gustafson), *The Sophisticated Investor,* and *Taxation of Nonrenewable Resources* (Lexington Books, 1981).